On Edge

**BACKROOM DEALING,
COCKTAIL SCHEMING,
TRIPLE AXELS, AND HOW
TOP SKATERS GET SCREWED**

JON JACKSON

WITH JAMES PEREIRA

THUNDER'S MOUTH PRESS

NEW YORK

On Edge
Backroom Dealing, Cocktail Scheming,
Triple Axels, and How Top Skaters Get Screwed

Published by
Thunder's Mouth Press
An imprint of Avalon Publishing Group Inc.
245 West 17th Street, 11th Floor
New York, NY 10011

AVALON
publishing group incorporated

Library of Congress Cataloging-in-Publication Data is available

ISBN: 1-56025-804-7
ISBN 13: 978-1-56025-804-9

9 8 7 6 5 4 3 2

Book design by India Amos, Neuwirth and Associates, Inc.
Printed in the United States of America
Distributed by Publishers Group West

WITHDRAWN

IN MEMORY OF
IAN KNIGHT

CONTENTS

∞

∞

Hotel Hi-jinx

MONDAY, FEBRUARY 11, 2002

S ALLY STAPLEFORD'S TYPICALLY calm British demeanor had turned as fiery as her red hair. I had never before seen anyone so angry. Maybe I was the first person she was sharing her anger with, or maybe it had ulcerated as she told others about the horror and injustice she had just witnessed in Salt Lake's Delta Center: the Olympic Pairs figure-skating judging debacle. Either way, she was wild-eyed and bubbling over by the time she happened upon me.

"Oh, Jon! Hello." I could see her fists clinched, but she got ahold of herself and added, "It's nice to see you. What did you think of the results tonight?"

Accompanying Sally were Britta Lindgren, her fellow International Skating Union (ISU) technical committee member, and a man I recognized as John Hall, the British member of the ISU Council. I greeted Britta, who introduced John.

"Hello, Jon. Have you met John Hall?" Britta asked.

"No, I haven't," I replied. "Nice to meet you, Mr. Hall. Jon Jackson," I introduced myself.

"A pleasure," replied the stately yet frail John Hall. John was in the later stages of a battle with cancer, and it had taken a toll on his physical appearance.

"So, what did you all think of the hack job those judges worked on the Canadians tonight?" I asked.

"What was going on down there? Were those judges asleep at the wheel?" Sally exclaimed. "How could they possibly come up with that result?"

"Yes, it's such a pity," Britta said with a slight Swedish accent. "Pffft! What are we to do, ya?" Then she turned to Sally: "Sally, I'm going to take John up to the room. I will come back down and join you for a drink. Will you be here?"

"I may run up to the room, but I'll come back down. Meet me in the lobby," Sally said, and Britta and John departed. Then she turned back to me: "Oh Jon, this is such an embarrassment to all of us. After everything we've done, all the education, the training, for all of skating, for the sport and for all of us. I just don't understand what could have happened. It will set back judging for years. What were those judges thinking?"

Hearing her disappointment only added to my gloom. "I can't imagine," I answered. "I was hoping maybe I had missed something. The judging *can't* be that bad. I'm just sickened by it."

Despite my exasperation with the outcome (the imperfect Russian pair team had been awarded a gold medal over the Canadian pair team, who had skated perfectly that night), this discussion with the Chair of the powerful ISU technical committee was a heady experience for me. I was a young Olympic-level judge, and it caught me by surprise that Sally cared about my opinion.

Sally continued to vent her frustration. "Clearly the Canadians were the best tonight!" she nearly shouted. "Still the Russians won. I don't understand it!"

"I know!" I said. "Somebody has to do something."

We both knew which of the nine judges had given which scores that night, so we started discussing the five judges who had gotten them wrong—Poland, Russia, Ukraine, China, and France.

Suddenly the hotel doors swung open. An arctic chill swept through the room and froze our chatter. In walked the pale, frazzled, and overly furred Marie-Reine LeGougne.

The French judge.

I flashed Sally a wide-eyed look, and turned my chin toward the designer furball with candy-apple red hair. Sally turned to me and whispered in a voice only I could hear, "She looks very embarrassed, Jon, don't you think?"

For a moment, Marie-Reine was unaware of our presence, surely lost in her own thoughts and demons. But then she spotted Sally. Her body reacted with a startled flinch and her stride quickened as she made her way deliberately and dismissively past us, toward the elevator bay. Sally shot her a look of disgust, a look that made it clear that she suspected Madame Marie was guilty of more than simply poor judgment.

Hoping to flee the lobby, Marie-Reine moved around the corner out of my line of sight. I heard a "ding," and assumed she had pushed an elevator's call button. The elevator, slow in coming, and perhaps in on the alleged "Western media conspiracy" to deny the Russians their gold medal, turned Marie-Reine into an unwatched crockpot. A few seconds' wait must have felt like a lifetime as she stewed in the uncooked juices of her raw emotions.

Sally and I resumed our conversation, though now in more hushed tones. I can't be sure that Marie-Reine overheard our conversation, but perhaps our whisperings, combined with Sally's knowing look, the anxiety stemming from Marie-Reine's guilt, and a mercilessly slow elevator were too much for the French judge. Anyway, she suddenly rushed from around the corner and began a full Napoleonic charge on the British Front, heading straight for Sally. In her rage, Marie-Reine had rendered me invisible.

Within inches of Sally's face, Marie-Reine screamed in heavily accented yet perfect English. "Ice dancing is ruining our sport!" she blubbered. "You have no idea! I must defend myself!" she continued, sobbing. "You don't understand! I had to do this! Gold for gold! This was for my Dance Team! You don't understand the pressure!" In a hysterical fit, she deliriously repeated these rants, singing like a canary turning state's evidence.

Sally, blessed with a British sense of propriety, moved Marie-Reine out of the public corridor. Had she not done so, there would have been many other witnesses standing near Marie-Reine's makeshift confessional.

As Sally and Marie-Reine hastened to a corner at the end of the hallway, I stayed put, where I could both see and hear all of Marie-Reine's admissions unfolding. Just then, Britta reappeared in the lobby and rushed to join the spectacular meltdown. But even a new witness couldn't quiet Marie-Reine as she continued her tirade. Try as they might, the two calmer women could not pacify the French irrational or get her to clarify her extraordinary outbursts. Yet I understood her perfectly well. "You must help us!" she screamed. "I had no choice." And then, le plus important, "It was a deal with the Russians!"

Stunned into silence, I took in every word.

A Feathered Fowl Takes Flight

*T*HE GREAT SALT Palace once occupied the heart of downtown Salt Lake City. The Salt Palace's size was monumental, with its name indicating its grandeur, at least in the eyes of a thirteen-year-old Mormon boy. Alongside the Palace, we had the world-famous Mormon Tabernacle and the golden bugle-blowing Moroni-topped Temple, all within the grounds of the Church of Jesus Christ of Latter Day Saints, or "Mormons" as they are commonly called. To me, that cool-looking temple really seemed like just another church.

Now the Salt Palace, that was a building! Beautiful and shaped round like a huge bass drum, a kid my age could only imagine how many millions of people could actually fit inside that structure watching a sports event or attending a tractor-pull.

My siblings and I really looked forward to any trip to Salt Lake. My hometown Centerville was a small rural community, with farms on every side of the condominium project my father was developing on the acreage of old wheat fields. Salt Lake City was the big city by every standard I knew. Parking garages, department stores, tall buildings, it was all quite impressive.

The drive from Centerville to Salt Lake City usually took my family about 25 minutes, depending on traffic, speed traps, or road construction. The trip can be made entirely with freeway driving or by frontage roads and surface streets, depending on your inclination. During that short drive, my siblings and I managed to drive my parents to the brink of insanity with our arguing, poking, fidgeting, and fooling around.

"Do you kids want me to turn this car around right now and take us all back home?" My mother was known to say on pretty much every outing. "I'll stop this car right now, and the next one to make a peep gets the first thump!" Of course she never did. I found her empty threats humorous.

Older than me by just 17 months, my sister Tami was known for her rule-consciousness. With two younger brothers close to her age, she would rather hang out with her girlfriends from church than attend family outings. She really just wanted to be left alone. And why wouldn't she? It didn't take Tami long to figure out that it was in her best interest to stay out of my way. Despite her repeated attempts to get even with me for some hardship I had already caused her, or just to get me in trouble for something that had happened, it was she who usually wound up taking the blame.

I was the second child, with a younger brother, Eric, and a fun little sister, Janica. Janica and I always got along the best, and she seemed to understand how to stay out of my way and in my good graces, simultaneously. Tami left Janica alone for the most part, devoting much of her day to thinking up ways to avoid me. Eric was a sharp kid, but not blessed with the quick wit to defend himself against my machinations. I found Tami's annoyance with me amusing, entertaining myself for hours by leaving little messes in her line of sight or purposely hanging up the phone when one of her friends called. That is if I wasn't listening in on the extension and reporting every word to my mother.

Tonight's trip was one of the promised good times at the Salt Palace to see the Ice Follies. My brother, sisters, and I were all giddy with excitement, and we literally bounced off our station wagon's shocks all the way into town. These were the old days, long before minivans tricked out with TV screens and Disney DVD. In my day, large, Partridge-sized families drove around in Mondrian-painted school busses. Why didn't we have one of those?

We were going tonight because my mom was on a new kick. Every couple of months or so, the scales of religious inclination around our house would shift one way or another regarding our involvement in "The Church." Mormons call their church "The Church," as if there were no other church worth the tithes they collect. I think my mom sometimes remembered my family's deep Mormon roots and, maybe through guilt, would at least try to keep one toe in the waters of Mormonism. She might also have been getting subtle pressure from my grandparents for shirking her role in bringing us up in the Church. Nevertheless, her new kick was the Monday night Family Home Evening.

Family Home Evening was a program started by Mormon President David O. McKay back in 1964 as a plan intended to strengthen families in the church. The curriculum was designed to assist parents in teaching the gospel in the home. Since then, that agenda has been emphasized by the Church, and they officially set aside Monday evenings for Family Home Evening.

To help neutralize the ills of the world, published church theory was: "The spirit of the times is worldliness. Hoodlumism is common . . . youth from recognized good families express their revolt in destructive acts. . . . Immorality, drug addiction, and general moral and spiritual deterioration seem to be increasing . . . [the church strives to] return the world to sane living, to true family life, family interdependence . . . to return the father to his rightful place at the head of the family, to bring mother home from social life and employment, the children away from unlimited fun and frolic . . . the family home evening will neutralize the ill effects . . ." (*Ensign*, Jan. 1975, pp. 3–4).

This teaching might seem a bit manipulative, fascist, and chauvinistic— or at the very least, archaic—by today's standards and economic necessity. But back then, my mom wanted us to have the opportunity to choose how we felt about the church and the programs it promoted. So for a few months, we made a pretty good stab at the Monday night Family Home Evening program.

On this Monday night, my parents decided to take us on a family outing. They got tickets and took us all to see the Ice Follies. I had no idea what Ice Follies were. My father had taken my brother and me to the Salt Palace before for the old Utah Stars basketball games, car and home shows, and the like—none of which I particularly cared for, but all of which were a thrill because they were held in the Salt Palace. A Palace! The home of kings and queens! Just who were these kings and queens, anyway, that needed a salt palace? The King of Salt?

As a young boy, the name "Salt Lake" or "Salt Lake City" had a meaning separate and apart from its individual words. To me, they did not mean the city next to the lake composed entirely of brine water and brine flies. Rather, they all ran together to mean a place: a downtown, the home of the Salt Palace and that Mormon temple. So when I would wonder about these kings and queens of salt, I didn't really think about the salt that comes out of a shaker, but rather about a mythical, fantastical dynasty that only an overactive 13-year-old mind might create.

The actual history of Salt Lake, which parallels my family heritage, is not so magical. Back in 1847, led by Brigham Young, the Mormon pioneers crossed the plains and arrived in the Salt Lake Valley in handcarts and covered wagons. This history held particular significance for my family because one of our ancestors was an original pioneer and eventual leader of the Church. The early Mormon pioneers traveled west, fleeing pitchfork-wielding mobs and the religious persecution that existed toward them back in Nauvoo, Illinois. They made their way across the heartland of the United States, painstakingly pushing or pulling heavily laden handcarts. Some of the Utah-bound Saints owned oxen or donkeys to help tow their families, *Book of Mormons*, and other belongings, but most pushed through this great pilgrimage fueled only by their own willpower and intense desire to survive.

The hymn "Put Your Shoulder to the Wheel" was a popular Mormon ditty written during that time and based on this trek. It holds significant meaning to any descendant of the original pioneers. While I am not much of a vocalist, as a young child I would gleefully sing along when this song was chosen at church, loudly belting out the chorus, as did the rest of my family, in homage to those who had founded the Church and the Salt Lake Valley. The lively chorus reads something like this:

> Put your shoulder to the wheel; push along (push along);
> Do your duty with a heart full of song (full of song);

We all have work; let no one shirk.
Put your shoulder to the wheel.

On rare occasions, this didactic song of praise would be sung "in wheel," or in rounds, where one part of the congregation began the hymn, then another part started at the second verse, and still another part started up on the third verse. It was great fun for a kid, and a nice break from the otherwise dull church services.

ONCE IN SALT Lake, we pulled into a parking lot and my dad paid for a spot. Oh my gosh, another ticket! "I wonder how I'll finagle it for my scrapbook," I thought to myself. "Tami will probably get it if I don't act quickly."

"Dad, do you want me to hold the parking ticket while we see the show?"

This brought a chorus of protest from Tami and Eric. By this time, they were all too familiar with my calculating conduct, and tried to cut me off at the pass. So to resolve the dispute, and still consistent with my plan, Dad gave the ticket to my youngest sister, Janica, all of four years old, to hold. I smiled to myself, knowing I could easily barter it out of her small hands. No, if I couldn't get it, putting it in the hands of Janica was the next best thing.

Crowding through the mobs of people, and up the ramps to the arena, we were overwhelmed by the displays of souvenirs being sold. My family, not poor by any means, was practical to a point that bordered on cruelty! My father's tight wallet and mother's zipped-up purse would not be pried open for these frivolous carnival delights. Popcorn and small-sized drinks, perhaps; T-shirts, baseball caps and glittered pinwheels emblazoned with the Ice Follies logo—out of the question. All that sparkle was simply not going to be part of tonight's show, at least not for the Jacksons. But that didn't stop us from trying.

"Mom, can I please get a T-shirt?" my older sister would ask.

"Nope." the speed-dial reply.

"Dad, will you get me a baseball cap?" my brother would plead.

"Nope." Parroting everything my mom said.

Soon we were all a chorus squealing pleases and why-nots, so my parents ultimately settled on a purchase of the official program just to shut us up.

Once we made it to our seats, we were each given a turn to look through the glossy, oversized promotional piece. Tami gave it a quick once-over but still managed to crinkle it up and smear it with her greasy fingerprints. My turn was next, and I gave her a mean look on account of her careless smudges.

As I opened the cover, I could see that each colored page was filled with incredible costumes and an assortment of beautiful people. Was this what we were going to see tonight? This will be amazing! Trying to take it all in, I must have taken too long looking at each page, and soon Eric, whose turn was after mine, started whining about it. I quickly finished and passed it to him, but wondering what the point was, knowing it had nothing to do with motorcycles, football, or fishing. Soon he and my younger sister had lost interest in the program, and it found its way back to my lap. But before I could lose myself again in its words and pictures, the show started.

The night began and ended with Las Vegas-style show girls on skates and, in my memory, it was over in a flash. Though the show was actually about 90 minutes long, I was mesmerized from beginning to end. It was just such a good time for me that, in every sense of the phrase, the time just flew by.

One Caribbean style-performance by a young African-American soloist was the showstopper. Its music was upbeat and lively and really had our toes tapping. He was very talented and nimble, but his bright, beautiful costume absolutely stole the show! He was completely covered in flaming orange, red, and yellow all billowing down his sleeves and pants. His routine was a crowd-pleaser, but his outfit would make Carmen Miranda smile a toothy pineapple grin!

All through the number, I could not take my eyes off this attractive, exotic black man and his amazing, flashy costume. I noticed that he was pictured in our program, though the picture did him no justice: Seeing him live was a lot better than Memorex! But I was thrilled to have the take-home memory.

It should be no surprise then that the program ended up in my scrapbook collection. Everyone else in my family had forgotten all about it as soon as the lights went dim; besides, I had it tucked down the sleeve of my jacket. Out of sight, out of mind, I always say. It would later serve as my connection to a fantasy world that rose up out of the finely tilled soils of Mormon farmland.

I never did get a chance to enjoy the parking ticket wasted in my younger sister's possession. Thanks a lot, Janica. Normally, I would have bartered it away from her in trade for something only a four-year-old girl could love and a thirteen-year-old boy no longer had use for. Surely she wouldn't have missed a parking ticket from a Salt Palace parking lot. Now, with the special Souvenir Edition Ice Follies Program, neither would I.

MY FAMILY, DESPITE its cart-and-wheel genealogy, was actually a non-conformist lot, at least by Latter-Day standards. Other than her lack of religious zeal, my mother was otherwise the typical seventies mom. Her hair was as big as the next mom's, and her day was just as full: meal planning, grocery shopping, house cleaning, clothes washing, and micro-managing her four kids. These were the halcyon days before the Prozac-clouded afternoons that would later creep over the Salt Lake Valley. Mothers performed their daily duties largely unmedicated and unfettered by daily doses of advice television.

A not-so-active member of the Church of Jesus Christ of Latter-day Saints, my mother believed that her home was her haven and her kids should reflect her values. While most Mormon mothers of that time taught their children about life in the Church (rules, propriety, and guilt), our mother's teachings were simply about life. She was a homemaker with a rebellious bent, instilling in each of us one of her more non-Mormon principles: individuality. "Why do you care what other people think of you? Be yourself!" she would often say.

In contrast, Tami was the "white sheep" of the family. By the time Tami was fifteen, she was very active in the Church. Every week, it seemed, there would be some new crafty project she had learned to create in her weekly young Mormon teenager's meetings. The Mutual Improvement Association, M.I.A. for short, was a weekly class for the mother-in-training, where young, impressionable teens and preteens learned to be good mothers and better wives. Essentially, women learned how to walk in the shadows of their men. Tami was determined to master it all. She cooked, canned, and crafted throughout her teenage years. Fortunately, every so often, the Church did allow the busy-bee Utah schoolgirls to enjoy themselves with some good-old fashioned Christian recreation—a "mixer" with the boys. One of those M.I.A. outings was a trip with 30 or so young girls and boys to a recently opened ice rink about five minutes from our house.

Recreational skating, snacking, and an hour and a half on the ice with just her friends—Tami was hooked. That night, she decided ice-skating would be her new sport. She enjoyed it so much that she convinced our mom to enroll her in a two-week learn-to-skate program. While she eagerly progressed through her lessons with a big smile on her face, I sat up in the stands with my mom and waited for her. Being a spectator was no fun for a hyperactive thirteen-year-old like me, particularly one with a special Souvenir Edition Ice Follies Program hidden under his bed.

At this time, I was a skinny and shorter-than-normal eighth-grader in junior high school. Always a stellar student, I was not otherwise involved in extracurricular activities. In a small town, the activity choices for teenage boys were few, and reeked with the stink of conformity: Boy Scouting; the rough-and-tumble of football, basketball, and baseball; and, of course, fishing and hunting. My father, a successful real estate developer, loved all those father–son activities, especially fishing. He even wore one of those ridiculous vests with hooked lures and fake fuzzy bugs stuck all over it. The pressure to participate in what I considered nonsensical activities came mostly from him. I dreaded when football tryouts rolled around each fall, and thoughtfully contemplated which medical ailment was going to afflict me just beforehand.

Fortunately, my little brother, Eric, loved anything associated with dirt, sweat, and gutting fish. Over time, I got more adept at avoiding almost all of Dad's fatherly demands, while Eric became his happy lapdog. My dad probably thought he was just being an interested father, trying to help both his sons become men the best way he knew how, interaction most boys would have been thrilled to get. Not me. I would exploit any possible opportunity where I could use my brother as a distraction to keep my father occupied, and could hardly keep a straight face when my school work, or, later, my skating, would interfere with my father's annual fishing trip. "Oh well," I would say, "maybe next year. You and Eric will have a great time without me!"

Clearly, I wasn't one of those boys carrying around baseball cards or tossing a ball in and out of a mitt to keep my brain blank. So, with nothing productive to keep me occupied, I sat with my mother, writhing with boredom, waiting for my sister to finish her skating lessons. After a few days of nothing to do but snoop under the bleacher seats for loose change, I soon begged mom to allow me to skate. She agreed, permitting me to skate around off to the side of the rink while we waited for my sister's classes to finish. Seeing that I was taking easily to the ice, she enrolled me in the Alpha class as my sister graduated to the Beta class. After three days of Alpha class, the instructor, impressed by how quickly I picked up the rudiments, advanced me into the Beta class. Once again, I was soaring to the head of the class.

When other boys my age were aspiring to be Joe Namath, Johnny Bench, and Pete Rose, I was yearning to be a male Carmen Miranda. It was kismet, although I had no idea there was such a word to describe my future in the world of ice, sequins, and bright lights.

Until I found skating, school had been the only activity where I clearly excelled. In the third and fourth grades, I was skipped into the higher grade level for advanced math and reading; had my sister not already been in the next grade, I would have skipped those grades altogether. But she was not about to have her little brother in the same grade with her in school. Sharing math and reading class were more than enough for her, and she let my parents know about it. Just like at school, on the ice, my sister was not pleased to have her tagalong younger brother sharing her skating lessons, and neither one of us was interested in sharing the spotlight in the arena.

If you want to learn about presidents and wars, you go to school. If you want to learn about God and sin, you go to church. Similarly, you would think that learning to ice-skate would take place at the ice rink, but that notion was lost on my mom. Instead, to supplement our lessons, Mom dragged us off to the library, where she checked out every single skating book and read them that same night. The next day, she boasted, "I can teach you this!" Reading us lessons from the books describing each maneuver, each point of grace, she had us practice in our socks on our slippery linoleum kitchen floor.

One afternoon after our lessons, Mom decided to join Tami and me on the ice, with a favorite book in hand. We assembled at one end of the ice arena, where she read out loud a couple of paragraphs as a refresher and began instructing us on how to master back crossovers, a move we beginners considered a first milestone. A back crossover is a maneuver that propels a skater backward across the ice surface; more importantly, it separates the talented from the ankle-wobblers. In the group-lesson scheme of things, we wouldn't learn this move until we were two levels higher, in the Delta class. My mother was determined that we learn it with her sooner than later. "So pay attention!" she said. She read a couple more descriptions to us and said "Now, let's try it."

Mom quickly abandoned her own back-crossover attempts and watched our unsuccessful efforts. "Don't pick up your foot, Jon!" "Tami, are you listening?" She continued to insist that we make an S with our right foot, while crossing it over our left. It was just not working. It seemed impossible to do without picking up a foot! Conceptually, with both feet side by side, one can't cross one foot over the other without picking it up and placing it there. "Mom, it's impossible!"

"No, it's not, Jon. It says right here that the right foot does not leave the ice."

My mother tried it with us again and declared, "It IS impossible!" We all then rechecked the book. Sure enough, it clearly said that the foot must not leave the ice.

The problem, I discovered quite by accident, was that we were trying to draw an S on the ice from a standstill. Tired of our unsuccessful attempts at the back crossovers, I started practicing the backward "fishes" that I had learned in my Alpha class. Backward fishes get their name as each foot creates a series of S's on the ice and together they create a "fish" pattern. Skating at a modest speed, I noticed that fishes are simply the S patterns I had been trying to create with my sister and mom only moments before. So, while backward "fishing," I slowly slid my right foot over my left. It worked! I then stepped my left out from behind, and S'ed my right foot over it again! Magic! I was skating backward!

"Mom! Mom! Look! I can do it!" I hollered. Once again, to the chagrin of my irritated sister, I was attracting far too much attention to myself.

$$\infty$$

I ADVANCED FROM learn-to-skate to the highest level, and was soon faced with the prospect of private lessons. Doree Ann Tateoka, a young, patient woman, had been my teacher for most of my learn-to-skate classes. After persuading my mom, who then successfully talked my dad into it, I began taking one private lesson per week from Doree Ann.

I soon realized, mostly from watching the other skaters taking private lessons, that taking only one lesson a week was never going to get me anywhere. I quickly learned the new moves Doree Ann taught me, and then practiced them all week. I mastered most of the early moves quickly and looked forward to learning something new each lesson. Yet Doree Ann was reluctant to teach me any additional maneuvers until I had clearly mastered the moves she had taught me—sometimes—weeks before. This pace was absolute drudgery and torture. One lesson a week was not going to keep me satisfied, and it was soon two. Then three per week. Then four.

Figure-skating has a way of sucking you in, family and all, without your realizing the amount of financial commitment you're making. One lesson a week turned into four; one public session twice a week soon became every day, then two public sessions, then private freestyle sessions, and so on. Skates, bags, outfits, and—later—travel, you and your parents are in for some serious coinage.

After about four months of the slow sucking sound of looming financial ruin, Doree Ann approached me about going to my first competition. It was a freeskating-only competition, one where I would not need to know my school figure-eights, which I had only recently begun practicing. Also, due to my age, it was a now-or-never moment for me, at least if I wanted to pursue the sport competitively. Even then, it was likely too late.

The competition was to be held in Great Falls, Montana, and would require that I learn a program set to music. I would also need a costume. Did I hear her say "costume"? Sold! Doree Ann promised to speak to my mother.

It turned out that my mother wasn't going to be the problem. My father, on the other hand, once learning of this unexpected expense, was not going to get sucked in so easily. His questions fell out in freeform, much like water from a faucet, but with the voice of the teacher in a Charlie Brown television special. "Just how much was this whole thing costing us, even without this boondoggle to Big Sky? And why? This was no sport for a boy. A costume? Not my son. It was bad enough that he was going off every day to the ice rink to dance around with the girls. Waa-waa-waa wah."

Despite my father's list of objections, somehow my mother came through, and we were off to the fabric shops to find me a costume. Picking out the "pattern" was not near as much fun as picking out the fabric. And the sequins! "Look at all the colors," I thought. So many textures, so many prints! I was having way too much fun in this strange ladies' world. But my fun soon came to a screeching halt as I was steered toward the plain black fabrics. Not the satins and sheers, just the plain black polyester gabardines. What about Mr. Carmen Miranda in the Ice Follies? Why couldn't I be him? I wanted red, or orange, or maybe even purple! I would have even settled for a nice blue. Maybe even a robin's-egg blue. But black? Blah. Who would ever notice me in that?

My mom could tell I was disappointed, but tried to explain, "Your dad will never go for anything other than black. Maybe we could sew some sequins on it to make it sparkle?" Ah, now she's making sense; a glimmer of hope. A language I understood. Glimmers rarely become flames, and this would be no exception. The sequins I got stuck with were as plain black as the fabric. My mom understood the course of least resistance with my dad and knew he'd ask during the project, "What are you doing?"

She knew she'd have to answer with what she herself probably thought sounded ridiculous, "Oh, nothing. I'm just sewing sequins on your son's skating costume." If the sequins were black, maybe he wouldn't even notice they were there.

∞

I soon learned that a skating competition has very little to do with the city it's held in, and yet everything to do with the airplanes, airports, taxi rides, hotel rooms, restaurant dining, and suitcase living that come along with it. Just into my teens, and already I was living the glamour jet-set life! Great Falls, Montana may as well have been Manhattan with me strolling Park Avenue swinging a Macy's hatbox from my wrist.

But Great Falls, lacking in bright lights and urban sophistication, made up for it as a rustic western cowboy town. Not that it mattered. I was still having a great time with my fellow Utah ice skaters, at the rinks, during meals, and in the lobby and hallways of the host hotel. Which is a good thing; the falls in Great Falls were not all that great!

Oddly enough, the old Great Falls ice rink was connected to the City Hall, with a laundromat and hardware store on either side. It was ancient, probably built by Lewis and Clark. And cold! The place might have been heated by a coal furnace, but the shoveler was on break. The northern Montana early spring weather was still quite chilly, and the temperature inside the walls of the rink was not much warmer. Instead of Plexiglas walls, this rink had rusty old chain-link fencing surrounding the ice, not helping to "warm up" the situation. Boy, had I been spoiled at the Bountiful Recreation Center back home!

On practice, I was still working to master an axel, a jump that was not coming as easily to me as did the other jumps. About half the boys on the practice were doing them just fine, the other half rowing the same boat I was.

Back in the hotel room, I was practicing my axel on the floor when my mom noticed and decided I should be practicing my whole routine. She started my music on a cassette tape recorder, and gracefully began to demonstrate to me how she felt I should present myself through my whole routine! I was laughing myself silly as I watched my mother dancing around the room, bumping into the beds and hotel furniture while she tried to teach me the importance of showmanship. In actuality, as a former Miss Ogden and Miss Utah runner-up—competing with dance as her talent, with music as a minor in college—she didn't look so bad and I should have been paying more attention. But I didn't get it. A little know-it-all, I just shook my head and said, "It's just music, Mom. It's only playing so I have something to do my tricks to. I need to practice my axel."

My poor mom. She tried in vain to teach me to keep my head up, to smile at the audience, to practice the preplanned arm movements of my routine to the rhythm of the music, but I wasn't listening. I just didn't see the point. This is a sport, isn't it? I needed to land my tricks, and do more of them than the other boys did to win. That's what this was all about!

As a preliminary competitor, the lowest of the many levels a young skater can progress in, my group would be among the first to skate. When they called us to the ice, the audience filled the stands with cheers and shouts for me and the other skaters: "Go, Jon!!! Yea Jon! Show 'em how to skate!" These rants and chants were repeated over and over by my mother and a group of screaming schoolgirls; and, all being from Utah, their enthusiasm would not be outdone by the skaters from other areas!

I soon noticed something else unsettling about this warm-up. The other four boys in my group could all do their axels. What happened to the boys in practice who were still struggling like me? Was I going to be the worst skater here? Wasn't riding in a taxi from the airport enough? What about the hat box?

As it turned out, the preliminary boys had been split into two groups, divided by age. I was the oldest and landed in the group with the "bigger boys," the ones who just happened to have been skating a lot longer than me. Try as I might, I could not land the axels in my program. I paid little to no attention to my music. My focus was ill-placed on those axels and my other single jumps, leaving little or nothing for performance. Not surprisingly, I finished fifth of five.

Ida Tateoka, Doree Ann's mother and a judge at the event (in fact, she was the highest-ranking judge in the region), came up to me after the massacre and pointed out that if I had been in the group with the younger boys, I would likely have won. Not one of them had even tried an axel. Some consolation! *Would have* won? Big deal.

This information solidified in my mind the concept that the boys with better jumps win. Period.

My mother tried to point out that if I had skated better to the music, looked up at the audience and judges, and put a smile on my face, I might have placed higher. But I knew better. I returned home determined to land that axel and get on to the double jumps. This was a sport, right? Who cares about the music?

One thing I learned for sure in Big Sky: I wanted medals, lots of them. If I couldn't have flashy Caribbean costumes, I was at least going to be covered in gold, and so I put my shoulder to the wheel and aimed for the stars. I was more determined than ever to succeed in this sport. My interest changed skating from a pastime for me to a passion. In this travel-the-world, sequined-covered sport, I had found my place.

I suppose my dad had his suspicions and did his best to object to every bugle bead along the way. Or maybe he was just as much in denial as I was. Maybe neither of us saw the obvious signs that I, as a young 13-year-old boy, was in love with the gayest sport in America.

How could I ever have known that my love affair with skating would lead me into an electrifying life as a judge, opening doors to an awesome world of travel and international friendships? Little did I know that my mentors would turn on me like wolves on a blind lamb, destroying my faith in the colorful world of Olympic ice-skating. Ironically, my involvement in the sport would begin unraveling on my home court in Salt Lake City, and all because of the value system that was ingrained in me as the oldest son of "goodly" parents whose moral values matched the teachings of their Mormon backgrounds. Who could have known?

> *Just over two years earlier, Russians Irina Rodnina and Aleksandr Zaitsev won the 1976 Olympic Pairs gold medal, her second, and the fourth consecutive Olympic gold medal for a Soviet pair.*

Pointing in the Right Direction

ACK IN CENTERVILLE, despite my last-place finish in Great Falls, I was somehow energized. I felt an inkling of self-confidence. The chance to go to Montana, without my brother and sisters, in some way made me feel special. Hopping an airplane for a midweek getaway was certainly not anything my schoolmates were getting to do. When I got back to school, I walked the halls of Centerville Junior High School with the confidence of a football quarterback. Well, not that confident, but a dose of self-respect was good for me, an otherwise reserved, bookish schoolboy.

After the school year, my training became more intense. That summer was my first experience with summer ice. I was essentially training non-stop, sometimes beginning as early as 5:30 A.M. Normally I did not get up that early, and would not have done so for the Second Coming, but I was determined to succeed this time: One way or another, I knew that I never wanted to feel like fifth place again.

The morning would begin with forty-five minutes of "patch training," skating nothing more than figure-eights. Patch training got its name because of the manner in which the skaters divvy up the ice into 24 numbered sections or patches. Each skater draws from a hat the number of a patch where they will keep their practice of the figure-eights to themselves, preventing chaos and run-ins. The center patches were more desirable, so it drove me nuts if I failed to select one in or around the middle.

An hour of freeskating followed patch work. I would usually get in two patch sessions and two freeskate sessions by noon. This was a major financial commitment for my family, as I was required to pay and sign a contract in the spring for ice time for the entire summer. At $1.80 per session, that worked out to about $7.20 per day, or about $35.00 a week, costing my family nearly $400 for the summer—and that was just for the ice time! My lesson schedule was also up to two patch and two freeskating lessons per week (about $60 per week), and I had to buy a separate pair of skates to do my figures with (an extra $300). With my family better off than most, I often wondered how other families did this. I would watch over the next few years as skating families hocked wedding rings, mortgaged homes, and declared bankruptcy, all in pursuit of figure-skating riches.

One way or another, my mom always managed to persuade my dad to make these extra financial commitments on my behalf without losing her wedding ring. One day after school, I learned of one of her tricks.

"Jon, your dad wants you to run over to the office this afternoon so he can teach you something," said my mother nonchalantly. She was never very good at nonchalant, and I knew immediately that something smelled, and it wasn't the rotting moss growing in the pond outside our door.

We lived in a condominium project called "Pheasantbrook" that my dad was developing. To keep his costs down, ever frugal as he was, he also acted as the primary sales agent. His offices were located in the converted garages of two adjoining "model homes" about two blocks away.

With fear and trepidation in my heart (Mom had provided little else to go on), I made the short walk to his office, sulking the whole way. I had been party to these dreaded little meetings with Dad before, and they almost never came out in my favor. They usually involved my learning to tie fishing flies, playing catch, learning to throw a football, or some other equally appalling activity.

I moped into Dad's office, and his secretary, Jeanette, greeted me.

"Hello, Jon! Good to see you," she said with a smile in her voice.

Then, without acknowledging my indifference, she said, "I'll let your dad know you're here. It's going to be great fun working with you!" Then she disappeared into Dad's office, walled off from the rest of the sales center.

Alone in the reception area, I stood staring at the huge miniature layout of the "project." It looked like a big Monopoly game board, but with little red (for sold), green (for available), and black (lived-in) dots instead of plastic little houses and hotels.

My mind went numb. Did she say "work?"

Go Directly to Jail. Do Not Pass Go. Do Not Collect $200.

I was an accelerated student at school, and excelled in mathematics more so than other subjects. I guess I was just a little bit too good at it, and perhaps overly entrepreneurial as well. These well-honed skills had caught the eyes of my parents, and sometimes their wrath, as on more than one occasion I had drained the piggybanks and pocketbooks of my brother, sisters, and friends with some concocted venture, the most profitable of which was charging them to play my Atari video game at ten cents a pop. My parents had evidently now figured out a way to tap my skills to help pay for my skate lessons and ice time.

Jeannette soon re-emerged and, upon seeing my miserable expression, pretended another big smile on her face, hoping it might be contagious, as she indicated that my dad was ready to see me. I walked into his office and, with another roll of the dice, I landed on the "Water Works" utility ($150) and began bawling my eyes out.

This would be indentured servitude—a whole summer of it, and likely the most traumatic event to happen in my young life. I couldn't think of anything worse. I was never going to have any fun again. My mind still racing and in hysterics before my dad finally calmed me down, explaining that it wasn't going to be *that* bad and not *that* much of a time commitment, and that I would have fun doing it.

He then produced a set of black plastic loose-leaf binders that made up his "books," and how each corresponded to a specific building in the development. I was to post entries depending on the incoming invoices Jeanette had scribbled notes on, in accounting code, for each unit. This scribbling might only have read "Building 22, Condo 2, and Drywall."

In Mom's negotiations with Dad for ice time, lessons, and skates, she had bargained me away as a bean-counter. As a result, as a soon-to-be 14-year-old, I spent my summer learning double salchows and double toe-loops in the morning, while learning and practicing certified double-entry accounting in the afternoon for my dad. I am amazed that he didn't also ask me to put together an initial public offering while I was at it!

That summer would set the playing field for the future relationship I had with both of my parents. My mother always, always, always finding a way to make sure that I would get in life what I wanted—no matter how—and my father and I finding something we had in common: business. I was finally relating to my dad on neutral ground.

The football, the baseball, or, worse, the fishing flies were no longer something I had to keep up on or begrudge him. When Dad would bring those topics up, I only needed to switch the conversation to business, and when the topic of figure-skating and sequins came up, my dad would do the same. We understood each other's mental limitations, and that marked the beginning of my adult relationship with my father—as the youngest accountant in Centerville, or possibly the whole United States!

My summer ice training soon paid off. I was now consistently landing my axels, double salchows, and double toe-loops. My parents, and Doree Ann, made the decision to move me up a level, from preliminary to sub-juvenile, as my advancing age was working against me. Most boys at the preliminary level are between seven and ten years old. Even at my new level, sub-juvenile, my competitors might be ten and eleven. At fourteen, I needed to advance quickly.

With loads of new jumps, a new program, and quite possibly the most dreadful and unfashionable of all my conservative costumes, I was off to California for the Central Pacific Regional Championships in Rancho Cordova, a suburb of Sacramento. My dad came along to accompany my mother, but spent his days looking over the condominium and planned-unit developments sprawling all over the Sacramento area.

The figure-eight portion of the competition accounted for fifty percent of the final overall placement. At this competition, I would demonstrate my figure-eights in front of the official judges for the first time. I had taken and passed the preliminary and first figure-eight tests back in Bountiful in front of three judges. For this competition, there would be a whole slew of judges, all lined up in their thick padded moon boots and fur coats, a sight not so unusual inside a Utah ice rink, with its cold winters and all, but in California? The mix of sunshine and pleasant weather outside, with people dressed for a pending blizzard inside, was certainly an odd sight.

For the figure-eights, I had an even more reserved outfit. I was dressed in my original black pants (from the Great Falls costume) and a little form-fitting black sweater. No sequins for the figure events. I thought it looked great, but I probably looked like an undertaker. Either way, as sharp as my mom and I thought I looked, the boy who won the figures was dressed smartly in "Polar Sport" gear—a brand of figure-skating warm-up suit that sent subliminal communication to the judges that these skaters were more "serious players." I decided then that I wouldn't skate figures again without the assistance of this sly appeal for higher marks.

I placed second out of four in the figure-eight competition. Getting the results from figures is a strange experience. While I knew how well (or poorly) I had skated, I could not possibly know how well (or poorly) my competitors had skated. Unlike freeskating, there was nothing to watch and criticize; no jumps, no spins, no falls, just lines across the ice that only the judges could see. So I essentially went out onto the warm-up, skated my figures, then, 30 minutes or so later, got my results—and, because they were not based on anything visible to the naked eye, they made no sense whatsoever.

Heading into the freeskate, my confidence was fairly stable. Second place was a good place to be, and I was only a few points from the lead. The freeskate is a program set to music, the portion of the event that is familiar to most people, as it is the portion that is watched on television. The freeskate routines are filled with difficult jumps, spins, and crowd-pleasing steps and movements.

During practice, I noticed that the other boys were doing the same jumps I was, with the exception of the fourth-place boy, who had not yet mastered any of his double jumps. However, the first and third Polar

Sport boys were doing the same moves; so, between us, the one who landed his jumps during the competition would be the winner. I also knew, from my Great Falls experience, that landing those jumps was the most important thing, so I was determined not to fall.

Skating once again to nondescript background music, for which I had absolutely no concern, I was now dressed in a red outfit, with a form-fitting vest adorned with a swath of gold sequins, looking very much like a little tin soldier or a Michael Jackson groupie. Perhaps my music was also military-inspired, like a march (just a guess). I truly have no idea. I do know, however, that I was in the ugliest homemade outfit of the group.

As I had planned, I made it through my program without a fall. I diligently concentrated on those jumps, careful to land them. However, just to make sure, I put my free foot down on the ice as I landed to guarantee I wouldn't fall. Well, I soon learned that putting your foot down to prevent a fall was just the same, in the minds of the judges, as falling in a heap—something I didn't know until my third-place finish was posted. I know now that any failure in a jump, no matter how small, earns no points toward the total score. My free-foot–assisted landings were the same as falls to the ice. Had the fourth-place boy not been such a disaster—skating like a deer on a frozen pond—I would have been dead last!

This placement was even harder to take (though I got my first medal, a bronze) because I felt like I lost because of something I did not know. No one ever told me anything about putting my foot down on the jumps. Simply "land the jumps!" is all I was told. How was I to know that it would affect my score?

Naturally, both my mom and I decided that my ignorance was the coach's fault! Surely it could not have been mine! Besides, why were we not clued in on these Polar Sport fashions? How could I show up to this big event with such a disadvantaged costume?

As far as we were concerned, we were paying out all this money and we were not learning the ins and outs necessary to win. I felt like a whipped dog. With our tails between our legs, we packed up and headed back to Salt Lake.

By the time we got to the Sacramento airport, we were already a self-made hysterical skating family—wanting to blame anyone and everyone, but primarily my poor coach Doree Ann (who, of course, bore less fault than any of us). We were ready to change coaches. I had my sights set on Kris Sherard, a coach from Bountiful whose skaters always seemed to win. However, fate would once again get in my way.

While in the airport waiting lounge, my mother struck up a conversation with a motley family also returning to Salt Lake from the same competition. She believed from their introduction that this family was Mormon Zion's branch of the famous Kennedy family tree. Charles, the self-proclaimed (yet never proven) relation to the well-known Kennedy clan of Massachusetts, along with his wife Rebecca (maiden name Zitting, a little green apple from a polygamist family tree), were the proud stage parents of a pair of rather talentless teenagers, Philip and Linda. The Kennedys were loners in the figure-skating world, yet, after a short dialogue, took my family under their wings. They detailed the reasons for their own kids' recent failure in Sacramento (Linda's hair wasn't appropriately pulled into a bun, according to one of the judges. Her hair!!??), and so we all commiserated together.

During their conversation, my mother mentioned her fears that I might be training with a sub-par coach. Charles Kennedy then launched into a diatribe over the local figure-skating political power and plots of the Central Pacific judging fiends Joan Burns, Barbara Meeks and Joyce Burden. We were all ears.

According to Kennedy, this "coven of witches," as he called them, schemed in the back rooms of the arenas and decided the placements of skaters before they even took to the ice. To me, it sounded like plain paranoia. To my mom and dad, it sounded furtive and clandestine at the same time. They were spellbound.

Every word that poured off Mr. Kennedy's tongue held them captive. His details of the secret behind-the-scenes judging were so fascinating and interesting! He warned that if I left Doree Ann for a new coach, it might not sit well with Ida—and her Central Pacific sisters were sure to find out. Though my skating was sure to improve, it was a dangerous move.

In Kennedy's eyes, Doree Ann just didn't have what it took to move a skater up the cutthroat ladder rungs of competitive figure-skating.

"There's no chance in hell any of these Utah kids will ever go anywhere!" he exclaimed. "All the kids that win, that are training for the Olympics, have been fine-tuned by the world's best celebrity coaches."

"A *celebrity* coach?" my mom asked, her eyes wide and spinning. "How do we get one of those?"

With that opening, Charles was off to the races on this next topic—celebrity coaches. He described several popular coaches with the skills and reputations necessary to get a skater beyond the confines of Utah politics and out into success on the Regional and Sectional levels. We had heard of Frank Carroll (coach of Linda Fratianne, 1980 Olympics), John Nicks (Tai Babilonia and Randy Gardner, 1980 Olympics), Carol Heiss (herself an Olympic gold medalist), Norma Saline (coach of Charlie Tickner, 1980 Olympics, and Barbara Roles (an Olympian like Carol), among others, but had never imagined ourselves at their caliber or with one of them as an option.

Lucky for us to have met these Kennedys, because—wouldn't you know it—they were coincidentally bringing their own celebrity coach into Salt Lake City directly across the border—Canadian champion Ian Knight (so we were told). We were impressed.

Although we didn't know an Ian from a Frank (he was, after all, a Canadian champion), we were star-struck from that minute on. However, there was a problem: According to Charles, Ian was coming to Salt Lake under an exclusive arrangement and contracted by him to teach only the Kennedy children. They had already signed the contract.

"Oh, but please," my mother begged.

"Well, I will have to bring it up with my lawyers." Charles cooed. "Why don't you call us next week? Let's get together for dinner and maybe we could work something out and your son could train alongside my kids."

That was the exact moment when Mr. Kennedy cast his net, pulled the line taut, and sunk the hook into my parents. From that moment on, anything a Kennedy said was good enough for Bruce and Sharol Jackson. Mr. Kennedy was a master at playing on our emotions—and one tough negotiator. Truth be known, he was looking for someone to share the cost of his "exclusive" contract. Charles Kennedy was a very wealthy man, and I was soon learning why. His negotiating skills were sharper than his last name, and his wallet as tight as the control he would soon have over this elite coach, Ian Knight, my parents, and, by proxy, my figure-skating career.

Part of Ian's strange exclusive contract was that he could only teach at Hygeia Iceland, an old ice rink with one wall open to the elements. This now-defunct ice rink was a 35-minute drive from our house. For me, it was another chance to get out of the backwoods every other day and into the big city for my lessons—but for my mom, it was becoming more than taxing. With three other children to transport to and from school, each with a host of sports and activities, the fact that she did this drive on my behalf for more than four months is miraculous. In Rancho Cordova, we had learned that skaters in California were driving two and three hours for practice; my mom and I considered ourselves lucky. My sisters and brother must have been confused by our use of this term, "lucky." The sacrifices skating families make, willingly and unwillingly, are beyond belief, and this would just be the beginning for mine.

Yet there was no discussion of going back to Doree Ann. Any discussion was self-confirming: "Jon's improving. We made the right decision." Well, technically, I was not improving at all, but we were too naïve about figure-skating to know that.

Every Monday, Wednesday, and Friday, my mom and I made that drive after school. I also still practiced at the rink in Bountiful before school, and again on Tuesdays and Thursdays after school. On the days I trained in Salt Lake, my mother spent her afternoons in a coffee shop gossiping and mudslinging with Rebecca Kennedy.

In the meantime, I spent my days on the ice with Linda and Philip. When Ian wasn't coaching one of us, he was coaching the other. I had never dreamed I would have so many private lessons, and I had no idea how my family was paying for it. This sacrifice, while making me feel somewhat guilty, inspired me to practice even harder.

I soon made friends with many of the other Hygeia Iceland skaters, but my primary friends were Linda and Philip, and our families became very close.

After months of us kids skating together, Rebecca eventually invited my family to join theirs for dinner to celebrate Linda's birthday at one of Salt Lake's finest restaurants. My mother was all too eager to accept. So the Jacksons joined the Kennedys for haute cuisine at the hottest shack in town, Le Caille at Quail Run. When we entered the restaurant, we saw the Kennedys in the waiting area and went over to greet them. Without saying a word to us, Charles threw his hand up in the air and gestured to the maitre d' that he was ready to be seated. Then laughing loudly, he shook each one of our hands, welcoming us to their little party.

We sat at a long table in the middle of the main dining room. Mr. Kennedy plopped himself at the head of the table and the rest of us scrambled to find seats as far away from him as we could. Mr. Kennedy was dressed in a threadbare suit and a dirty old hat, which he wore throughout the dinner. A heavyset man, he walked with a limp and was blind in one eye (though you would be hard-pressed to say which one it was). When he addressed you, he would sternly peer into your soul with his one good eye and raise his bushy eyebrows to the cadence of what you said.

Mr. Kennedy was always certain of what he wanted, and was never shy to ask. He barked pushy orders throughout the dinner at the overly-bosomed waitresses, often simply pointing to his empty water glass or holding an empty bread basket in the air until it was filled. When it was time for the waitresses to serve the salads, with a wave of his hand, he forced them to stand in silence next to our table, holding their serving trays up over their heads, while he muttered his blessing on the food.

I was sitting next to my older sister, doing my best not to break out in full laughter as Mr. Kennedy meandered through a prayer like none I had ever heard. When growing up, we had learned to pray privately or at least in silence, certainly never for show, and certainly not in restaurants. "O Lord!" he belted out, as the entire restaurant went silent and turned toward our table. He was sort of a Baron Munchausen character with a badly behaving Santa Claus act.

My family wasn't the typical Mormon family who ate all their meals at home; rather, we ate out more often than in, and, when dining at home, it was more likely to be takeout than home-made. Nonetheless, eating out for the Jacksons was certainly a different experience than eating out for the Kennedys. At La Caille, dining apparently involved pulling up to a building that more resembled a Swiss chalet than a restaurant, and being greeted by a valet driver who takes your car away while you are ushered into a beautifully decorated dining room with waitresses dressed in costumes rather than uniforms.

Le Caille was one of Salt Lake City's finest and most beautiful restaurants, with everything perfectly appointed, right down to the swans gliding across the pond outside the dining-room windows. "Figure-skating has taken me here!" my mind quickly noted, once again tabulating the benefits of this sport.

Our host was a man of enormous wealth, and he made you painfully aware of his money and power. While one could be sure of Mr. Kennedy's cash flow and his contacts, no one knew exactly what he did for a living. The rumors began to swirl around him, and he was never one to refute any of them. In fact, he may have even started the rumors himself. Once, when we were waiting for him on a visit to his house, he came into the room apologizing for the wait, "but I simply could not get Prince Zia off the phone." Prince Zia. Of Pakistan?

On another occasion, the ringing of a telephone interrupted us. Rebecca disappeared to answer it in another room; then, reappearing, announced "Charles, its Jacqueline. I told her you were with company, but she said it can't wait." Jacqueline? Jackie O?

Whether it was a concerted effort of smoke and mirrors, or part of the concocted mystery that is Charles Kennedy, I will never know, but it mesmerized my parents. The rumors in the ice rink had it that Charles had lived as a bachelor for nearly twenty years when he first came to Salt Lake City. During those twenty years, Mr. Kennedy had befriended a group of polygamists, and from this group he would buy his first and only wife, Rebecca. She was a teenager when she married him, the story goes, sold like livestock and forced by her church leaders to marry Charles. True or not, bought and sold, Rebecca was fiercely loyal to Charles and very much in love with him.

The closer our two families became, it seemed the more control Kennedy exhibited over my skating. The only person who felt more controlled than me was our elite celebrity coach, Ian Knight.

Ian was a handsome man in his late thirties when he came to town, but he didn't look a day over 29. He joked that hanging out in ice rinks all his life had preserved his youthful exterior. He raised cockatiels on the side for extra money. His hair, a ginger red, was cut in a close-cropped military crew. He was animated and flamboyant, some would say effeminate, behavior that was considered "gay acting" everywhere but Salt Lake, which hid its head in the sand about the entire topic of homosexuality. Ian's sexuality went widely unnoticed and seldom discussed. For the most part, everyone simply believed or pretended he was straight.

After a few months commuting to Hygeia Iceland, my mother drew the line. The drive was becoming too much for her. She begged Mr. Kennedy to allow Ian to travel to Bountiful to teach me. Reluctantly, Kennedy agreed to give this one inch, just this one time. However, off his short leash, that inch would soon become a mile, as Ian reveled in his newfound freedom.

IAN DIDN'T WEAR ice skates, ever. He simply marched around the ice in his snow boots, barking orders and directions. Most coaches wear skates and chase their skaters around the ice. Ian usually stayed near the sideboards, with a cup of coffee in one hand, and a wry sense of humor to help keep the rest of us warm.

When coaching my skating, Ian directed his first line of attack on my jumps. He didn't like them, disassembled them all, and put them back together incorporating an "old style" of jumping technique with the landing leg held in front—rather than "stepping up" onto the landing leg in mid-air. This technique was outdated, but Ian clung to it like an old friend, and the Kennedys, my parents, and I didn't know any better.

So there I was, jumping around like Sonja Henie with an errant free leg. I am sure that Ida Tateoka and the other judges were concerned over what was happening to my skating, but what could they say? Judges largely stay out of the coach's business, unless asked. Ian never asked; and, having fired Ida's daughter, my parents and I didn't dare ask either.

When I did learn to land the jumps with Ian's antique technique, he immediately put me to work on all my doubles—loops through axels—even though most skaters usually learn one new jump at a time. Because of this, my practices were littered with discouraging falls. When I was able to stand up, it was only because I had "cheated" the jump—a poor technique wherein some of the rotation is actually done on the ice once landed. I could soon land all my doubles in the "I'm still standing" sense, but the jumps were plain and simply under-rotated, old-fashioned, and of very poor quality. Not that I would figure that out until later.

With an arsenal of difficult (albeit poorly executed) jumps under my belt, Ian went about finding me a piece of music to skate to. He sought my input, but I honestly didn't care that much about music; it didn't make that much difference to me.

One night, while I was out playing with the neighbor kids, my mom came out running to get me. "Jon, come in, Ian's on the phone," she said.

Ian explained that he had found the perfect music and wanted to play it for me over the phone. He had already aired it for my mother, and she loved it. Though it was like listening to a transistor radio at the bottom of a swimming pool, I listened anyway and approved his choice, still not giving it much thought. I later asked my mom where Ian said he had found the music, but she had no idea. Ian never told her, and never told me. Nevertheless, we liked it well enough, and that was good enough for me.

As it turns out, Ian had been to a screening of a very controversial movie earlier that week, *Midnight Express* starring Brad Davis. Utah conservatives later banned the movie because of its sexual content—not a surprise in a state that also banned Culture Club, Prince, Miss Piggy, and Olivia Newton-John—but with Ian's connections to the gay underworld, at the time unknown to us, he had managed to find a screening of it.

Midnight Express is the true story of an imprisoned young man (Bill Hayes) caught attempting to leave Turkey with hashish in his possession. The tale unfolds with him locked in a brutal Turkish prison, experiencing all sorts of violence and forced sexual acts. In the end, the young man escapes when he rams a cruel guard into a coat hook as the guard prepares to rape him. The movie is extremely intense, though mild by today's standards, but in the late '70s it was considered extremely racy.

I didn't learn the origins of the musical score until years later. When I did, I got a good laugh off the naughty joke Ian had played on my parents and me—a person he clearly realized was a young gay man trapped in his own Turkish prison of self-denial.

I premiered my new "Midnight Express" program later that summer at a competition in Redwood City, California.

"I LIKED YOUR program!" Rudy Galindo, one of my young competitors, said.

"Gee, thanks." I replied. "I liked your jumps."

Rudy and I had just completed a practice at the Ice Palace, a run-down old dump in California just off the El Camino Real. While there were many skaters on the ice, Rudy Galindo was the only one from my group that I would be competing against in the following days. Of course, while practicing, I couldn't help but check out the competition—and things didn't look too good for me. How would I ever beat this talented little hotshot at this otherwise meaningless summer competition in July of 1979?

Rudy didn't miss a single jump the entire practice.

"I'm Rudy," he had said. "Your name is Jon? With no 'H'? How come?" The future U.S. Champion, then all of eight years old to my fifteen, asked an awful lot of questions.

"I don't know," I replied. "It's just how my parents decided to spell it." Just then, my mom came over to remind me to wipe off my blades. "Rudy, this is my mom," I introduced.

"Oh, hi. I'm Rudy." Then he added, "I thought you were Jon's coach." His assumption wasn't very surprising, as my mom was by the baseboards the entire practice. Ian Knight, my actual coach, was conspicuously absent at the practice.

When we had boarded our flight in Salt Lake City with the rest of the Utah skating contingency, Ian was a no-show. We had no choice but to go on without him. When we landed in California, my mom called Rebecca Kennedy. Ian had been in hot water with the Kennedys ever since his arrival in Salt Lake, and he was in trouble again.

"Rebecca, do you have any idea where Ian might be?" my mom asked.

The Kennedys hadn't traveled to Redwood City for this competition, as there were no other Pair Teams scheduled against whom they could compete. I knew from subtle comments I had overheard earlier in the

week that Ian was happy they wouldn't be coming along. I couldn't hear
Mrs. Kennedy's story unfold over the phone, but my mother's response
indicated it didn't look good for Ian.

"Why, what's happened?" my mother exclaimed. "Is he all right?" That was
usually her automatic reaction, typically assuming the worst had occurred.
She was anxious as she listened to Rebecca's detailed response.

"A DUI? He hit two girls in a crosswalk?! He's in jail? Oh, no! He's
going to miss Jon's competition!" my mom moaned.

Further explanation followed, and I was becoming disturbed
as well.

"What do you mean? He's not coming back to Utah? This doesn't have
anything to do with the 'problem' we discussed earlier, does it?"

As a former national champion, he must have been somewhat of a
minor celebrity in Canada, because he had a prima donna temperament
matching his affected and effeminate personality. Ian wasn't accustomed
to taking orders. He was finding it increasingly difficult to work under
the watchful and restrictive eye of Charles Kennedy, and he began
to act out his aggression over it. Over the months, Mr. Kennedy had
become increasingly interested in Ian's personal life, and he didn't like
what he saw.

The "problem" to which my mother referred to in code, knowing that
I was listening in on her conversation but not knowing I was an ace
code-breaker, was Ian's supposed homosexuality. If true, the Kennedys
would be having no more of Ian Knight. In addition, with a restriction
in his contract that prevented him from teaching anyone other than
the Kennedy children (except for me, his only other pupil at the time),
if they fired him, the Kennedys could run Ian out of town.

"But what about his engagement?" my mom said. It had recently
become known, even though there was no official announcement, that
Ian was getting married. "You wouldn't want to ruin his chances of getting married, would you?" Mom quickly came to Ian's defense, using a
charade that even she didn't believe, though, at the time, I had readily
bought into the idea of my coach's "wedding."

A few weeks earlier, at the peak of the Kennedys' grumbling about Ian's
rumored homosexuality, Kris Sherard—another skating instructor—
showed up at the ice arena to teach her students with a very noticeable

diamond ring on her finger. When asked about the ring, Kris was very coy, saying only "a friend gave it to me." It was no secret, though, that Kris Sherard and Ian had become very good friends.

Upon getting permission to teach me in Bountiful, Ian began spending more and more time there, and, soon, more and more time with Kris. Their friendship to us skaters looked more like a relationship we were used to seeing between two adults of the opposite sex.

While Kris was coy about the ring, she let one of her students—the local arena gossip—know that it was from Ian. Within minutes, all of us knew, or thought we knew, that Ian and Kris were in love.

The ring trick worked, at least on me—and, I thought, on my mom. I had heard rumors of Ian's homosexuality and of the trouble it was causing him with the Kennedys. I certainly didn't want to believe Ian was gay. My indoctrination included the belief that being gay was a terrible thing and that homosexuality was evil. At fifteen years old, my denial of Ian's sexuality fit nicely with the denial of my own.

Immediately, I relayed the good news of Ian and Kris's engagement to my mother, prompting her, of course, to call the Kennedys. Charles and Rebecca greeted the news with nothing but skepticism. My mother, of course, pushed the cold facts as she saw them. She didn't want Ian run out of town any more than I did. He was a wonderful man, and a great coach for me, and I was responding well to his instruction, even if he was a Canadian, and even though my jumps were last year's model. He was fast becoming my best friend, certainly the one person in my life, outside of my family, who I spent most of my time with.

We would later find out that in response to Ian and Kris's unannounced engagement, Mr. Kennedy hired a private investigator to follow Ian around. The investigator learned, over the course of a few weeks, that Ian was in fact gay, frequently visiting a Salt Lake gay bar. My mother wasn't privy to these facts until after we returned to Salt Lake from the California competition.

Nevertheless, in this moment, the all-important day of my competition, the reality of the situation was that my coach was in jail awaiting bail by either Kris Sherard or, worse, Charles Kennedy. At least he wasn't in Turkey!

It was no wonder then that Rudy thought my mother was my coach.

All during practice, she was sitting low in the stands, and then running rinkside to give encouragement and instruction, just like a coach would. The other mothers sat quietly, high in the bleachers, or gossiped over coffee in the lobby.

"No. My coach is Ian Knight. Have you heard of him?" I asked of Rudy. "He was a Canadian National Champion!" I said, parroting the exaggerations of Mr. Kennedy. I often bragged about this fact as if it were my own accomplishment.

"Ian who? He's Canadian?" Rudy quizzed. "Maybe you know my sister, Laura? She's going to be a champion," changing the subject while expressing a wide-eyed younger brotherly wish.

"No, I don't think I know her. You have a sister that skates too?" I replied. "Is she as good as you?" I regretted saying it as soon as the words came out of my mouth.

"Oh, she's much better than me!" Rudy replied. "So you think I'm good? I've been working on my jumps, but sometimes they're just not there."

About this time, my mom dragged me away from the conversation to go back to the hotel. "Well, I'll see ya later, Rudy. Good luck!" I said as we left.

"Good luck, Jon without an H," he responded.

On my way back to the hotel, my mom relayed to me some very good news. "Everyone is watching you skate. They are all talking about you and the way you skate your program." Mom was trying to be encouraging, and she knew that the thoughts of other people were good motivators for me, even though she was unsuccessfully trying to teach me, and my brother and sisters, not to care what other people thought.

She continued: "Mrs. Signorella thinks you're a breath of fresh air, a real talent with a natural feel for music. She loves your program and was thrilled when you practiced it twice so she could see it again."

"Who is Mrs. Signorella?" I replied.

"She owns the ice rink! And her daughter is a champion!" my mother responded, clearly impressed. Stella Signorella, the daughter, was a regional champion. Although a relatively minor accomplishment, it was very significant to someone who had never obtained a championship at all. Had my program really impressed Mrs. Signorella? Ian and I had spent so much time perfecting it.

For months, he had drilled me on rhythm and movement, how to move with the music, to really listen to the music and skate to it. To my annoyance, and to the annoyance of the other skaters in practice, Ian would stop my program as soon as he felt I wasn't listening to the music, and would make me start again, sometimes only five or ten seconds into the program. My lessons often ended without my getting through even half of the program. Ultimately, I caught on to the ideas Ian was teaching me, even though I felt ridiculous expressing them at first.

Working with Ian to develop this program felt to me like embarking on the creation of something unrelated to sport. He first made me listen to and understand the music—what it was trying to achieve emotionally. He showed me how the song slowly built and then came back down, before the climax, all while hiding its true meaning from me. We spent many practice sessions putting together movements that matched the music, something I had never done before. When I worked with Ian, I learned to enjoy playing with the music and the movement with him.

The beginning of the *Midnight Express* theme song started with three extended, electronic-sounding booms, followed by the upbeat disco thump of the movie's theme. My skating started with three prolonged positions, one outward for the first boom, one inward for the second boom, and the third outward again, in perfect time with the music. Then, when the disco started, I was out of the blocks. I began by skating backward for momentum around the end of the rink, then turning forward, striking my arms opposite each other in a full disco pump to the beat of the music as I made my way down the ice into the corner to execute a very poor example of a double lutz. That was the problem. No matter how "refreshing" Mrs. Signorella, or anyone else, considered my music and my skating, my jumping technique was still very poor: old-fashioned technique meets under-rotation.

Yet Ian insisted that my jumps were coming along, and that my musicality would someday make the difference for me.

When Ian got sprung from jail, he finally showed up in Redwood City. I was already on the ice for my last practice before the actual competition, skating once again with Rudy Galindo, the little jumping phenom from San Jose.

"Why can't I jump like that?" I said to Ian, after giving him about ten minutes of silent treatment. I mean really, just whom did he think he was getting drunk when he was supposed to be teaching me in Redwood City?

"You will, you can, Jon. You just need more practice," Ian replied. "Rudy has been skating for years. You will get it. Now go do your program. I want to see what everyone is talking about."

Oh, I guess you ran into my mom, I thought skeptically as I skated over to put on my music.

Ultimately, my disco program and matching silky beige outfit, with its dark-brown-roped and low-cut V-neck (fabulous, by the way—though I'm still not sure how my mom got it past my dad), didn't come close to matching the effortless jumps of Rudy Galindo. Similarly, my mother's plea to the Kennedys wasn't enough to save Ian.

Within weeks of returning home, Ian, with his vintage silver Corvette, cockatiels, and green-card engagement, was on the fast rail out of town. That his homosexuality was the cause of his demise wasn't lost on me.

It was a sad day for me when Ian left. He had become my best friend, a fellow artist in the creation of a magnificent program. I still couldn't jump, but I didn't know any better, so I certainly wasn't blaming Ian. With Ian's departure, I commiserated with Kris Sherard, who had also lost a good friend, and began my campaign to get her as my new coach.

Even so, with Ian gone, the Kennedys' stronghold grip on my family tightened. I soon learned that the recently defected Protopopovs, the famous Russian Olympic champions who had fled Soviet rule for a new life in the United States, would be coming to town to coach Philip, Linda, and me for a couple of weeks while Charles searched around for a new celebrity coach.

AFTER A COUPLE of weeks of secrets and hushed conversations, the Jacksons and Kennedys set out for another family outing. The Protopopovs had just arrived in Salt Lake, and Charles had secretly arranged two hours of late-night private ice at the Bountiful ice rink. Kennedy also managed to have the rink shut down tighter than Fort Knox.

My dad, my mom, and I, with sisters and brother in tow, arrived a little after the practice started. Charles and Rebecca were already there, this time with their extended relations that made the rink look like a Brigham Young family reunion. Numerous broods had come together to witness this event; screeching children were everywhere and hanging all over Mr. Kennedy and begging for the candy he kept in his pocket, which he ever so often handed out for their affection.

Despite the Kennedy spectacle, my eyes focused on the ice. Ludmila Belousova and Oleg Protopopov, the defected husband-and-wife pair team from Russia—and the originators of the famous "death spiral"— were standing before us, about to perform.

Just weeks earlier, Charles had phoned my mom, indicating that the Protopopovs were defecting from Russia. He told her to write this confidential information down, put it in an envelope, then go to the post office and have it time-stamped so she could someday say she knew about this momentous event in figure-skating before it happened. How did he know? Who knows? Whatever connections he had that gave him the information were the same connections that had brought the Protopopovs to town, and they would soon be teaching us to skate!

I watched as the Protopopovs effortlessly glided across the ice—no, *floated* across the ice. It was like living in a dream. I had never seen anything so mesmerizing. They never spoke to one another, seemingly reading each other's minds instead while skating.

It amazed me how they spent much of the practice doing stroking and footwork—easily more than half. The simple movement across the ice, in various positions, used a variety of edges and turns, gaining speed, slowing down, and all so lightly and silently. (I wouldn't see this type of movement on the ice again until much later, and then by only one skater, Michelle Kwan—her movement on the ice, her edge quality so perfect. The ice becomes a whole with her—masterfully.) It is so difficult to do, yet the Protopopovs made it look so easy. These Russian pair skaters had "it." Where did *it* come from? The Russian dynasty in pairs had begun with this team, and now it was apparent why.

I couldn't sleep when I went to bed that night. I simply couldn't believe that anyone could skate like that. It was like nothing I had ever seen. This is what Ian had been saying—the effortless movement, the ease of glide! How was I ever going to learn this?

The Protopopovs stayed in Salt Lake for just under two weeks. They mostly practiced, or gave pair lessons to Linda and Philip. I also got a lesson or two from them during their stay, though I was so completely star-struck that I don't remember taking advantage of the situation to learn anything they might have instructed me.

The week after they left, I met my next "celebrity" coach. His name was Gilbert Sosa, a freeskating specialist from the Midwest. He brought a few skaters with him. It must have been part of his negotiations with the Kennedys—negotiations Charles must have lost. It wasn't like Mr. Kennedy to share his coaches.

Gilbert's imported students consisted of a young, buxom blonde girl from Albuquerque named Tara who competed at the senior level, and two junior-level men, both a few years older than me. Martin from Austin, Texas, was fairly good, yet nondescript. Chris, the other boy, from Naperville, Illinois, wasn't quite as good as Martin—but he was drop-dead gorgeous! I nearly fainted when I met him. Perfect dark-brown hair, combed back in the feathered look of the day. He had a flawlessly chiseled face and a warm, inviting smile that could melt raw steel. I was in love the moment I met him.

When Gilbert gave me lessons, often he would have Martin demonstrate a jump or spin for me. I would usually ask if Chris could show me too! Any interaction with him made me want to dance like Snoopy around the rink. I was always thinking up little presents I could bring him, or questions I could ask him about himself to get him to have a discussion with me. I could hardly keep myself composed whenever he would talk to me, but he didn't seem to mind.

Gilbert began helping me by fixing my jumps, explaining to me that the Sonja Henie hop had gone out years ago! He was a true technician, and in a very short time corrected my technique. Soon, I was actually fully rotating my jumps. However, when he later tried to change my music, I put my foot down! My program was a masterpiece by Ian and me. I wasn't changing my program. Now, if Chris had asked me to change it, and mentioned how utterly ridiculous I looked doing my homo-disco routine, I would have changed it in a Tigerbeat. I would have even skated to "Turkey in the Straw" if Chris had said so. But sadly, Gilbert didn't have that kind of control over me.

The regional championships were soon approaching in Belmont, California, and Gilbert wasn't looking for a fight over the music. He could always tell the other coaches that it wasn't his choice, or that it was too late for him to change it. No matter what he told them, I still loved skating to it!

My memories of Belmont are mostly a blur. I do remember getting fourth place in figures, but I have no memory of actually skating them. Sitting fourth of seven skaters, I was smack in the middle of the pack. A good freeskate would move me into third and earn me a medal; a bad skate would drop me back with the bottom feeders.

Luckily, I had a great freeskate. Though my technique was adequate, it was not as good as the other boys. I knew my program was better, and my expression superb, but would it win the day? Gilbert wasn't confident.

A fellow skater's father, Jack Searle, wrote down the scores as the judges read their marks. Then, after about five minutes of analysis, he presented me with the bad news. I would be fifth in the free skating. It was going to be very close—only the first-place boy had strong scores. For second through fifth, it was very close, but in the archaic manner in which figure skating placements were determined, through broken ties and total majorities, according to his figures, I wound up with the short end of the fifth stick.

I wasn't happy; my heart sank into my stomach. How could my figure placement help? I wanted so badly to hang on to my fourth-place finish. Maybe, somehow, Jack had made a mistake. It was possible! Maybe he wrote down the wrong numbers.

When the accountants posted the scoresheet, I nearly passed out. I looked again to be sure and then ran to the restroom, locking myself in a stall, and began crying like a baby. Soon, my mom was yelling into the restroom through the door at me.

"Jon, get out here! They are calling you for the pictures! What are you doing in there? Hurry up and get out here!" she called.

Somehow, in the mystical, magical way of individual scoring, the combining of each score for each figure, and the freeskate, for each judge, and then figuring out an entire new result, unrelated to either of the results in the figures or the freeskating, I had landed in second place!

Jack was correct; I was fifth in the freeskate. The marks were all close—the judges in disagreement—but when all the scores were combined, there I was in second place! It was too good to be true. I would later find myself working with Jack Searle in the accounting room at a competition held in Bountiful. I was intrigued by the scoring system for my sport, and determined to get to the bottom of its whacky math.

Back at the hotel that night, I studied the result sheet for hours. Would someone discover the certain mistake? Would they take my medal away? There were no answers to questions only time could answer, but maybe I really deserved it.

I returned home with a big grin on my face and my first title: the Central Pacific Intermediate Men's silver medalist! It was too good to be true. That skate resulted in a silver medal and a berth in the Sectional Championships held in Great Falls the following month. This time in a brand-new, double-surface arena, with no chain-link fence!

On arrival in Great Falls, I immediately felt a difference. This was a "Sectional" championship. It was a privilege to be there, and the coaches and skaters acted that way. Their clothes were nicer, their manners were more refined, and the competition itself had a sense of order.

I knew I had "made it" the next morning when, being seated for breakfast, I looked over to see Tai Babilonia, the famous National and World pair champion, eating with her mother. It was like spying on a movie star! Later in the week, after skating good figure-eights and an acceptable freeskate, I finished near the bottom of the pack.

One night, one of the skaters told me that there was a mafia family in the rink in Great Falls to watch their daughter skater. Immediately, I wanted to know who. Unfortunately, this particular canary was only going to sing so much. It was the mafia, after all. He wasn't going to go there. He left me to my own devices to figure it out, saying only that she had a "very Italian-sounding name."

Back in the privacy of my hotel room, I shared this tidbit of intrigue with my mother—who, upon hearing it, went ballistic! "An Italian-sounding name?!" she cried. "That is so stereotypical! Who told you this? That is the most ridiculous thing I've ever heard." When I tried to tell her that it was true, she looked at me as if I was crazy, and told me never to repeat such a racist comment ever, ever again.

Later, as she was looking through the program of skaters a bit too carefully, I asked her what she was doing. She answered, "Oh, just seeing if there are any skaters here from Las Vegas." Right, Mom, so much for stereotypes!

When we returned, confident from mingling with those lucky enough to have qualified for the Sectional championships, and a few who went on to the Nationals, we would soon learn that our luck had ran out.

Gilbert Sosa was too good to be true. In less than three months, he had turned me around as a skater. Less than three weeks later, he was gone. He went home, as did his students, for Christmas break, and never returned. Kennedy had run another celebrity coach out of town, though I would never learn why.

Back at the rink following New Year's, no Gilbert, no Chris, no Martin. I never got to say good-bye to Gilbert, nor did I get to say good-bye to Chris. I was doubly crushed.

A few months later, I would watch on television the Winter Olympics in Lake Placid, New York, as Linda Fratianne was denied the gold medal by a German, Anett Potzsch. Anett had won the figures, but her freeskating was dark in comparison to the Hollywood flash and smile of America's charismatic Fratianne. *How could it be?*, I wondered. More of that funny math, I supposed. How unfair, though. It was crystal-clear who the best skater was. The best skater received the silver medal, and did so very graciously, proud to have won a medal in front of her home crowd.

I also watched, with the rest of America, as Tai Babilonia and Randy Gardner, defending World Champions, withdrew because of injury. I felt immediately the sacrifices they and their families had made to get them on that ice in Lake Placid, as I was experiencing them myself. To have it all come to down to one injury, at the wrong time, was more than I could stomach. I was sick for days.

> *Soviets Irina Rodnina, with her husband Aleksandr Zaitsev, march to the now-familiar beat of the Russian drums, claiming the Pairs gold medal at the 1980 Lake Placid Winter games. It is her third Olympic Gold Medal, his second, and the fifth consecutive for the Soviet Union.*

Beads, Buttons, and Bedazzlers— My Life in Sequins

HE ICE SURFACE of the Cottonwood Heights Ice Arena on Salt Lake City's southeastern foothills is possibly one of the best in the world. The arena sports huge glass windows on its southern end that perfectly frame the picturesque Wasatch Mountains in the background. Because of these beautiful windows, the natural lighting is excellent, in complete contrast to the fluorescent lighting used in most arenas, and with those mountains! It is truly spectacular.

The first time I skated there, the ice rink was brand-new and part of a large recreational complex with indoor and outdoor pools, including a diving pool with boards and high platforms, racquetball courts, and the like. Because of its newness, in taking advantage of the latest ice-rink technology, it was a warmer arena, both on the ice and for the spectators up in the stands; its only disadvantage to me was that it was a 45-minute drive from my house.

I was skating there one day, to take a lesson from the Kennedys' new coach, Philip Grout. I say the Kennedys' coach, because my parents and I had already decided that enough was enough. I needed stability in my training. Besides, the 35-minute commute to Hygeia Iceland had been bad enough. The commute to the Cottonwood facility would take an extra 10 minutes, and that was excuse enough to stray from the Kennedys' grip.

Finally, my dream to take lessons from Kris Sherard, Ian Knight's best friend, would be realized.

As a courtesy to the Kennedys, my mother agreed to drive me down a few times to try out the new rink and their new coach. "Maybe you will change your mind," the Kennedys must have said, likely furious that the marionettes had worked loose from their strings.

I went through the motions of this "try-out" for about a week, but my heart was back in Bountiful with Kris. Kris and I had something in common: Both of us had been taken in by Ian, each in our own way, and the Kennedys had taken him from us. I would never forgive them for that, and neither would Kris. For that matter, I wouldn't figure Ian would either—at least not before his death a few years later.

Admittedly, skating on the Cottonwood ice surface was a thrill. I've gone back to that rink several times since, usually as a judge or referee, and I still enjoy the feeling of openness from those gargantuan glass walls of mountain-filled beauty. Anyway, at the time, they were tempting, but not tempting enough. While I remained friendly with Linda and Philip, my involvement with their parents would be very limited once I began taking lessons from their bedeviled Kris Sherard.

I later found out that when Kris had first come to Utah, the Kennedys had tried to hire her, again on an exclusive basis, to coach Linda and Philip. Mr. Kennedy offered to pay her very handsomely for such a contract. She had her own "celebrity" status, a contemporary of Dorothy Hamill, who she had bested on occasion. The deal fell through when Kris learned that in addition to teaching the children on the ice, her duties would also include dressing them in the morning, getting them to school, and then to the ice rink. She would be the Kennedys' own figure-skating nanny. In all likelihood, Charles might have had his good eye out for a second wife and wanted to give Kris a test drive, but that's another story.

The coach/skater relationship between Kris and me was exactly what I had dreamed of right from the beginning. I had wanted for so long to take lessons from her, and finally to be doing so was extra motivation for me to work harder. The growth spurt I was going through at about that time gave my back and legs the strength they needed to perfect my doubles and my double-jump combinations. In no time, Kris had me skating faster with stronger jumps.

One of the first things Kris did was to scrap my "Midnight Express" disco program. She instead selected music from the movie *Mutiny on the Bounty*. It was much stronger and much more masculine than any music I had skated to previously. Kris assembled my program differently than Ian did. First, we laid out the jumps and spins, then we added in footwork, connecting steps, and finally arm movements. Thanks to Ian, I had a sense of why figure skating was performed to music—I realized it wasn't simply background noise, but rather part of the whole performance, something to be skated to and interpreted.

Though my new program was put together from a technical standpoint, I still attempted to interpret the music, and Kris encouraged my personal development on that part of the program. With Kris, however, it was all business: speed across the ice with strong jumps. The men didn't win figure-skating with amazing choreography; according to her, they won with their strength.

I had once again entered the Big Sky Championships and was going to try out my new program there; but, for financial reasons and to my disappointment, I had to withdraw a few weeks before the event. Skating was becoming very, very costly for my family at this point, and my dad decided that we needed to be more careful of how we spent our money. I was disappointed not to be going, and very depressed on the day the other Utah skaters were leaving for the airport.

I made one last attempt to go.

"Mom, I just counted all the change in my jar" (a large glass water jug that I had purchased at a garage sale for 50 cents a few years before). All the quarters, dimes, nickels, and pennies I collected from my side ventures ended up in this jar. "I think I have enough to pay for the plane tickets if you and Dad could spring for the hotel."

My mom smiled, and, just like that, we packed and were off to the airport. My willingness to part with even a plugged nickel made my mother realize just how important this competition was to me and how upset I was to be missing it.

We stopped by the ice rink, quickly grabbed my skates, and headed to the airport. The slick new blue costume we had started assembling wasn't yet finished. Having withdrawn, there was no rush to get it done. My tan disco blouse and chocolate brown trousers would get one last run.

My dad, though not happy with this sudden change of events, drove us to the airport, but was silent the whole way. Never ones to accommodate a buzz-kill, my mom and I couldn't stop talking. "Oh, it's going to be so much fun! Kris is going to be so surprised! I can't wait to see the look on her face! What will Janet and Kathy say?" seemingly repeated eighty times.

My dad dropped us at the curb, slowing down barely enough to allow us to jump out of the car without getting hurt, and then sped off without a good-bye. Undaunted, we hustled to the airline counter where, after a wait in line, we ran into a roadblock we could not pass.

"I'm sorry; it's too late to buy a ticket on the flight to Great Falls. The plane leaves in 45 minutes. You're too late." said the unapologetic and unhelpful service agent on the other side of the counter.

Despite my spontaneous outburst of tears, and my mother's ever-increasing loss of patience with first the ticket agent, and then her supervisor, we could not manage our way onto that plane. "Mutiny on the Bounty" would have to wait until summer.

THAT FOLLOWING JUNE, I turned 16 and finally received a driver's license. My dad gave me his collectible '65 Mustang convertible. It was painted powder blue, a color that even I would have liked to change. But according to my father and his fellow avid car collectors, the original color on a classic car should not be changed. What was he thinking? My dad gave his figure-skating son a baby-blue convertible Mustang? Sometimes, even he was oblivious! To make matters worse, I immediately applied for a vanity license plate that read "I Skate." All through high school, I drove that car with its baby-blue irony and license plate to match.

The car was important for a number of reasons. My schedule in the summer had intensified, and there was no way I could have done it without wheels. I was working at "Utah's Fun Spot," an amusement park called Lagoon. I loved that job, and Lagoon loved me. I made employee of the month and set the all-time high skee-ball record. I worked there until late at night and then trained early in the morning, right up until I needed to be at Lagoon again. I literally got off the ice, changed into my white shorts and light blue Lagoon logo T-shirt, and sped to work. I didn't even have time to shower. It must have been miserable to work with me and my dried-on sweat that summer. I didn't have a clue about deodorant—and a number of other things, for that matter.

I learned years later that many of my fellow employees were getting to second base, and further, in the Haunted House after closing—and, worse, that some of the boys were getting beyond second base with other boys! I say worse, only because I missed out on it. I was too preoccupied with skating to notice most anything.

Mid-summer, I skated at the Copper Cup, Bountiful's summer competition, in an event called "Open Men," which essentially combined all the boys from the different levels into one event. Still, there were only three of us. Many times, I would enter a competition only to find that no one else had entered against me. There were simply too few boys in the sport at the time. Skating against someone from a lower level was no challenge for me, and skating against someone from a higher level was no fun. Still, the practice of skating in front of an audience in costume made it worthwhile.

My costume for "Mutiny on the Bounty" was navy blue with very simple, yet elegant, beadwork down the sleeves and around the neck. It was by far the best-looking costume I ever wore. It showed off the improvements I had made, as did the simple music of *Mutiny on the Bounty*. I skated great, but finished second to Michael Stephenson—from Great Falls, Montana, no less—who opened his program with a perfectly executed axel, double toe-loop, double toe-loop combination. I was impressed!

With little or no pressure on me during that competition, I asked Jack Searle, the parent who had calculated the results for me from the stands in Belmont earlier that year, if he needed any help in the accounting room. Jack was the chief accountant for the competition. He said he could use my help, probably figuring I would be good at making copies, or sorting paper clips, not knowing that I was practically ready to sit for the CPA exam, having already worked my dad's books.

I was eager to learn all about this system of accounting, but most importantly its flaws. It must have flaws, I reasoned: If I could place fourth in the figures, fifth in the freestyle, and still end up second, something had to be wrong! What about Linda Fratianne? How could that happen?

I threw myself into learning the complex, mysterious, smoke-from-the-chimney-of-the-Sistine-we-have-the-results calculation system. The scoring itself is simple and universally understood: two scores, one for technique, and one for style. Both rated on a scale of six, with the famous 6.0 representing perfection. However, a skater gets, from those simple scores, marks from anywhere from five to nine judges, who then determine a consensus majority winner; but the subsequent placement is too complicated to explain here. Let's just say it's not easy to follow for a reason. Complex is exactly how figure-skating officials want it. There is power in information. Those who understand it have the power, and those who don't are at their mercy. The coaches, the skaters, and certainly the parents are at the mercy of the officials. It's a 6.0 for them. Perfect!

HAVING FURTHER MASTERED accounting, I was right back at practice. While I enjoyed working in the accounting room, I would have preferred to compete against boys at my own level. Kris soon found the answer: The Colorado Championships in Colorado Springs had a reputation for attracting a number of boys. So off we went to Colorado.

Because the opportunity to skate against other boys was so rare, Kris wanted me to enter more than just the freeskating event. Colorado also had a "Compulsory Moves" event, which, like the Short Program the seniors and juniors were skating, had some required elements, though it wasn't skated to music. I could use my same costume and I didn't need a new program.

When I first saw the entries for the championships, written on something mailed to us about a week before the event, I was excited to see that I would be skating against seven other boys! My excitement turned to dread, however, when I saw one of the names: Eddie Shipstad. Everyone in skating knew of the Shipstad family, famous for "Shipstad's and Johnson's Ice Follies." Great! I would be taking on one of skating's most famous family monarchies!

"Oh, Jon, you worry too much," Kris assured me at practice. "He's no different than you."

"Yeah? Well, I bet he was born with figure skates on. He's probably skated his whole life!" I responded. How could I ever compete with these people? At this point, I'd been skating for less than three years. My late start was always going to be a problem, and I didn't need a little hotshot to remind me of it.

When I arrived at practice in Colorado, my uncertainties only got worse.

"Jon, I'd like you to meet Eddie's coach, a friend of mine," Kris began. "Barbara, this is Jon Jackson. Jon, this is Barbara Roles." Barbara Roles! Oh, my God! She's the Olympian! She was the celebrity coach that Mr. Kennedy had told us about!

Of course, I couldn't say much more than "Hello," with my tongue knotting and head spinning.

Well, it makes sense, I thought; of course a skating sovereign like Eddie Shipstad would have a celebrity coach! Why wouldn't he? How am I ever going to compete with this combination?

I had as good a practice as I could under the circumstances. I could hardly concentrate, and when I did, it seemed that little Eddie was popping a perfect jump, one after the other.

Kris could tell I was rattled, and did what she could to calm me down. Just before the warm-up for the compulsory moves, as I was eliminating my lunch in the bathroom, in what was becoming a nervous ritual, I just told myself that it didn't matter. I was used to losing, so who cares? Just go out there and land those great big new jumps.

I not only landed the jumps, I landed myself in first place!

I don't think I had ever been more excited in my whole life. That exhilaration, and what must have been the first suggestion of confidence in my jumps, led me to skate one of my best free programs as well. However, Eddie would get his due in the freeskating, finishing second to my third. He was a master of not only the jumps, but also the footwork, the spins, the connecting steps—I was simply outclassed. He was a well-oiled machine. Still, I beat him in the compulsory moves—and, more importantly, I skated a perfect freeskate program. The summer ended on a high note.

∞

THE SUMMER SEASON ended at Lagoon. I had loved working there, the hustle and bustle, the crowds, the entertainment, and the whole atmosphere of fun. However, what I would miss most was the bills in my wallet and the change in my pocket. While I could go back to the boring grind in Dad's office, I realized I liked working around other people.

Luckily, a well-timed job opened up at the ice rink. John Miller, the rink manager, knew that I had spent the last two summers working at Lagoon, so he approached me about taking the job. It was part-time, three evenings a week and Saturdays. My responsibilities would include passing out rental skates, monitoring the public sessions, filling in at the snack bar, cleaning, and so on. It was the bottom-rung job at the Recreation Center, yet I was thrilled to climb on!

My junior year of high school started out on the right foot. I had signed up for all the honors classes at school, AP history (a class I took with seniors, just to keep me sharp), and I enrolled once again in debate. As a sophomore, I had teamed up with an enterprising little gal, a year older than me, and together we had held our own against the more experienced teams.

I was still excelling at school, with nearly straight A's, and winning debate tournaments, and this year I focused on an individual speech event called "Extemporaneous Speaking," or Extemp in debate vernacular. Extemp involved putting together a five- to seven-minute speech within 30 minutes, and then successfully delivering it to a judge or group of judges. Generally, they provided us with three topics to choose from, and then we raced through a stack of *Time*, *Newsweek*, and *U.S. News and World Report* magazines quickly to master a subject, or at least get to a level where we would speak intelligently about it.

Because of the pressure I had already experienced with skating, my nerves rarely got the best of me in Extemp. Speaking in front of one or maybe three other people was nothing compared to skating in front of hundreds, so I didn't have a problem jumping right up and making a collected delivery.

The pursuit of debate took me to various high schools around the state, usually on weekends, as well as to Arizona State University in

February for an interstate high-school debating junket. I had missed the event as a sophomore; I did not intend to miss it as a junior.

My success at these tournaments had the regrettable consequence of leading to my father's congratulations, and his subsequent attempts to get me to quit skating altogether to focus more on my schoolwork. I was already making straight A's; how much more focus did he think I needed? Balance, Dad!

He persisted. "You are so talented at debate. You're doing so well in school, isn't it time to give up skating?" my father would greet my every success. I think he even once offered to buy me a new car if I quit. I should have gotten the new car for successfully doing it all, not for downsizing!

The bribes parents offer to get their kids to give up the sport are notorious, and with good reason. I was making $3.25 per hour, working part-time, yet spending over $10,000 per year in pursuit of this go-nowhere sport. That's how my dad saw it, anyway. I was going nowhere.

He'd say things like, "What are you going to do when you are successful at this, Jon? Join the 'Circus on Ice?'"

"Holidays on Ice!" I would correct, and "No, I'm still planning on going to college." But I was really thinking, "Oh, those fabulous costumes! Touring the country!" I knew that would not be an option once I finished high school.

Early in the school year, my mother and I had joined a carpool with another skating family, the Blackburns, to attend the Central Regional Pacific Championships, a 14-hour drive away in Fresno, California. I would compete at the Novice level, one level higher than last year's Intermediate, and two levels below the Olympic-level Seniors.

Despite having competed several times, my pre-competition jitters never went away; that nagging feeling of nerves and breathlessness when an athlete gets a case of the butterflies. Butterflies—such an agreeable name for such an uneasy feeling!

I never had any butterflies in my stomach. Not even so much as a moth. My stomach always felt more like the spin cycle on our old Speed Queen with a wet, lopsided sleeping bag inside. The churning would start hours before I would ever take to the ice in a competition—gurgling, bubbling, and fuming, with unimaginable nausea. Without fail, during the drive to the rink between our house or hotel, my face would turn shades of green, my lips blue, and eyes all red. My mouth was so dry that it felt like I had been chewing gym socks through the night. Nothing could calm me. I would try to read signs or billboards along the way to get my mind off my misery. Naturally, we would happen upon a sign for a Roto-Rooter or a Long John Silver's fish hut, and my stomach would do a somersault. By the time we got to the rink, I was faint and weak-kneed, my head absolutely empty. I never had my wits about me before competition time, and at this important event in California, that inattentiveness almost ended my skating season.

THE JOURNEY TO Fresno was a long jaunt for anyone, and, as usual, I was sick to my stomach the entire trip. The event itself would last a couple of days; on the first day, despite my upset biology, I scored a very respectable second-place finish in the Novice Men's school figure-eights.

The next day, the Blackburns, my mother, and I left our hotel together for the rink.

When we arrived at the ice rink, I grabbed my little blue-beaded costume—which, even on a hanger, looked like it would fit a doll—and my gym bag and jumped out of the car. My mother joined me as we walked into the Fresno ice arena, while the Blackburns headed to a mall.

I assumed that my mom had grabbed my skates. She assumed I had. Once inside, and about to get myself ready, I suddenly realized that my skates had been left in the trunk of the Blackburns' car.

I had no idea what to do. My face started to sweat and my mouth went dry. Frantically, I searched for Kris, my coach, who immediately tracked down the event referee, Bill Munns, to let him know what had happened.

During a second-place finish in school figures the day before, I had impressed Mr. Munns with my manners when making my selection for the patches of ice to skate my figures on. I politely satisfied his every request, and patiently waited for his permission before starting. Most skaters obliviously head to their starting positions as soon as their names are called. Linda Leaver, a judge on my event from Salt Lake City, tracked down my mother afterward to let her know that the judges were talking about me, and her report was favorable.

When Kris found Mr. Munns, her pleas to give me extra time fell upon sympathetic ears. Munns agreed to delay the competition until the Blackburns returned.

"Can he do that?" I asked Kris.

"Jon, if the judges like you, they can do anything they want!" As it would later turn out, that was the understatement of my life in figure-skating.

In case Munns changed his mind, my mother began frantically calling all the Fresno malls, looking for the Blackburns. No luck. I was sched-uled to skate some fifteen or twenty minutes into the event after the mandatory five-minute warm-up. Had the competition started on time, I would already have missed my warm-up, and if the Blackburns were even a few minutes late, I would miss my freeskate altogether. What do you say to a mall operator when you call to find three people shopping in a mall? "Hey, do you think you can help me find my friends? They look like Ken and Barbie, with a daughter to match. Their name is Blackburn. Would you check, please? Yes, operator. I'll hold." Click.

Eventually, the tardy Blackburns arrived 45 minutes after my event was originally scheduled to begin. However, that was no problem for Munns or the other judges. They had already made up their minds about me. Mr. Munns even allowed me plenty of time to get my skates on and loosen up a little bit before officially starting the warm-up. I skated around the five-minute warm-up with my head in a completely different place. For the second time in my skating career, I experienced the feeling of self-confidence, this time more so than the first. I would later learn that true confidence feels the same as false confidence.

I came off the warm-up composed and unruffled, but by the time my name was called, some four skaters later, I was already in the men's room, bent over the toilet, orally relieving myself of the tension that had once again built up inside me.

From inside the stall I heard the announcer decree, "And now, repre-senting the Utah Figure Skating Club, Jon Jackson!" Wiping my mouth off with tissue paper, I hustled out of the men's room and out onto the ice. On the way, my bewildered coach was both calling for me while simultaneously giving me last-minute advice and reminders, none of which I heard in my oblivious state.

As I reached my starting position, a sense of calm again washed over me. "They like me," I again remembered. "Mutiny on the Bounty" began, its cadence slowly building to an intense and powerful rhythm. I started my movements, opening with a double flip jump. The next thing I knew, I was finishing the program. I knew I hadn't fallen because there was no snow on my knees, but I couldn't remember executing any of the jumps or spins, or even interpreting the music. I had skated perfectly. Confidence is a wonderful thing. Confidence would bring me my first gold medal, and the title of Novice Men's Regional Champion. I had finally arrived!

In addition to the gold medal, another thing of significance came about from my taking lessons from Kris Sherard. Because I now had an "acceptable" coach in the eyes of local Utah figure-skating politics, the Utah judges now spoke to me again. They came up to me to give me compliments after I skated, or to offer advice, to explain why I might have failed a test, or to congratulate me for passing. I had previously received this kind of behavior from Ida when I was taking lessons from Doree Ann. During the entire time I was with the Kennedys, I didn't have that interaction. Not one judge uttered a single word to me, at least not that I can remember. Ida, I could understand. Blood is thicker than water, and we had spurned her daughter. Nevertheless, why the change with the other judges? Those judges, including Ida, were once again free with their remarks and their friendship once I was taking from Kris and out of the Kennedy stronghold.

A person's actions do speak louder than words. I am good friends with many of these judges now, and I am certain that they believed they had treated the Kennedy family no differently than any other skater. However, I experienced their actions along with Linda and Philip; there were no words of encouragement from them. I know that their behavior was not kind at that time, though I've come to realize that they did not intentionally mean any harm by it. Nonetheless, I made a vow back then that I would never treat another skater poorly simply because I didn't like his or her coach, or his or her parents.

As a sixteen-year-old young man with a cute little car and a driver's license, my family's influence was slowly slipping out of focus. Working at the recreation center, going to debate meets, training before and after school, and still somehow finding the time to get my homework done, I had less and less contact with my family.

∞

BOTH MY PARENTS came with me to Culver City, California, just outside of Los Angeles, for the Pacific Coast Sectional Championships about one month after the Fresno competition. Southern California is a great place to be in late November. The weather is still warm, while the snow is already falling back in Salt Lake.

My dad spent his days touring the various building projects in the Los Angeles and Orange County areas, scoping out the latest and greatest in planned family developments. My mom and I spent our days at practice hanging out with the other skating families.

I still couldn't land my double axel. I could do all the other jumps with my eyes closed and in combination too, but the double axel was like a card trick with no sleight of hand. The other competitors were split 50–50. The ones who could do it were also trying low-level triples, but without much success. The others, like me, would be putting it into our programs even though we knew we would likely fall on it.

In the compulsory figures, I was doing quite well. There were four figures to skate, the last being the "loop." The loop is a small figure-eight, about one third the size of the other figure-eights, with a difficult, accelerating 360-degree oval at the top of each of the two circles that comprise the figure-eight. They are easier for some skaters, more difficult for others. I was known as a skater who had good loops.

After each figure-eight was skated, the results were posted showing where each skater stood in relation to the others going into the next figure. I was always superstitious about looking at these "tentative" results, because I did not want to jinx a good result or get down over a bad placement when my focus needed to be on the next figure. On this occasion, one of the other skaters, unaware that I did not want to know, passed me and said, "Congratulations, Jon, you're in second place!"

Three figures over, and I was in second! Oh, my gosh!

So, for the first time I went over and checked out the ordinal sheet. I knew my way around the mysterious and complex scoring system by now, and looking over the ordinals, my second place looked pretty solid. I even had a first place or two.

This was fantastic! I had just skated a beautiful double-3 serpentine figure-eight, and it was quite impressive to me, so it was nice to see that it impressed the judges as well. My back loops were excellent. I looked forward to showing the judges that the double-3 was no fluke.

Proudly, I skated to my starting position. I looked at the referee for permission to start. After his nod, something must have gone wrong as I went on to lay down the crummiest outside back loop I had skated in my life! Jinx! My overly analytical mind played games with my body, sending all the wrong signals and mixed up impulses as I skated that loop.

I fell from second to fifth place and, in doing so, planted myself in the sucky first warm-up group for the free skate. My chances of earning a spot to the National Championships disappeared the moment I looked at that result sheet.

"Mutiny on the Bounty" would play one last time, and I would wear my blue-beaded costume one last time. I skated nicely up through the double-loop jump, when, unexpectedly, my blade slipped out from under me on the takeoff. Splat!

That was probably the worst way to fall, mostly because it takes you so much by surprise. Every skater gets used to falling on the landing of a jump—but on the takeoff? This was the first time it ever happened to me, and it happened right in front of the judges. Strategically, my double loop is staged front and center as one of my best jumps, and I went crashing right into the baseboards at their feet.

Though the physical recovery happened quickly, my mental recovery was not so fast. I have absolutely no memory of skating the rest of the program. However, because of an ever-meddling Charles Kennedy, who secretly videotaped the performance, I know that I went on to make another poor attempt at a double axel, landing short of the rotation and on two feet, when a one-footed landing might have earned me the points I needed. I completed the rest of the program perfectly, but the look on my face revealed my lack of any thought: No one was home.

∞

BACK AT THE Bountiful ice rink, despite my dreadful showing at "Coasts," I began to focus on the next season. Pacific Coasts were going to be held on my home ice in Bountiful the next year, and I was determined to make it. Rather than hold back in Novice for one more year, a common practice among most skaters, I chose to move on to the Junior level. While the competition would be much more difficult, it wouldn't pose a problem if I could improve over the next year at the same rate I had improved the last.

I immediately went to work on passing my sixth figure-eight test, a process of learning a whole new set of figure-eights, and then my Junior freeskate. Once the pressures of the season were gone, my double axel came along immediately, and it soon became one of my more consistent jumps.

I then set out to master a triple. I knew I would need one, if not two, to be competitive that year at the junior level, so I began working simultaneously on the triple toe-loop and the triple salchow. Right away, I knew that these difficult triple jumps were not going to be mastered as easily as the doubles.

During the winter of my junior year, I got on a bus with my fellow debate-team members and headed to Arizona State University. On this trip, my repressed sexuality would become a difficult devil to denounce. On skating trips, I was accustomed to traveling with girls—all girls. Even the fathers, on most occasions, stayed home. On this trip, however, I was traveling with both boys and girls, about 30 kids, with only two or three chaperones.

There were four boys or girls assigned to a room with two beds per room, so we would all be sharing. You have to be kidding, I thought. Sleep with a boy? This could be Heaven, or this could be Hell.

I had skipped gym class since the 9th grade. My parents and I had convinced the school officials that my fitness requirements were being met on the ice, and that I could use the extra hour for practice. So every day I left school an hour earlier than everyone else and went straight to the rink.

Because of this, I was not accustomed to even being in a locker room with a gazillion naked adolescent boys; but in the motel room, my three roommates were apparently more than comfortable with this, and were naked when they got up, got showered, goofed off, chased each other around, and wrestled, before finally putting on their slightly too-small suits and crooked neckties.

I was completely aghast. No, shocked! I had no idea that this typical male, adolescent behavior was going on and I had been missing it! Seeing them in action really for the first time was so exciting for me! I felt completely out of place, yet right at home at the same time.

I did what I could to hide my "discomfort," and went about getting into my fancy duds without disrupting their horseplay or my line of vision, and most importantly, without drawing attention to myself. I didn't want to get ready too quickly and miss the show. For God's sake, they were in the shower, three at a time, soaping, splashing, joking, frolicking, pinching, and sudsing! I wasn't going anywhere. "Girls Gone Wild" has nothing on unsupervised teenage boys.

But what did all this mean? It was actually quite easy to rationalize in my mind. My whole life, I didn't ever fit the typical male roles—but I always so desperately wanted to. I was interested in these three naked, adolescent schoolmates because I wanted to be one of them. So comfortable in their sexuality, and in their bodies, that they held no inhibitions about their interactions with each other. For them, they were each the same: sexually aroused by women, but entertained by men.

They enjoyed intimate encounters with girls, and the company of other young men. I enjoyed the company of girls, and intimate encounters with . . . uh . . . well, I don't think I knew that yet—or did I? No, certainly it couldn't be that. I enjoyed the company of girls, *and* the company of young men. I wasn't intimate with anyone. I just wasn't good at being in the company of young men, yet. There it is! I just wanted to be like them. I admired them so that I could model my life after them—nothing sexual about it.

"I'm not gay," I told myself. I can't be gay! I'm not like that. No, I simply like to look at good-looking men, and boy do I, but it's only because I'm looking for the perfect person to emulate.

I would have bought any rationalization at that point, at any price. It was all too much information in that Arizona hotel room, information that I was not yet ready to assimilate—particularly in the mornings, then again before bedtime, or any time in the hotel room for that matter.

The students who did poorly in the debate meet had plenty of time left over after the initial rounds to spend at the hotel swimming pool. My desire to be with the "rowdies" in the pool could not overcome my overachieving ambition, so while they carried on in the water, I fought my way into some semifinal or final round.

Ah, finally, the ride home on the school bus—back with both girls and boys, when the boys could go back to acting like jerks and the girls acting like they thought it was funny.

One of the chaperones, an eccentric woman, brought a deck of tarot cards with her on the bus and read them for some of the students. When it was my turn to have my cards read, she asked me to mix them up and place them in a red velvet cover. After I did so, she carefully removed the cards, and began turning several of them over, one by one, placing them in some mystical pattern. Once she had about ten or so cards in place, she silently studied them.

All at once, she looked up, peered straight into my eyes, and said, "You are too young; I can't read these cards for you. You are not ready."

Suddenly, you could have heard a pin drop. The other students watching went silent, but then perked up. "What is it?" "Is he going to be murdered?" What could this tarot-card reader possibly know about the most bookish, overachieving do-gooder on the bus?

If there was one way to pique a classmate's interest in me, something that was beforehand not apparent, this tarot-card reader found it without even trying. She repeated, "I can't tell you," staring straight into my eyes—and at that moment I knew what it was.

I went back to my seat and thought about it the entire night. She knew. She didn't say it was terrible, she just said she couldn't tell me. I was too young. Then why did she know? Why did I know? Moreover, how was I going to change it? She had to be mistaken. She doesn't know that I like boys only because I want to be like them. If I could explain it to her, she would understand; but did I dare mention my theory to her? Maybe she will forget.

Now, halfway through my junior year of high school, I knew the truth, though I was desperately trying to suppress it. I was gay. I was a great

student, but I was gay. I was an accomplished debater, but I was gay. I was
a figure-skater who wore sequined outfits, but of course I was gay!

I WENT BACK to Great Falls in late March, this time to try out my
new program at the Junior level.

To my surprise, there were several men entered, both from the United
States and from Canada. During practice, sizing up the group, I realized
that I had the confidence to win. I was as good as, if not better than,
every boy at the practice. My double axel was solid, and my weak triple
salchow was on par with the other boys.

Because it appeared to both Kris and I that I had a chance to win, we
decided to put my focus on two good, solid, clean double axels. I would
not do the triple, instead replacing it with a double, when I performed
my program for the judges. In other words, we decided that the triple
salchow would "come out" of the program.

But I couldn't stop myself from wondering, when would I? "Come
out," that is. Do people really do that, and if so, why, and to whom? I
had so much to learn, and so much yet to understand. Why did Ian
have to go? I could think of a million questions to ask him at this point,
and not one of them had anything to do with double toe-loops or triple
salchows.

On the day of the skate, Michael Slipchuk, a Canadian, would execute
the same strategy Kris and I had planned. His triples came out, leaving
him with two solid double axels.

Kris informed me of the development, as I had not been watching
his skate, and it confirmed that our strategy was correct. I would start
with a mindless double lutz (I could do it with my eyes closed, or so I
thought) and follow it with two "three turns" to regain speed and my
first double axel.

When the music started, I was thinking only of those two double
axels, primarily on the first. I must have had my eyes closed on the
double lutz, thinking ahead to the double axel, because suddenly I found
myself "splat" on the ice. The fall was so unexpected that it stunned me.
Without thinking (again), I got up, did one "back three" to gain some

speed, and threw myself into the all-important double axel. Thud! It turned out to be a double fall.

Well, realizing immediately that I had just blown this competition, again, and within the first 30 seconds, I went about the rest of my program without a care in the world. Oddly, when I skated without a care in the world, I really could skate!

My jumps were all solid, the second double axel executed to perfection. I didn't even hear the roar of the Utah skaters when I hit it. What did it matter at this point? I finished the program, literally a perfect program, the two falls notwithstanding, and got off the ice in tears. I had blown it big-time.

"Wow that was quite a skate!" Kris stated. How nice of her to try to make me feel better.

"I fell on a double lutz!" I screamed at her.

"But everything else was so perfect! The double axel was fantastic," she replied calmly.

"You didn't see me fall flat on my butt?" I sassed back.

My little smart mouth got me a very stern lecture from Kris Sherard. She grabbed me by the back of my costume and dragged me to the changing room, and gave it to me good, yelling at me for being such a baby and too much of a perfectionist. "You're a great skater and you don't even know it!"

Sheepishly, I agreed to apologize for my behavior, but only if I wasn't right about finishing in last place.

Thanks to some wacky accounting, I had a healthy helping of crow to eat as I accepted the bronze medal for a third-place finish. Some of the judges had even given me second place. I guess the judges, like Kris, looked beyond my fall on the double axel to see the skating I had done well. I liked the bronze medal, but hated to be wrong.

IN THE SPRING of that year, the Utah Figure Skating Club held its annual ice show. I had skated in these dreadful "shows" in the past. They were really more of a recital, put together for family and friends to come see a year's worth of progress in the skaters.

This year, Doree Ann Tateoka, my first skating coach, was the director and choreographer of the show; in this role, she sparkled like a diamond.

The title of the show was "Broadway on Ice," and it would turn out to be the best ice show ever presented in Bountiful and in the whole state of Utah. It might have been the best amateur show in the country. It was that good. People still talk about that one ice show, and Doree Ann deserves the credit, because it wasn't the skaters, it was her.

We had been skating in terrible ice shows for years, and would continue our streak once again the following year, but in the spring of 1981, "Broadway on Ice" made every one of us feel like figure skating stars.

Doree Ann chose me for a solo. My regional title would look impressive in the program (Novice Men's Champion!), and at this point I was one of the better skaters in the club. The music Doree Ann selected was "I Can Do That," from the Broadway musical *A Chorus Line*.

The finale of the show was set to the song "One," also from *A Chorus Line*. For this number, the entire cast wore silver lamé tuxedos with matching hats. The number started with a difficult pinwheel maneuver, and finished with a spectacular kick-line down the ice. It was a perfect ending to a perfect show. It brought the crowd to its feet. It was also a perfect ending to Doree Ann's figure skating career. Out with a high kick, she had proven herself a master and decided to hang up her skates for good. She headed straight to Park City, where she managed the affairs of Mr. and Mrs. Debbie Fields while they traveled the world selling high-priced cookies.

IN THE LATER part of the summer, I traveled to Sun Valley, Idaho to compete again at the Junior level. I persuaded my parents to let me go up two weeks early to live in the dorms with my friend Lesliegh Anderson, who had spent the summer training there. She had arranged for me to have some odd job in the afternoon, to help pay for the costs of the trip and to make up for the loss of income I would have from being away from my job at the recreation center.

The two weeks I spent with Lesliegh and several of her new friends was a complete blast. I don't think we made it to our patch practices even once! We did manage to make it to the freeskate a few times—most of the time exhausted from lack of sleep. There was a lot of drinking going on during those two weeks, and I suspected marijuana use too.

The first night of drinking, I told them that they were breaking the law. They broke out laughing. Was I serious? I quickly covered and laughed with them, but after that they knew not to let the Utah saint see them smoking pot!

I was still pretty strait-laced, so I did not take part in the drinking games, though I sure enjoyed being around the partiers. The pot—well, if it was there, they were all very careful to keep it out of my sight, but I really wouldn't have known the difference, even if Cheech Marin and Tommy Chong had pulled up in a van and handed it to them.

Lesliegh also introduced me to her new boyfriend, Doug. She had fallen for him early in the summer, and when I met this hunky guy, so did I! He was a total babe! Because Lesliegh and I were such inseparable friends, I was also going to be spending a lot of time with Doug, and I could hardly wait.

My "dates" with Doug included two weeks of partying, lying out by the pool, missing practices, renting bicycles, wading the golf-course streams, looking for errant golf balls, eating too much at Louie's, the legendary Ketchum pizza parlor, sneaking into the ice shows, and sleeping on the most uncomfortable cot in the world. Oh, yeah, Lesliegh was there too.

At the end of it all, I needed to compete against three other very good and very accomplished skaters. Three that likely hadn't spent the previous two weeks slacking off.

During the competition, I landed the opening double lutz (this time I actually gave it some thought), but then fell out of my double axel.

"Shit!" I said, way too loudly. Oops.

Did the entire audience just hear me say "Shit"?

"Did Jon Jackson just say 'Shit'?" the entire audience must have thought to themselves.

The judges coolly glanced at each other, as if to say, "Did you hear what I heard? Ummhmm. Okay, just wanted to make sure."

I don't remember the rest of the program. All I could think about was how I had used bad language and bad judgment at probably the most inopportune time. The judges penalized me for it, dropping me into fourth place.

When I got off the ice, Kris had a big smile on her face. She pulled me close to her and whispered, "Did you just say 'shit'?"

When she saw the mortified look of confirmation on my face, she broke out laughing. I couldn't help but laugh as well. This was the relationship that she and I had developed, coach and skater.

Kris knew me better than anyone else and was determined to make a good skater out of me, but was thrilled to see me coming out of my shell. The coach/skater relationship is the most important key to a successful skater. The coach is the last person to speak to you before you take the ice. They spend hours with you beforehand, preparing you psychologically, and weeks and years beforehand preparing you physically.

In the seconds before you start your program, right when your mind needs to be in the right place, they say a few words and send you out to your starting position. How well they know how their skater's minds work, how well they choose those words, and how much trust the skater places in them, has made the difference in Olympic gold medal performances. Compare for instance Debi Thomas and Tara Lipinski.

Who knows what Debi's coach said to her just before she took the ice as the overwhelming favorite in Calgary? Whatever he said, it wasn't the right thing. Debi was lucky to hang on for bronze.

Consider Tara Lipinski at the 1998 Olympic Games in Nagano. She was to skate after the overwhelming favorite, Michelle Kwan. "She held back. It's yours if you want it. You can do it!" or something similar must have been the last words of Richard Callahan and Megan Faulkner, her trusted coaches. Whatever they said, it did the trick. Those coaches pulled out of Tara the performance of her life, and an upset that shocked the world.

The whole coach/skater relationship dynamic is just that important. After my series of coaching changes, I was finally developing a positive dynamic with Kris Sherard and learning the value in it. Unfortunately, I would also soon learn that once damaged, this relationship can never be repaired.

∞

I STARTED MY senior year of high school still working part-time at the recreation center. I had a number of Advanced Placement classes, having earned college credit for my junior-year history class. I was determined to get more college credit this year.

My guidance counselor breached the subject of college early in the year: "So, it looks like you are preparing for college."

I responded yes, even though it wasn't a question.

"Do you want to go to BYU [Brigham Young University] or the U?" "The U" referred to the University of Utah.

I really hadn't given this decision much thought up to this point. I knew that my grandparents and parents had gone to the U. I also knew that I didn't want to go to a Mormon school, although, having never touched alcohol, a cigarette, or even a sweater-and-bra-covered breast, I was at least as morally qualified as most of its applicants.

"The U." I responded.

"Okay. Here's the application. You also qualify for a Presidential Scholarship. Fill both of these forms out and bring them back with a check for the registration, and we will submit them for you with the other applications," she said, as if she were instructing me on how to make a fruit salad.

In less than two minutes, this woman had decided the direction of my scholarship. Though I had the grades and the test scores (a perfect 36 on the math portion of the ACT) and could have gone to just about any college in the country, those options were never presented to me by my part-time high school guidance counselor. She just assumed everyone in Utah would want to go to a Utah school.

My parents never questioned the decision to attend the U. They must have been flat out of money after four years of shelling out the dough for my skating. Scholarship to the U? Enough said!

The Central Pacific Championships were held in Berkeley, California. The host hotel was the stately and historic Claremont Inn, which sat on a hill above the UC Berkeley campus. Just dropping down the hill in the morning for a croissant and Coke was a thrilling experience for me. I had never even tried a croissant, let alone one fresh from the ovens of a quaint French bakery. Luckily, they also sold Coca-Cola on tap, the breakfast of Mormon champions, usually found in a Big Gulp cup or a Maverick Gas Station super-sized plastic mug. My morning ritual usually included a Big Gulp and a doughnut, followed by practice. In Berkeley, it was a large Coke and a croissant. I was moving up!

At the Junior level, I was outclassed. My double axels were solid, and I could land my triple salchow, though inconsistently. The other four boys had solid triple salchows and toe loops and were working on triple loops, flips, and lutzes. Additionally, they all had been at the Junior level for two or three years.

My only hope was to do well in the figure-eights, though they had at least two more years of practicing these figures than I did. My usually admired figure-eights did not compare to the expert tracings of these experienced young men. I finished fifth of five.

While I was waiting to be called to the ice for the short program, another competitor named Craig Henderson struck up a casual conversation. Sensing my nerves, and trying to make me feel better, he said "Hey, not to worry, not one of us placed well our first year of Juniors. You need to give it two or three years." It was nice of him to say, I guess. If his comment was meant to psych me out, it didn't work. I skated perfectly, landing both my double flip, double toe-loop combination, and a beautiful double axel, but I finished fifth of five again.

The long program was more of the same. Great skate—missed the triple salchow, solid on both double axels, and again, a solid fifth. Did anyone feel sorry for me? Nope. They were too busy feeling sorry for the person who finished fourth, who had held back in Juniors for a third year but still did not qualify for the Sectional championships. No matter how bad I felt, there was always someone worse off.

They held the closing banquet in the ballroom of the Claremont Hotel. I was starting to socialize with kids my own age from California and had a great time with many of them. As one might expect, the conversations eventually turned to sex.

"Did you hear that that pretty judge from Utah is sleeping with Eric Tanko,* the U.S. Figure Skating muckety-muck?" I hadn't. I was shocked.

"What are you so shocked about? How do you think she got her

---

* Not his real name.

judging appointments? Besides, you knew he was sleeping with Damon's mother all last year, didn't you?"

"No, I didn't."

Soon, gossip of previous years filled my ears, as these skaters found a newbie with whom to rehash all their sordid stories. A certain local female coach was sleeping with the influential Slick Hardwood* from the East Coast, this parent was sleeping with that Eric Tanko, this married male judge slept with that married male coach, that coach is sleeping with that skater, and so on.

It was too unbelievable for this goody-two-shoes, but I took it all in nonetheless. And surprisingly, I can't think of one liaison mentioned that night that did not later turn out to be generally considered true.

Much later, as a judge, I would hear about or see circumstantial evidence of these types of affairs firsthand, all the time. The most interesting side of the sport is behind the scenes, I was learning, and I hadn't seen much of it yet.

Returning home, I had come to accept my fifth placement. My parents did not feel the same way. The worst part of this fifth-of-five finish was that my parents again "blamed the coach," an ability they had mastered all too well under the tutelage of Charles Kennedy.

When we returned home, my mother contacted Russell Sessions, a young man who had recently "turned pro" and was teaching at the ice rink. Russell was a local boy, who had some modest success on the professional circuit, winning a silver medal at the World Professional Championships in Jaca, Spain.

I remember this for two reasons only: First, the local club officials wouldn't let Russell skate in our annual ice show. "No professionals allowed" was the official reason, even though professionals had skated in the show in the past. The real reason: they were jealous of his success. They didn't want Russell stealing the limelight from an amateur guest star they had flown in to headline the show.

Local residents recognized hometown hero Russell Sessions, and surely the club would have sold more tickets and made more money. Yet club officials would not allow him to skate. It would have been his

---

* Not his real name.

last chance to skate for his home town, and the green-with-envy skating busybodies squashed his chances. I learned early on the distrust and resentment between volunteer skating officials, most of whom had never set blade to ice, and those skaters who made money from their trade, the "professionals."

The second reason I remember Russell's title was, not surprisingly, his costume! It had tiny racing lights charged by a small battery pack that was sewn in. It was like having the Las Vegas Glitter Gulch stitched right into his outfit. The Golden Nugget on ice! It was really too much . . . and I loved it!

Nonetheless, Russell's fine taste in over-the-top, outrageously fashionable costumes would not overcome my desire still to have Kris as my coach. It fell on me to tell Kris, by the way, and she fought very hard to keep me. I knew she was right, but I had my marching orders, and I stuck to them, bawling the whole time.

After two or three weeks of my finding fault with everything Russell was trying to teach me, my mother got a phone call. She wasn't happy when she hung up.

"Russell tells me you're misbehaving. He says if you don't start cooperating and treating him better, he won't teach you any more. If he drops you, then what? Who do you think is going to teach you?" my mother scolded.

"Kris," I responded. "When can I call her?" This was not the answer she wanted to hear, nor the "kind-of-sass" she expected from me, and she promptly sent smarty-pants to his room.

I was back with Kris by the week's end, but the tight bond that we had developed, the ever-important and ever-so-delicate coach/skater relationship, was forever broken. Fixing it was impossible.

I was soon to graduate from high school. I was accepted at the only college I applied to, the University of Utah, and my mind slowly gravitated to a path better suited to my talents. I spent the entire winter and spring as a teacher's assistant for the debate coach, G. R. Burningham, as did a classmate, Todd Leishman. Todd and I were the stars of the debate team, so good old G. R. let us get away with murder that spring. We spent nearly every hour not in G. R.'s classroom, but at the local Arctic Circle, guzzling coffee (we were pretty high on ourselves for breaking that Mormon rule!), discussing politics, planning for college, and enjoying each other's intellect.

I skated in the annual ice show, this time to the Beach Boys' classic "California Girls." Somehow, my mother consented to the most outrageously inappropriate costume ever worn by a figure-skater (make that a male figure-skater). It was a sleeveless navy blue midriff-cut body shirt adorned with bangles and beads of every color. I looked like a fruitcake. I could have been wearing the mop that cleaned up an all-night New Year's Eve party. My tiny chemise was an unholy mating of pre-Flashdance fashion and a post-mugged hooker. I wouldn't have been allowed in a gay refugee camp.

I skated out in mere tatters of clothing, barely a spaghetti-strap tank top really, with sequined bedazzlers catching even the dimmest of light. Way, way too much glitter for a soon-to-be eighteen-year-old boy, and I loved every tacky, flashy inch, err, centimeter of it.

I didn't sign up for summer ice that spring, and, with graduation from high school and a change in my daily routine, I let the skating go. It was, in the end, anti-climactic. After the change of coaches, my heart just wasn't in figure-skating any more, and it was apparent that Kris's wasn't either. Certainly she sensed that my mind was elsewhere in our practices. As an experienced coach, she saw it coming long before I did, and I think she did everything she could to make my transition out of the competitive arena of ice-skating as easy as possible.

I graduated from high school with high honors, was named Sterling Scholar for Social Sciences (and would later learn that I was missed out on the more important General Sterling Scholar because of the horrible, homophobic, ignorant principal—something confided to me years later by my debate coach). My focus had changed away from the ice and on to academics.

> At the 1964 Winter Olympic games, the Russian dynasty in Pairs figure skating found its genesis in Ludmila Belousova and Oleg Protopopov, who debuted a dangerous and never-performed move, the aptly named "death spiral." They would earn their second Olympic gold medal four years later, and it would also be their last. It would not be the last for mother Russia.

You Put Your Left Foot In

S MY FRESHMAN quarter at the University of Utah approached, I needed to generate some cash, not just burn through it. Having just turned 18, I spent the majority of the summer working again at the Bountiful Recreation Center. In order to augment my working hours, I registered for an advanced lifesaving course and certified as a lifeguard. I worked between 50 and 60 hours a week, about half the time on the ice-rink side of the complex, the other half out by the pool.

Many of the other lifeguards were former competitive high-school swimmers, so most already knew each other from school or swimming meets, and had become close friends, doing things together after work. It wasn't long before they started including me in their after-hours fun.

On Friday and Saturday nights, and sometimes during the week, the ex-swimmers invited me to join their "reindeer games." I soon learned I was a fish out of water with this exciting new aquatic group, because most of their parties centered on drinking like fish. This was something I did not do, more because I considered myself an athlete, Mormon

upbringing or not. So at first, I avoided their parties. The last thing I
needed to add was "laugh and call him names" to my already awkward
socialization. Poor Rudolph!

Eventually I made up my mind that I was missing all the fun, so I
started saying yes. I wound up having a great time even though I wasn't
drinking. I did feel a bit awkward at first, and even more so when certain
established relations started pairing off and disappearing into the back
rooms. That was my cue to split. While I could handle the alcohol, I
wasn't about to find myself in the awkward position of having to swat
away a teenage girl I had little or no interest in.

When fall classes began at the U, it wasn't long before I actually fell
in love with a girl for the first time. She was in my freshman English
class and I spotted her the moment I walked in on the first day. Her
name was Victoria, or Vic for short. She had a great smile and a sweet
disposition, and I was immediately drawn to her.

Vic was a sporty petite girl with short dark hair, preppy clothes, a
string of pearls, and Vuarnet sunglasses hanging around her neck. It
was love at first sight, although it took me about three weeks to get up
the nerve to ask her out, and once I did, it took me another five dates
before I dared to kiss her.

On the night when I would finally make a go at this kiss, I met Vic
out with her friend Teresa at Gepetto's, a student hangout and pizza
parlor. I was already seated when the two girls arrived. Teresa was carrying a pillowcase-covered bundle tucked under her arm. She looked
like a member of the Symbionese Liberation Army with her secret bag
of what could have been live rounds or a case of grenades. As she slid
into the booth, without explanation she pushed the bundle under the
table. After a little small talk, we placed our order, and suddenly out
popped a can of beer from Teresa's bed linens. Teresa passed a cold one
to Vic, and then offered me one.

I was completely stunned and horrified, and the look on my face
must have said so, because Teresa started to apologize starting with a
sheepish "Oops."

"Ah, don't worry, Teresa, he doesn't care if we drink, do you, Jon?"
Vic said to Teresa.

"Uh, well, normally no, I don't care, but in a restaurant? And you brought your own? Aren't you afraid of getting caught?" I replied, thinking that Salt Lake Vice might storm the place any moment.

Vic giggled as Teresa brought the beer back out and popped one open. "No. We don't worry about that, Jon. We drink here all the time. Everyone does. What are they going to do?" Teresa prodded.

After dinner (surely narrowly missing arrest), we took two cars to the west side of town to attend a punk rock concert being held in an industrial park. When we arrived, it was apparent that there would be a lot more drinking, as Teresa swung the pillowcase again over her head and screeched a bloodcurdling "Woooooo!" at us when she got out of her car. The concert—and I use that term very loosely—nearly deafened us all, as we seemed to taunt death or dismemberment by some of the city's more criminally aware.

Once inside, everyone around me continued to get sloshed. For the life of me, I couldn't see the point. If this is how people acted when they got lit, it held absolutely no appeal to me. If they could only see themselves on camera, I imagined many of them would stop themselves and ask a friend, "Do I really act that stupid?"

When we were leaving, I opened the car door for Vic and after I closed it, I heard the now wasted Teresa yell out from behind me, "Kiss her!" as I was getting into my side of the car. So, even though my date was a drunken sticky mess, I took her home and before she went into the house, I kissed her.

After all that worrying, all that nervousness, it just happened, and it happened for about five or six minutes! Tongue tangling and tonsil hockey! Then I said goodnight, and I left. Just like that.

On the drive back to Bountiful, my mind splintered. "Well, that's it. It was nothing. It was nothing? Oh, no! It was nothing! Where were the fireworks promised in the movies and television shows like *Love, American Style?* Why didn't I 'feel' anything?" I asked myself.

The disappointing realization that nothing magical happened to me when kissing a beautiful girl made me wonder once again if I would ever be physically attracted to girls at all.

Then I had another paralyzing thought, "What if she could tell?"

∞

VIC AND I continued to date throughout the fall, doing our best to end each date with an obligatory make-out. However, if I felt Vic wanted to go further—more than a tongue wagging—I would just take off, making up some excuse why I needed to get home.

In the meantime, I found myself surrounded by beautiful young men at school, but I was doing everything I could not to notice them. Sometimes I just couldn't help myself. Sometimes I daydreamed and boy-watched in the Union Building, rationalizing that I was trying to pick out the exact person I "wanted to be just like." The rationalization was the same as before, but I was starting to enjoy myself much more. I hadn't stopped to realize that in morphing myself into 50 different guys every hour, I was never actually grasping who I really was.

In the winter, I took Vic out for some ice-skating in Bountiful. I introduced her to my family and skating friends, and was satisfied with the looks of approval and thumbs-up received from them all.

"Thank goodness. I knew he was straight!" I hoped they were all thinking.

One person who wasn't buying into me was Vic's father. I later learned that he said after meeting me, "Vic, he's gayer than a picnic basket!" If I had known that, I would have been devastated. At least there were no comparisons to Liberace.

Winter quarter, Vic signed up for Economics, not because she had an interest in the subject, but because I would be in the class with her. It was fun having a class together; someone to cover me if I couldn't make class and to discuss class topics with.

Over the Easter break, Vic went on vacation with her family to Hawaii. When she returned, I simply stopped calling her. Our relationship ended without any discussion, without any fight, no exchange of harsh words. It was just over.

Worse, I stopped going to class. I saw her across the auditorium when I had to show up for the final, but I didn't speak to her. I was very embarrassed by my actions, but, at this point, I didn't know what to say. It was easier to just avoid the issue and move on.

When the spring quarter rolled around, I was careful to avoid the Union Building at times when I believed Vic might be around, but otherwise went about my business as usual. I continued working many hours at the Rec Center.

When all the skaters left once again for the Big Sky Championships, my longing to skate resurfaced. I genuinely missed the travel and the camaraderie that went along with being a competitive skater.

Shortly after the skaters returned, a younger skater named Barbara Howard approached me about skating again, this time as an ice dancer. She had done well in the "solo dance" competition, but was not going to go anywhere without a partner.

The great Torvil and Dean, British and Olympic Champions, had popularized ice dancing. Who could ever forget their famous Bolero free-dance routine at the 1984 Olympics? Ice dance is performed entirely without jumps. It relies strictly on movement, intricate footwork, and interpretation of the music. Admittedly its challenge intrigued me.

I thought about it a long time and initially said I was not interested. Eventually, because of her persistence and her offer to pay for all the lessons, she persuaded me to try out ice dancing.

We would be taking lessons from Kent Weigle, a former National Dance Champion, whose comfort with his sexuality only seemed to aggravate mine. I had taken lessons from him years earlier, and left him because I didn't appreciate his unkind but honest words. He said I wasn't going to make it in singles, given my age, and that I should focus on ice dance. Here I was, just a few years later, not having made it in singles, and now pursuing ice dance.

Barbara and I spent most of the summer practicing when we could. There was not much ice time available exclusively for ice dance, a few hours Monday night, and maybe an hour on Saturdays. So, on the other days, we would practice during public sessions, which worked out well during the summer months, because most of the public was busy with outdoor sports.

At the end of the summer, we traveled to Sun Valley to compete. It was just like old times, with one exception. I had turned 19 that previous June, and the drinking age in Idaho just happened to be 19. I was already easing up a bit on my stuffiness, so in Sun Valley I had lunch with some of the non-Mormon parents of the Utah skaters and ordered a strawberry daiquiri on the veranda of the world famous Sun Valley Lodge. I suddenly found out why all my classmates in college were drinking. Wow!

We skated. We won. I did not go to Sun Valley for the competition, however. I hooked up with some of my former singles competitors who were still skating, and together we went out on the town. Scott Williams, Scott Kurtilla, and Rick Verberg either were still competing or in Sun Valley skating in its infamous Saturday Night Ice Show.

We didn't have dinner until after their performance. Now that I think about it, we didn't really have dinner. We started at the Pioneer Saloon in Ketchum, Idaho, and proceeded to barhop back to the Sun Valley Mall, where we ended up at a bar called the Orehouse.

Oddly, Scott, Scott, and Rick were all straight guys. Odd only because everyone thinks most male skaters are gay, but the ratio of gay men to straight men approaches equilibrium. There are still more straight guys than gay ones, even in the gayest sport in America. By comparison, in other sports it more closely resembles the general population. So while in skating, the gay population was close to 1 in 2, in other sports, it might be 1 in 10 or 12.

We drank until the bar closed, with more than one of us falling off our barstools. It was a wonderful night of male bonding. I used my "lost" relationship with Vic as subterfuge when the topic of conversation turned to girls, and never felt the least bit uncomfortable with these guys. I had learned to drink, first with skating parents and then with skaters themselves. It was a great ending to a great summer.

Back in Utah with my sophomore year at the university under way, and still working at the ice rink, I started hanging out more and more with the lifeguards. I continued skating with Barbara, but after winning the regional title at the Intermediate level, my heart just wasn't in it. The challenge of intricate edge work and musical interpretation never fully materialized. At that level, our attention was on monotonous ballroom-style pre-set waltzes and tangos. I just couldn't do it any more. I broke the news to Barbara. Strangely, her mother, with whom I was very close at that time, seemed to take the news harder than Barbara did. I suspected that skating was answering needs of hers that were not being met at home. My suspicions proved correct when she and her husband divorced soon after.

Divorce is very common among figure-skating parents. It is a time-consuming sport, taking the mother and child out of the family circle for hours each day, and multiple days and weeks throughout the year. For some mothers, the marriage may already have been in trouble, and the skating serves as the escape they need. But for most, it is simply a strain that even the best marriages have trouble surviving.

For straight male judges and officials in the sport, these high rates of divorce, and large numbers of women away from the family unit, provide plenty of opportunity for philandering. Interestingly, the interviews and biographies of the high-ranking male officials seem to reveal this common thread. The reason they give for getting involved in figure skating is the opportunity to be around "all those girls." "Why did you join Holiday on Ice," one of them might be asked? "To be one of the few boys around all those beautiful young women," was the common response.

Later, these single, straight skaters became officials, married and had families. But the same temptations that drew them to the sport in the first place continue to present themselves at the out-of-town competitions they attend. They find themselves as one of maybe just a few straight men, amongst hundreds of women. Affairs between straight and very married male officials and also married female officials, skating mothers, female coaches, and even sometimes a skater, are rampant. It's really just a matter of numbers. Two or three eligible men (eligible defined by their sexuality, not their marital status) surrounded by upwards of four hundred women. You do the math.

One of the most abused opportunities for these dalliances is the National Championships, and halfway through my second year of college, that circus came to Salt Lake City. Well, with all the fur, it seemed like a circus or maybe a traveling zoo. It was January of 1984, and Salt Lake City hosted the National Figure Skating Championships, the qualifying event for U.S. skaters going to the Sarajevo Winter Olympics. That event exposed me to the glitz and glamour of elite celebrity figure skaters and their fur- and jewel-covered officials, and I was on the hook again.

The freeskating events were held at the Salt Palace in downtown Salt

Lake City. The figure events, which were skated prior to the freeskating and worth 30 percent of a skater's final score, were skated at the Bountiful Recreation Center.

The Bountiful Municipal Center of Recreation had accumulated many names over the years: the BRC, the "Rec Center," the "Bubble," or, to local skaters, simply "Bountiful," as in "Kent teaches at Bountiful on Monday evenings." The athletic complex is made up of an Olympic-sized figure-skating and hockey arena, an outdoor pool that is covered in the winter by a huge, white bubble of air, two racquetball courts, a sauna room, a steam room, and a sparsely filled basement known as the weight room.

For these National Championships, the weight room was transformed into the judges' room, where judges (who were treated like visiting monarchs at this competition) could relax before and after their events. The room included a spread prepared and brought in by some of the city's finest chefs. The judges' room is also where judges could congregate after watching practice sessions to digest and trade the latest information they had learned over a cup of coffee, a glass of champagne or other mixed drink, a hot bowl of soup (compliments of one of the sponsors, Campbell's) and a plate of Mrs. Fields cookies. Still, to this day, the 1984 National Championships are remembered for their free, fresh-from-the-oven Mrs. Fields cookies by both skaters and officials.

The figure events attracted virtually no spectators. There was no excitement at all in watching them. To give you an idea, each skater performed a selected figure-eight (or serpentine—three circles instead of two). They skated each half of the figure three times on each foot, for three tracings on the ice (or six tracings for "paragraph" figures—those where the entire "eight" were done on each foot).

After each skater completed his or her figures, the judges would examine the markings on the ice and give a score. After the judges' marks were held above their heads and read to the empty arena, the next skater performed his figures. After all skaters had completed their figures, the monotony started over, with the next selected figure being skated, until, in all, three figures had been skated by each skater in the event. The figure events would go on endlessly over the course of several hours, which seemed like days, leaving the skaters and coaches with nothing to do but watch the ice dry.

It is striking to me that the most interesting thing about these otherwise boring figure events was how well the judges were dressed—well, overly dressed, really.

In Utah, most people don't wear fur. I realize Utah's supposed to be a winter wonderland, world-renowned, according to its ad campaign, as having the best snow on earth. However, it's not Siberia. People don't live in igloos.

Utah is the land of parkas, overcoats, moon boots, and galoshes—except for the week of the National Championships. Nearly every one of the judges showed up each morning at the Rec Center in a full-length fur coat. These same judges would judge the freeskate performances later in the week at the climate-controlled Salt Palace, where not even a sweater would be required, so the figure events at Bountiful were their only chances to show off their pelts.

The parade of animal-skinned judges also included some of the men, with a few judges even having fur-covered boots. I had seen my fair share of fur-covered judges, usually rare at most of the events I skated in; but at these Championships, it was overwhelming.

Even more fun on the people-watching scale was the opportunity to see the American Olympians, both on and off the ice. Soon-to-be skating celebrities like Scott Hamilton, Rosalyn Sumners, and the brother/sister pair team of Peter and Kitty Caruthers behaved like regular folk outside the rink, and tore it up on the ice.

I remember being mesmerized by many practices, the most exciting of which had Kris Sherard's cousin Jimmy Santee in the same practice as Scott Hamilton. Jimmy was a recent Junior and Novice titleholder. He was gunning after the favored—and now famous—Scott Hamilton. The practice I watched had triple jump after triple jump, fired off in rapid repetition, and at both ends of the ice. This was the first time I had watched this level of skating, head-to-head, with so many elite skaters. Even though I was only a spectator, it was mind-blowing.

After the National Championships, Ida Tateoka, Doree Ann's mom, traveled to Sarajevo to judge the Olympic Games. This was a big deal in our local skating community. We even had a big dinner to give Ida a proper sendoff. The thought of traveling halfway around the globe to a figure-skating event was exciting enough, but to get to go to the Olympic Games? Wow! I was completely overwhelmed.

After the Sarajevo games, Ida returned and filled my ears with stories of her Olympic travels. Perhaps seeing the delight in my eyes, she told me I should think about becoming a judge. As it turned out, U.S. Figure Skating was seeking younger, progressive judges from the skating ranks, intending to improve the dated image of the current judges. Ida told me that I fit the bill, so I was excited to learn more about the chance to become a judge.

The prospects of former skaters judging current skaters appealed to my sense of fairness. I hoped that I might prevent some of the ridiculous results that I and many other skaters felt we were subjected to from judges who were out of touch with the sport, most of whom had never landed a double axel, and certainly not a triple jump. These judges were from an era when figure skating was about the figures and freestyle was considered the rebellious stepchild of the sport. Though now it counted for only 30 percent of the score, many judges still preferred the discipline of the figures, and were not too happy nor familiar with the judging of the freestyle, or so we skaters thought.

I told Ida I would think about it. While the opportunity to travel was appealing, being a judge in figure-skating was strictly on a volunteer basis. Not only would I never be paid for my time, but also I would be expected to pay for my own expenses during a period of "trial-judging."

Trial-judging is a method in which former skaters, and sometimes parents of skaters or mere fans, and anyone else with deep enough pockets and an interest in figure-skating, can become a trial judge. They go on to become judges after being taught to "think like judges," rather than like skaters or spectators. The trial judge sits behind the actual panel of judges, and practice-judges the event, "turning in" his or her marks for review. Later, in what can only be called indoctrination, the trial judges meet with some of the official judges to learn why he or she may have seen things a little differently, and how to see them like the real judges the next time.

The figure-skating judges' education is one almost strictly learned by emulation. By attending test sessions and competitions, a trial judge watches and marks the skating alongside the actual judges. After the event, the judges discuss with the trial judge his or her marks, provide feedback, and evaluate the performance of the trial judge. When the peer judges feel that the trial judge is ready for an actual appointment, a promotion is made. If a trial judge does not see things the way the official judges see things, then he or she will not be promoted until he changes his errant ways—a process that encourages judge cloning, creating the same bad judging habits that existed before.

At the time Ida approached me, I was also considering becoming a coach. I liked the idea of an opportunity to make a little extra money while in college, at an hourly rate that far exceeded what I was making as a lifeguard or cashier. On occasion, when one of the Bountiful coaches couldn't make a learn-to-skate class, I had filled in, and I actually enjoyed working with the students on the ice. I knew I didn't want to be a coach long-term. On the other hand, the short-term financial benefits would help pay for some of my educational expenses up through graduate school. At the time Ida approached me to be a judge, a parent asked me to give her daughter, Danielle Dimeo, private lessons. Danielle was cute as a button and loved skating. I was almost as drawn to teach skating by the preciousness of this young child as by the prospect of the dollars in my pocket.

In the end, Ida talked me into taking a philanthropic view of things. I decided to try out the judging end of the sport for a while, reasoning that if I didn't like it, I could always start coaching later.

I began by trial-judging the low-figure and freeskating tests. In Utah, the test sessions were usually held on Sunday mornings, generally very early. It wasn't long before I was traveling to California to trial-judge competitions.

Making my way as a judge from Utah in the California-controlled Central Pacific Region was not so different from making my way as a skater from Utah. Californians dominated this region, and outsiders were not welcome. The powerful California judges wanted little to do with a twenty-year-old Utah rube fresh out of the skating ranks. Also, I was more at home with the skaters and coaches (who were closer to my age and shared common interests) than with judges. I spent a considerable portion of my free time with them.

What I failed to realize at first was that this new accelerated program was not very popular with the existing judges. They saw the skater-soon-to-be-judge as a threat to their positions, their power, and their coveted invitations to travel to events. Additionally, all of these judges had spent years, if not decades, earning their appointments. They resented that a select group was being given an express ride through the system.

This attitude by existing judges was more pronounced in some regions of the country, with the Central Pacific region being at the top of the pile of discontent. Interestingly, this region, my region, had then and still has today the reputation for having some of the worst judges in the country. Those bad judges were threatened, and for good reason.

I would learn of these feelings of ill will when Ida submitted my application to become a "low-test" judge under the accelerated program's reduced requirements. Ida also submitted my application to be admitted into the accelerated program. Keep in mind, Ida was the highest-ranking judge in the region and very well respected. Nonetheless, my application to become an accelerated judge was turned down. Interestingly, however, my low-test judging appointment was approved.

Now, this made no sense whatsoever. If I was not an accelerated candidate, then my few months of trial judging, with minimal amounts of experience, would not meet the standard requirements to even submit the application. So I could not even meet the minimum for submission, forget approval, *unless* I was accelerated. I was being approved as though I were an accelerated candidate, yet being denied admission to the club. It was almost as if to say, "Ida, we will give him this one low-level appointment out of respect for you, but for all future appointments, he must meet the traditional requirements." The Central Pacific judges were going to have no part in the rapid advancement of the first skater in their region to take advantage of this program.

As it turns out, I was denied acceptance into the accelerated program on a technicality. The requirement for acceptance was that the prospective candidate had passed their seventh figure test and Junior freeskating test. The requirement was a nod to the fact that a skater with that high a level of experience had developed a technical expertise that would not require them to spend a decade in the trenches with parents and other non-skaters who knew nothing about the sport.

I had passed the Junior freeskating test, and the sixth figure test, but not the seventh. Ida, in a very diplomatic and gracious manner, went over the heads of the Central Pacific judges, appealing to bigger wigs, and got my acceptance into the program. I had the basic technical knowledge meeting the program's intent. Without Ida, her diplomatic pull, and her reasoned thinking, I might still be a low-test judge, if a judge at all.

I was just scratching the surface of the resentment in the Northern California area. The California judges didn't know me. What they thought they knew of me (special privileges), they didn't like. Therefore, while I won that initial battle—or, I should say, while Ida won that initial battle—the war was just beginning. I would not win the war until securing support from other parts of the country.

In any event, in the early fall of 1984, I received my first judging appointment and my admission to the special club. However, other things were going on in my life during that time as well.

AT THE END of the spring quarter, I was promoted to an assistant manager, which paid a lot more, and gave me a regular part-time schedule in the evenings, making my life a heck of a lot more enjoyable. I also still worked as a lifeguard, cashier, or skate monitor to pick up additional hours.

With all that extra money, I decided it was time to get my own apartment. I was living as hand-to-mouth as one could, with my parents picking up the cost of my tuition and books. I lived on fast or frozen food, both of which I loved. I was raised on the three main food groups: pizza, cheeseburgers, and burritos. My venture into the frozen-food section of the grocery store was my attempt at "eating healthy." It also meant I wouldn't need dishes, pots, pans, or even dish soap!

Sometime during that spring semester, my dad moved out as well. My mom called me and told me that she and my dad were getting divorced. It went without incident, really, something they both knew was inevitable as we kids grew older and they grew further apart. The only child it had any real impact on was 13-year-old Janica. I had my own developing life at the time, so I didn't fully grasp the impact that a divorce would have on a young child. Her father was moving to Omaha, Nebraska, and now she would only see him a few times a year.

The divorce was amicable, as far as divorces go, with my mom securing a small property settlement and alimony and, most importantly, a monthly stipend for each child as long as we were in school, through college. This meant for me that my tuition and books would be paid until I graduated—something I didn't appreciate that much at the time, but for which I will forever be grateful. Both to my mother for negotiating the deal, and my father for paying it, without question or resentment, even though, with my continued involvement in skating, I took the leisurely five-year approach to college.

The following summer I continued working at the Rec Center as an assistant manager in the evenings and a lifeguard during the afternoons, and though I wasn't making a lot of money, I managed to pay my bills, and still managed to party—a lot.

I was hanging out a great deal with a strictly platonic girlfriend, Sherri Morris, whom I had skated with years earlier. She had been a talented skater, but her parents' divorce put an end to it. Prior to the divorce, Sherri would go to skating competitions without her father knowing about it. "She's at her grandmother's for the weekend," her mother covered for her in her absence. When the bills came in, Sherri's cover was blown, and I'm sure the white lies told in pursuit of a skating dream did little to help keep that marriage together.

Sherri liked going out as much as I did, but neither of us was yet 21, the legal drinking age in Utah. We would usually drink at my apartment before going out, then head to Salt Lake's underage and underground dance club, the Maxim.

The Maxim was everything a closeted, young gay man could want in a dance club. Many of the men were gay, but most were not open about it. The girls were there to dance, and hope that the person who caught their eye might be straight, or at least still pretending to be, even if only for a few weeks.

The club-goers wore all sorts of bizarre outfits, mostly in shades of black. The popular music at that time was "new wave," a then-modern offshoot of punk rock. Depeche Mode, New Order, Bronski Beat, and the Psychedelic Furs were on heavy rotation. Their fans and my fellow club-goers did everything they could to emulate the popular artists. Some danced on stage or atop loudspeakers, lip-synching their favorite tunes in outfits and makeup in mimicry of their idols.

It was edgy music, and a surprisingly edgy Salt Lake scene. In addition, the club atmosphere served as a springboard for many closeted gay men to begin dealing with their sexuality. I had my demons well hidden. My years in figure-skating had taught me what happens to gay men: getting run out of town, ending up in the clink with DUI's, and living an isolated, hermit's life. That was my thinking at the time, based on what I saw and what I was told.

I spent that entire summer in the company of straight women and closeted gay men, listening and moving to the beat of fabulous music, dressing up in outrageous outfits, and staying in the closet all the while. Hmm . . . lots of straight women, closeted gay men, fabulous music, and outrageous outfits? Wow! Going to the Maxim that summer was a lot like hanging out in an ice rink!

Also that summer, a close battle between Kem Gardner and Wayne Owens was heating up for the Democratic nominee for the next Governor of Utah, and Angie Harwood, a friend of mine from the Recreation Center, got me involved in the campaign. We would be walking the streets and hitting the phones for Kem Gardner, a Salt Lake businessman.

Despite all our efforts and a well-run noble campaign, we ultimately lost that battle. The opponent, Wayne Owens, was simply too loved and well-known by Utah Democrats for his role in taking down Richard Nixon. Nevertheless, I loved the political experience. That fall, I changed my major to political science. This shouldn't be a big deal—changing majors. Everyone did it, but maybe not as often as I did.

I had started school pursuing math, my field of expertise, at least according to the standardized testing. Then, when jobs in computers began to take off, I changed my major to computer science. "It's the plastics of your generation," my dad enthusiastically encouraged.

Once in the engineering department, I realized I was very, very, very much out of place. Was socializing not allowed, or do these people just not know how to do it? Homework that can't be completed *during* class? Late nights, very late nights at the computer lab? Physics lab topics that cannot be understood without perfect attendance? This major was not fitting in with my deep-rooted lack of study habits. While I had over-achieved in high school, I had done so without much of a book crack. I did my homework at school, during lunch breaks or recesses, or during class. Computer Science required homework and studying outside the classroom. This was not going to be for me.

A quarter or so later, I was in pursuit of a business degree, where I found the classes to be about as challenging as walking a straight line. While Accounting 101, with its complex double entries, was sending most of my class into fits, I was either napping or doing my homework through the lectures. Child-labor laws not withstanding, that indentured servitude with my father had paid off! And, because the established common ground with my dad was all things business, when I took management and finance classes, they seemed almost second nature. My sophomore year of business studies had literally become a cakewalk.

Therein lay the problem: There was no challenge in it, and certainly no excitement. Now, politics—that was another story!

During the fall of my junior year, I started going to weekly lectures organized by the Hinckley Institute of Politics, listening to local, state, and sometimes national policy wonks rattle on about new and interesting political topics. It was challenging from an academic standpoint and fascinating on a philosophical level. It reminded me of my days as a senior in high school, playing hooky with Todd Leishman back at the Arctic Circle.

I also continued pursuing my trial-judging, traveling back to Fresno— home of my Novice Men's title—to trial-judge the Central Pacific Championships. There I would violate nearly every unwritten rule of judging decorum.

The judges, by and large, are a little older. Plain and simple. The volunteer activity of judging figure-skating events requires time away from job and family. Naturally, it falls to those without jobs or family responsibilities, or retirees. Certainly, there are wealthy homemakers sprinkled here and there, usually one with few or no children, and the occasional business owner, able to make his or her own vacation schedules, but the majority of the judging flock are retirees.

As a twenty-something, I had no interest in socializing in the judges' room with people so much older than me. I was still working at the recreation center; I knew all the Utah skaters, coaches, and parents. So, while the other judges retired to the smoke-filled judges' room for caviar, canapés, petit fours, and Tom Collinses, I would dart off to the stands to sit and socialize with my friends. My occasional visit to the judges' room was only to grab a bite to eat, and then I would get out of there as quickly as I could and go get some real food with people I wanted to hang around with.

The only time the other judges really saw me was when I was trial-judging alongside them, or afterwards when they were criticizing my performance.

I also soon learned that popularity among the skaters and coaches was not a pathway to a successful judging career. "The judges are not to fraternize with the skaters, parents, or coaches!" I was continually reminded. Even so, I was not dissuaded by these warnings.

By the end of the week, Jack Searle, who was also there trial-judging and sharing a room with me to help keep down expenses, let me know that after the events on Saturday night, I needed to come by the judges' hospitality room to socialize. What did he mean, "Needed to?" I was already on my way into the shower, with plans to change my clothes and run off with Kris Sherard and some parents for dinner and drinks.

"Why do I need to go to the judges' hospitality room?" I asked.

"Because you won't ever be promoted if you don't make friends with the judges," Jack responded.

Then he followed with, "They are all talking about how you don't fit into a judge's mold, are too immature, and are running off with the other skaters."

"But my trial-judging was excellent, Jack. I nailed just about every event," I responded. "They'll give me my appointments when I earn them. U.S. Figure Skating is looking for good judges." I actually (and incorrectly) believed this.

"But good judges are determined by existing judges," Jack responded.

As a skating parent-cum-judge, Jack knew that his advancement would come very, very slowly. He hated to see me held back simply because I had little in common with the other judges. He was one of the few who seemed to sincerely care about my advancement.

"If you don't find some common ground with them, they will see you as an outsider—as a skater. You need to make them think of you as a judge," he said.

Jack gave me a lot to think about, though I dashed out the door to meet my friends anyway. As usual, I was having a great time, a mini-vacation, associated with a sport I loved, and sharing great times with good friends. Was I really going to have to give up on the good times to advance? I didn't think so, and I couldn't have been more wrong.

At the 1984 Sarajevo games, Russian pairs Volova and Vasiliev won the gold medal, the sixth Russian Olympic gold medal in a row in what was becoming one of sport's great dynasties.

From Athlete to Official

*B*ACK IN SCHOOL, and back at the Hinckley Institute of Politics, I applied for an internship with the Utah State Legislature. I was accepted to a full-time position. I spent the entire winter quarter working from early in the morning until late in the afternoon for three different legislators. The experience of operating within the legislative process was fascinating to me. I also continued to work evenings at the Rec Center, as an assistant manager, which, with the small stipend I received from the internship, helped keep my head above water.

I also continued to carry on too much over the weekends with Sherri at the Maxim or with the lifeguard crowd. I was like a wild dog off a leash with my drinking. I wanted to try it all, and usually overdid it. After all, I had a lot of catching up to do.

Then during the spring quarter, I landed a job as a paid intern working for the University of Utah's Department of Continuing Education at their Bountiful campus. I took a semi-leave of absence from the Rec Center to have the time both to do the internship and to remain enrolled full-time in classes. It was a semi-leave of absence, because I continued to pick up shifts whenever they called. I never wanted to be too far away from the lifeguards!

Because of this internship, I learned about some courses I could take in Bountiful at night that would count toward my graduation. I wanted to be supportive of their programs, so I enrolled in one of their night courses—a pottery class.

I wasn't optimistic about my abilities for this class. In previous art classes, I had been a terrible student. My inability to draw so much as a stick figure with reasonable competence frustrated me.

I needed to access the right side of my brain. With numbers and statistics—the left-brain occupants—I was on top of the world. Hand me paint, markers, or brushes, and I had nothing over the cave-dwellers.

I don't know what made me think I could do anything with clay. I don't even like to get dirty, and playing in the mud for the sake of art seemed more like an exercise in patience. Nevertheless, I was determined to round out my skills and develop a more complete identity of myself, despite my self-perceived creative block.

The class included the study of old pottery and clay pots of the ages, origins, clay options, glazes, and stains. There was also paper homework (which was mostly memorization and regurgitation), and for those portions of the class I did really well. However, the major part of the class was sitting at a pottery wheel, keeping the damn thing spinning at a constant speed while attempting to mold clay into bowls, mugs, and vases.

Our final exam involved creating a piece of pottery without the use of the wheel. We were given a lump of clay and two weeks to make our *objets d'art*. I had no idea what I wanted to make.

During that time, I was asked to judge an event in Phoenix at their annual Fiesta Skate competition. I was a lower-level judge and wasn't used very much, and so I had plenty of free time on my hands in Phoenix. I would've liked to have spent that free time lounging by the pool in the warm Arizona sun, but the transportation provided from hotel to rink was only once each day, so I was trapped at the ice rink all day long.

Stuck at the rink, I decided I would make the best of it by spending time with some of the judges in the judges' room between events. The judges I remember from this competition smelled of Aqua Velva and

Jean Naté. Among them were World War II vets, either with war stories that might interest a John Wayne movie fan or older women who knitted socks, scarves, or embroidered doilies. I was not yet 21, and in the judges' room the closest person to my age was already collecting Social Security benefits.

What I did learn, to my surprise, was how interested they were in *my* life. They had all been 21 once, after all, most had been to college, and one way or another each had come up through the trial judging ranks. Even though some seemed to resent the inroads I was making into their exclusive little club, a younger judge with new ideas and enthusiasm was perhaps refreshing to them. So, despite my inherent lack of interest in their lives, we seemed to find plenty of things to talk about. Me!

As we talked, I realized that I was actually becoming interested in them. Many of their pasts were fascinating, and I came to enjoy learning about what some of these judges did with their lives when they weren't judging others.

In my own judgment, I had wrongly stereotyped these judges into an "old folks" category and assumed that we had nothing in common. It was a revelation to me as a person, and it was certainly the first step toward access into their worlds.

Between events and socializing with the bald and bluehairs, I wandered the shopping mall connected to the ice rink. One of the mall stores sold pottery among other things, and, because of my concurrent class in that area, I spent a lot of time in that shop. As I browsed the various pieces, I was amazed at the mastery of the craft that these "professionals" or artisans had produced.

Where my work and that of my classmates seemed rough and/or asymmetrical, the pieces for sale in that shop were all so smooth and perfect. Except for one piece. It was a tall vase, with pieces of dowel-shaped clay poking out randomly from its sides. The owner of the shop explained to me that the artist was trying to emulate the prickly look of the familiar Arizona cactus.

This artist's little creation wound up serving as the inspiration for the "final" in my pottery class.

Back in class, with the assignment of our final project, we were given our glob of clay and expected to find the beauty hidden within. That

Arizona artist's work and her artistic motivation were on my mind. Where her vase was tall and slender, and designed to hold flowers, I had created an oval-shaped vessel, more suitable for a potted plant. Where her vase had its "cactus spines" sticking out its sides, but blending seamlessly into the work, my creation was made by forming rows of rolled-out clay, with the ends of the rolled pieces sticking out the sides as a continuation of the layer. The randomness of the inspiration piece was replaced in my work with a very orderly ascending angle. So, I actually ended up with something Southwest-looking, unique and original, a wonderful plant pot—and, best of all, I got an A!

Back in Phoenix, while spending my days with the judges, I spent the evenings again with Kris Sherard and a coaching colleague of hers, Todd Kaufman, from San Diego. Kris, Todd, one of the skating moms, and I would all go out each night for dinner and drinks. While I was still 20, Arizona had a lower drinking age, so I indulged myself.

Todd was a little older than I was, probably in his late twenties. He was dark-haired and physically fit—a former pairs skater; a handsome hunk in every sense of the word. I had a schoolgirl's crush on him from the moment I met him, and wondered why I had never met or even seen him before in my skating circles. I got the impression that he was also gay and more comfortable with his sexuality than I was.

I was also incredibly shy about making any kind of gesture toward him, but secretly hoped he would make a move on me. I was still so deep in the closet, and probably sent him a host of conflicting signals, but I did my best to spend as much time with him as possible, under the protection of Kris and "Mrs. Skatermom" as our chaperones. Near the end of the week, I sensed that Todd was finally taking an interest in me, and instead of being thrilled, it scared me to death, so I backed off, and surely ruined any chance of scoring even a kiss off this attractive man.

On the last night of the competition, we were all four again in a car returning from some restaurant or another, with the two women in the front and Todd and me in the back. Todd suddenly slid his hand across the seat and held mine the rest of the way to the hotel. I never recoiled, but probably left my hand there more out of fear. His hand was soft but firm, and his touch made my heart race. Just this simple act was way too much for me; once we parked, I ran straight to my room after saying a quick good-bye.

As soon as I was in my room, I regretted having left that "missed chance" in the back seat of the car. I would not get a second chance with Todd; he died a few years later from complications associated with AIDS.

I was sharing my room with another very gay late-thirty something judge from the Los Angeles area. He was in the room watching TV, and noticed my agitation when I returned to the room. He gave me the standard "Hey, I didn't see you in the judges' hospitality room" greeting that was wearing very thin after hearing it for the third or fourth straight night.

Resigned that my crush on Todd had ended with nothing more than a tighter grip the moment I darted out of the car, I sat down to watch television with that poor judge who I was apparently not spending enough time with.

After a few minutes, I turned to him and asked, "Why do people care whether or not I go to the judges' hospitality room? It's almost as if someone is keeping track."

"They are!" he snipped, as he grabbed the remote and turned off the TV, getting straight into bed, and leaving me still sitting there in the dark.

"They're keeping track?" I thought to myself. "What's up with that? Here I have all of these other issues going on in my head, and someone is tracking whether or not I meet the judges for a cocktail in some hotel-ballroom-cum-smoked-filled-lounge?" And here, on the last night of the competition, I had earlier looked back and felt that I was making some headway with these people, socializing with them all day at the ice rink. A huge gesture on my part, at least I thought so at the time, but apparently it was not enough. One step forward, two steps back.

I spent that summer again pursuing my usual activities. I was managing the Rec Center during the evenings, lifeguarding during the day, picking up an occasional cashier shift, and I started teaching tennis lessons in the morning.

I had played tennis competitively years before. The summer programs sponsored by the recreation center included golf lessons, tennis, and other sports unrelated to the actual recreation complex. The city was short on tennis instructors, as Angie Harwood, the girl who recruited me into the Kem Gardner for Governor Campaign, had just graduated from the U and was moving to Washington, D.C. She had taught the tennis courses every summer until then, and her departure left an opening for me to fill.

I loved teaching the tennis lessons, even though the first lessons began at seven in the morning. I taught four consecutive hour-long lessons to a handful of six- to 12-year-olds at various levels of competency. The classes ended around 11 A.M.

It seemed like every day, promptly at 11, there would appear one parent or another to discuss their child's progress with me. Even if the child was in the 7 A.M. class and had been gone for three hours, the parent, usually the mother but not always, would suddenly reappear wanting to badger me with questions before I could get out of there.

Now, keep in mind, these classes were $20.00 for two weeks of daily lessons, ten total, in a very low-budget recreational program. The key word here is *recreational*. Moreover, even though I was teaching various levels, even the advanced class was merely an "advanced" beginner class.

What exactly did these parents have in mind? They wanted to know things like whether I thought their child showed any talent. Did I think Susie was good enough to go on some day to play professional tennis? Does Danny have what it takes to get to Wimbledon?

At first, their questions were a shock to me. These kids and I were just having fun on the court. I was more a babysitter with a tennis racket, than a tennis coach with any concept of what kind of talent was needed to "go all the way."

I would try to steer the parents down a different path and respond, "Well, is Susie enjoying the lessons? Does Danny like to practice in the afternoons?" I was attempting to help the parent see that this was more important than any predestined glory (and it must be predestined if they were expecting me to see it after three one-hour group tennis lessons).

But my questions were lost on them. "Susie likes lots of things," they would respond. "I want to make sure that we spend our time and money where it is best spent, on her talents." Or, "Danny is good at so many things; we just want to make sure he finds his true calling." Mormons, even tennis-playing Mormons, always seemed to have a "calling."

To this day, I cannot understand how figure-skating coaches deal with the parents and all their grandiose hopes for the future. "Is my kid going to make it?"

Of course, as I advanced as a judge in figure-skating, similar questions would find their way to my ears, from parents who had the guts to bother a judge with such a question (most are afraid of the judges, so it wasn't very often). Their questions always made me equally uncomfortable. Maybe I should have learned to read tea leaves, or asked that tarot-card reader from my debate years for lessons to help predict what the future held for Suzie and Danny, because they seemed more like a couple of bowlers than skaters to me! But, of course, that's not what the parents wanted to hear.

I finally turned 21 early in the summer, and was now eligible to drink legally, and eligible for membership into Utah's private clubs and bars, complete with a plastic membership card. In Utah, the archaic drinking laws of that time required that to have an alcoholic drink, one had to be a member of a "private club." Membership was very, very exclusive. The private clubs were only open to those of very privileged means, the standard for membership being an extra twenty-five bucks and a valid driver's license. Very exclusive indeed.

My weekends drifted away from the Maxim, and on to Salt Lake City's adult clubs. The Dead Goat Saloon was my bar of choice for cheap beer ($2.50 a pitcher) or the Collector Club at Twelve Oaks for dancing. The crowd I was hanging with didn't change much, just the scenery. It was still me, Sherri, a few lifeguards, and the occasional random friend, out on the town.

Despite all this partying, I managed to make it to every 7:00 A.M. tennis lesson. When someone else was paying my bill, I wasn't about to disappoint.

NEAR THE END of the summer, I finally connected with a group of judges who not only enjoyed my company, but who didn't put any pressure on me to do anything extra to hold favor with them. They never made me feel unwelcome, as a former skater, an advancing-too-fast judge, or a college kid who simply wanted to hang out with skating friends rather than judges. As soon as this happened, I found myself preferring to hang out with them rather than my skater friends, both in the judges' room and in the hotel hospitality suite. These amazing people were judges from the midwestern section of the United States.

I first met the midwestern judges at the Colorado Championships, held earlier that year in Denver. It was a large event. There were many skaters, and two ice surfaces going at the same time to handle them all, and many judges as well. Ida managed to get me invited. I was likely the youngest of the judges, certainly the lowest-ranking.

The Colorado judges took me under their wings. They were interested in me, without being overly interested. They didn't seem to have an agenda, either for themselves or for me. I was there to judge, and they appreciated the time I was volunteering to help.

It was such a stimulating experience, and one very different from my experiences on the West Coast. I met judges like Bonnie McLaughlin, Virginia Mount, Gay Barnes, and Beth Graham from Colorado, Shirley Hague from Minneapolis, Bette Todd from Indianapolis, and a whole slew of other kind and sincere judges. Kind to each other, and sincere in their interest in the sport.

I remember laughing aloud during one event I was judging, sitting between Bonnie and Bette, two good friends who loved to chat even when the event was going on! It wasn't so much what they were talking about, just the fact that they were talking at all!

On the West Coast, if a judge dared even sneeze while on the judges' stand, his or her file was noted, with punishment imposed swiftly and furiously after the event. By contrast, the midwestern judges always chatted each other up. During warm-up, between skaters, it didn't matter.

There is a strict rule for not talking during the event, which is why most judges could pass for wooden Indians. Avoiding conversations on the judges' stand is accepted protocol; to do otherwise might give the appearance to the skaters, to the coaches—or to network television, for that matter—that the judges are in collusion.

So, with a clear understanding of why the rule was in place, Bonnie and Bette ignored it. They would be the last judges simply not to "call it like they see it." Their reputation was for being strong-minded and straightforward. Even if the coaches or skaters saw them talking, they would never believe in a million years that this duo was discussing their marks. Even if they were, neither one of them would ever be swayed by the other's opinion.

So there I was, sitting between their exchange of bon mots, feeling very uncomfortable, believing that eventually a referee would come by and smack their heads with a ruler.

The referee never did intervene. Their chatting had nothing to do with the skating on the ice, and it would have nothing to do with the result. No harm done, no interference, and that was the midwestern approach to everything—at least it seemed so in the judging of those championships, and I would later find out that it was true in the entire midwest.

The midwesterners were not the least bit uptight about any of the rules. The bottom line for them was whether the skaters were fairly treated, and whether the judging was accurate. If you needed to trade an event so you could catch an early dinner with friends from college, you'd hear, "I'll take that event for ya. Have a good time!"

Not once did a judge ever try to manipulate me into doing more (socializing with the judges, going to the hospitality room, and so on) or less (don't fraternize with the skaters, why do you hang out with the coaches?). They really couldn't care less what I did or who I did it with. The attitude was very refreshing.

Around this time, I met Joe Inman, an openly gay judge from the Washington, D.C. area. Loud and flamboyant, Joe was a heavyset man who spoke with exaggerated animation and fluttery arms to make his points. Later, when I saw Nathan Lane in *The Birdcage* with Robin Williams, I thought of Joe Inman. Joe was friendly and always a good time. Like watching a cartoon, I found him funny and entertaining and looked forward to his Looney Toon antics and hearing his wild stories when I saw him in the judges' rooms "holding court" between events. Joe was a musician in the military, a position which required him to "fit in," so at the figure skating events it seemed important for Joe be noticed in a crowd. He was never at a loss for words. Although Joe was from the D.C. area, our paths would cross many times in the future.

Also at the Colorado championships, another judge, Virginia Mount, struck up a conversation with me and, before I knew it, I was up in her room with two other judges where Virginia taught me to play bridge, an ability that would later come in handy both at and away from the ice rink. Years later, I often wondered if I was being invited to a skating competition because of my judging skills or my bridge-playing skills. Sometimes I hoped it was the latter! The bridge-playing judges are simply a whole lot more fun.

I returned from Colorado excited about judging again. I had made some new friends and, for the first time, felt welcomed into the "club" of judges. The Pacific Coast officials acted like snooty members of an exclusive country club with its dues to be paid, its rules to be followed, enforcing stiff penalties for getting out of line. The midwestern judges treated the other judges not as members of a stuffy club, but more as guests at a neighborhood barbeque. Come as you are, have a great time!

I sowed the seeds of some lasting friendships that week, and found myself in Colorado often thereafter, judging advancement tests and competitions. I'm certain that by the time I received my National judge appointment, I had judged more often in the state of Colorado than I had judged in all of the Pacific Coast states collectively.

DURING THE FALL of 1985, my pursuit of politics landed me an internship in Washington, D.C., working for the Committee for Education Funding. I earned twelve hours of credit for more than a forty-hour workweek, and received a $400-per-month stipend. How was I supposed to live on $400 in Washington, D.C.?

To make ends meet, many interns live with six other interns in two-bedroom apartments out in the suburbs, and commute to work.

It was an interesting fall. I shared a bedroom full of three single beds and a bathroom with two male schoolmates, one an old friend, fresh from his Mormon mission to Japan, Todd Leishman. Todd was no longer drinking coffee, but neither was I (I went back to the Coca-Cola of my childhood). The other bedroom had four single beds, and four women sharing one bathroom. Every time I started to feel cramped, I just thought of those poor girls!

It was a fun group of students in a naturally fun environment. We hung out a lot with the interns from BYU, who also lived in the same apartment complex we did. Of course, the BYU students' living arrangements were not coed, and they were not crammed into small spaces. The boys were with the boys, and the girls with the girls. Two to a room, two to a bathroom. Then again, the BYU Cougars were always a more civilized bunch than the Utah Utes were! However, they didn't know how to have near as much fun. (Well, a few of the girls did. It seemed if they weren't getting into trouble, it had a way of finding them!)

My internship was near Embassy Row; so, unlike my roommates, I was not "on the Hill." It seemed as soon as I arrived and settled into a regular working arrangement (arriving at 8:30, lunch at 12:00 noon, and leaving at 5:00), all hell broke loose at the Capitol. At least it did for those involved with saving education funding.

The Graham-Rudman-Hollings Act was introduced into Congress, and it had a huge following, as a way of dealing with the out-of-control budget deficits of that time. It was, in its simplest form, an across-the-board cut of nearly every educational program.

"Nearly every program" are important words in the lobbying business. Does that mean someone is exempt? Some programs are not being cut? As a lobbyist, it's your job to find out how you get your programs into those exempt groups, and if you can't, how you stop the bill?

I soon found myself on Capitol Hill every day. I was up at 6:00 A.M. so I could get a place in line for that morning's most important hearing. When Susan Frost, my boss, would show up at 8:30, she would take my place in line and give me the day's instructions. I would then end up in a less-important hearing taking notes, or distributing information around the various House and Senate offices, or I might find myself back in line as a placeholder for a hearing later that afternoon.

It was an all-out effort for our office to stop that bill, coordinated by Susan Frost, a former aide to Ted Kennedy. I was impressed by her Kennedy connection, especially on those occasions where we would be walking the halls and run into Senator Kennedy, and he would stop to say "Hello," and Susan would bend his ear about the bill.

As busy as I was, pursuing and participating in the politics of the day, I managed to find time to judge some figure-skating events as well. Ida had called a good friend of hers, Florence Sifford, to ask her to "take care of me" while I was back East, and Florence did just that. From time to time, I would get a phone call or message from Florence about a test session at this or that rink, and was I available to judge? Unfortunately, I usually wasn't, but on several occasions I was able to help her out.

When I was able to judge, Florence would pull up in front of the Oakwood Apartments in Alexandria, Virginia where I lived, usually at some ungodly hour like 5:00 A.M., in an old Dodge Duster, and would chauffeur me off to the ice rink, where I would judge a few tests. She would wait and then transport me on to the Metro station, where I could jump a train and still make it to work on time.

Florence was one of the most devoted women I think I ever met during all my time as a skating judge, and that is saying a lot. She had a true love for the sport and for the skaters, and it showed not just in her words, but also in her actions. I don't think there is a skater alive who is from the Baltimore/D.C./Virginia area who does not know and have a kind word to say about Florence Sifford.

At one of those test sessions, I met a former skater, Alice Lampit,* who was also in the accelerated program. She had just received her Intermediate appointment, and I was very, very surprised to learn that she had been trial-judging for less than six months.

"How did you get your appointment so fast?" I inquired.

"Well, I'm in the accelerated program. I was told you were in on that as well," she replied.

"Yes, I am," I said, "but I didn't get my Intermediate appointment for a good eighteen months, and even then it was a battle."

"Well, that's crazy! All of us on the East Coast have been moving along at about the same pace. Do you know Rob Rosenbluth? I think he just got his Gold appointment. He has only been judging for about two years."

---

* Not her real name.

"Two years! He has his Gold appointment? Wow! That *is* accelerated," I reacted, a bit enviously.

"Who is your monitor? Maybe you're not being pushed along fast enough," Alice stated unknowingly.

"Ida Tateoka is my monitor, and she is already in hot water with the judges in my region for pushing me so hard! It's definitely not that," I countered defensively on behalf of the woman who had taken a motherly role in my development as a judge.

"Oh, that's right. You're from out West. I had heard they were against you . . . oh, I mean the Accelerated Program." And with that, we marched out to judge the same test, Alice with her new appointment, and me with mine. I couldn't help but think, "Out West they're against me?"

In D.C., I had plenty of opportunities to find plenty of male role models. I was constantly people-watching, trying to find that perfect man who I wanted to be "just like." Okay, I was slowly accepting the fact that I wanted more from them than just to be like them; and miles from home, I finally had the guts to make a move.

At one of the cocktail receptions on the Hill, BYU Julie (middle name: Trouble, last name: Southern Charm) introduced me to someone named Mark who she clearly suspected was gay. She evidently supposed I was too. It was obvious in the way she introduced us. She winked, giggled, and quickly slid away.

I was immediately smitten by this guy's preppy good looks. We made some small talk, both slightly uncomfortable by the obviousness of the situation. I found out a little bit more about him. He said he was from Pittsburgh, worked in the Dirksen Senate Office Building, and lived just off the Red line. After a moment of deafening silence, we both looked around and found a reason to excuse ourselves.

Not ready to give up just yet, I stalked him, err, I mean, I thought about him and what he had said for he next several days. I figured that if he lived on the Red line, and worked at the Dirksen, he would likely have to arrive at Union Station sometime around 8:30 A.M. and walk across a well-worn pathway through the adjacent park toward the

Dirksen. All I needed to do was retrace those steps, and I was bound to run into him. After a few tries of being coincidentally at the right place at the right time, my detective work paid off, and I did happen to run into him.

"Hey, aren't you Mark, from the reception?" I asked feigning surprise to have bumped into him.

"Yeah. Hey! It's Jon, right?" he replied, thrilling me to no end. He remembered my name!

"Yeah! Hey, it's funny running into you. It was nice talking to you the other night, but I didn't get a chance to ask you . . . um, I was thinking it might be nice maybe to get together for dinner sometime. If you have a free night, " I said, probably very nervously. His response, after a muffled chuckle, cut short my hopes to date him.

"Well, so Julie figured me out, huh? Yes, I'm gay, but please don't confirm that to her. I would love to go out with you, but I have a boyfriend back in Pittsburgh, so I think it would be best if we didn't," came the crushing blow.

With my heart in my stomach, I responded, "Oh, don't worry about Julie. She doesn't know. At least she's never said anything. I just rather hoped you were. She doesn't know about me either, so mum's the word."

And with that, my first attempt at a boy/boy date evaporated. I never ran into Mark again, accidentally, incidentally or otherwise, but I often still wish I would!

I left Washington with a sense of independence. Upon returning home, I did not go back to work at the Rec Center. Instead, I found a job as a waiter at a new restaurant that had opened in Salt Lake City called Cravings. I found a two-bedroom apartment and shared it with two girlfriends, one of whom had gotten me the job at Cravings. I lived less than five minutes from the U and about five minutes from work. Living and working in D.C. had been a vitalizing experience. It motivated me to do better in school and refocus my energy on pursuing a career.

In late January, I finally met a guy who would eventually be my first boyfriend. One evening, I was walking down the street after work on my way home and I noticed a good-looking, dark-haired young man walking the other direction on the other side of Main Street. As he noticed me, we made eye contact and he stopped. We stared at each other for a moment, and then he crossed the street coming toward me. Curiously, I turned around and walked back toward work. As I walked past him, he was unmistakably checking me out.

"Hey there," he said. "What's going on tonight?"

"Hey," I casually responded. "Not much. I just got off work. I think I forgot my wallet, so I'm headed back over there." I had to think of something to explain my abrupt change in direction.

"Really? Where do you work?" he asked.

"At Cravings, just around the corner." I responded.

"Ah, okay. Well, maybe I'll see ya later." And he stayed right there as I walked around the corner, all the way back to Cravings (about a block), and was still there when I walked back.

"So, did you find your wallet?" he quizzed with a smirk on his face, as I walked by again.

"I did, actually. Thanks for asking," I responded.

"Well, good, you can buy me a beer. My name is Greg," he said as he reached out to shake my hand.

"I'm Jon," I responded, grabbing his hand with a big smile on my red face.

And with that, we jumped into his silver Subaru Legacy and hightailed it to a 7-Eleven like a couple of winos. While I thought we were probably going to a bar, he thought it would be more fun for me to buy him a six-pack and a sack of doughnuts and then head back to his place. After waiting this long for my first boy "date," I wasn't about to question where I bought his beer, or what he washed down with it.

Greg lived in a one-bedroom basement apartment near the University. He invited me in and was a perfect gentleman. He was also an officer in the Air Force. Boy, was I impressed with that. After a beer or two, he leaned over and kissed me. At last, here were the fireworks! It was all so natural and comfortable to me, and so right. I stayed the night, never thinking about where I was or what time it was, or where I was supposed to be.

Greg and I started seeing each other regularly. I introduced him to my group of friends, on a very slow basis, and he introduced me to his, usually arranging to meet up accidentally somewhere, wherein the charade would begin.

"Hey, I think that's my friend Greg from school. Do you guys know Greg? Hang on a second, I'll see if I can get him to come meet you." And so it went, in our closeted way: We introduced each other to our circle of friends, as though the other were just a casual acquaintance.

Greg's circle was much rowdier and crazier than my friends. Most of them, like he was, were from out of state, came to school in Utah for the skiing, and partied like crazy. Oh, and most of his friends were fraternity brothers in Sigma Nu or Pi Beta Gamma.

Greg was my introduction into the world of fraternity house partying, and I loved every Animal House minute of it, though we never actually partied at the frat house. Greg's friends were mostly seniors, so they lived in various apartments around campus, and on a good night, we would drink at all of them. There were always plenty of women around, and in front of me, Greg was not shy about trying to get them to go out with him. Then, after flirting with them all night, and drinking too much, we would go back to his place and sleep together.

Greg and I rationalized our sexuality by claiming to be bi-sexual. We continued to date girls, he more often than I, but we both did so throughout our relationship. We stopped using personal pronouns in our conversations, opting instead to describe someone as a "person," as in "I was out with this person from work till about 2 A.M."

I would later move into my own place. Greg and I bought a golden retriever together, and named him Bailey. Bailey lived with me because Greg's apartment did not allow pets.

I continued hanging around my same friends, though slowly Greg's crowd became more familiar, particularly in the spring when the snow melted. Greg's friends loved to play golf. And, at the University of Utah, students played nine holes for $3. And despite that being a great deal, it was not uncommon for students on the tee of the ninth to jump over to the tee of the second, and play an extra seven holes, or 16 holes, for the same $3.

There was a period of about five weeks when we played golf every afternoon. Usually, someone rented a cart, and at the first hole we filled the cart with a cooler of beer. After 9, 16, or 23 holes of golf, gin martinis followed our beer drinking until we passed out. We would get up in the morning, hung over, miss class, and do it again. Sometimes work got in the way, but we never let classes put a damper on our game. Honestly, I don't know how I passed my classes that quarter. I'm sure I nearly failed out.

Fortunately, at one of the golf-day after-parties, I drank way too much gin and got very, very sick. I didn't make it to class the next day, nor did I make it out onto the links. I stayed home all day, sicker than a dog.

To this day, I haven't touched a drop of gin, and on that day, I finally broke the every-day golf cycle.

AFTER A LONG winter, and a nearly nonexistent spring, summer finally rolled around and I took a job waiting tables at Oceans, a fine seafood restaurant located in South Salt Lake. The tips were better at Oceans than at Cravings, largely because the menu prices were higher, though I was working the lunch shift. Still, 10 percent is 10 percent.

Utahns aren't known for their generosity when it comes to tipping, and it was typical to wait on an entire family of 10 with highchairs and booster seats, and a huge fishy mess that looked like bombed Beirut when they were finished, only to find a dollar in dimes stacked under the debris. At $2 an hour plus the tips, I'd have to turn a lot of tables if I were ever to make a living waiting on families.

Working in a restaurant where most of the waiters were gay and closeted made me feel right at home and more comfortable with my own double life. It seemed like the norm, at least in the restaurants of Salt Lake, was to be gay, silent, and invisible, so I did my best to blend in and not raise any suspicion about my sexuality. It wasn't any different in figure skating.

Between school and restaurant side work, I was invited to judge Salt Lake's local competition, the Copper Cup, and traveled twice to Colorado to judge two of their summer competitions. I failed, however, to get an invitation to judge in Sun Valley. I was still not getting invitations to judge the numerous competitions held all summer in northern California. Not that I cared that much. I was really enjoying the friendly Colorado judges, and their bridge games, just fine. At one point, I was even considering moving to Denver after graduation just so I could be in a better region with more enjoyable people to be around.

The judging was starting to suck me in. Just as skating as a young kid had caught me like a trout and slowly reeled me in without fully understanding the sacrifices or expense, now too did the judging side of the sport. Making life decisions—such as moving to a new city—for an obsessively compulsive volunteer activity is more common than one might think, especially in figure skating.

I changed jobs again at the end of the summer. I had been working the lunch shift at Oceans, but had been promised a dinner slot once school started. Without the shift change, I wouldn't be able to take the classes I needed to graduate. The week before school started, I got the bad news from management.

"We think you're a great waiter, Jon, but at night we only want women serving," he said.

I knew of one male server working the dinner shift, so I asked why the exception for him.

His answer blew me away. "Well, to be quite honest, he's straight."

Aside from that plainly sexist and discriminatory statement of bigotry, I realized that everyone around me already knew what I had publicly ignored. I still hadn't admitted my same-sex attraction, yet my manager decided I was gay.

This was my first barefaced experience with homophobia, or was it? How could it be homophobia when I hadn't even come out as a gay man? Can a person be homophobic toward someone who they just *think* is gay?

I later learned that the asshole manager who made that comment was gay himself! How can a person be both homophobic and gay? I would later experience first-hand, in the skating world, that instances of homophobia by gay men toward other "suspected" gay men are not unusual at all.

IN THE FALL, I was assigned to judge my first qualifying competition, the Central Pacific Championships, being held once again in Belmont, California. Coincidentally, it was held at the same rink where I had won my Intermediate Men's silver medal. I was determined to make a good impression and finally to make friends with those damn California judges.

I felt like I had started making a good impression. If it hadn't been for all the bland, old-people food, a great Chinese restaurant a few blocks from the rink, and a Wendy's Hamburgers across the street, I would have made an even better one! I spent my mealtimes at either Wendy's or the Chinese place, and then quickly returned in time to socialize in the judges' room as best I could. Each night, I also went reluctantly to the hospitality suite at the hotel to try to get to know the California judges.

When I first walked into the hospitality suite, I overheard one of the ladies, surrounded by a group of other judges, telling a story with extraordinary detail and receiving enormous praise from her audience. I went in for a closer look and saw that the woman holding court and getting all the laughs was Joan Burns, who after Ida, was the highest-ranking judge in the entire region. She seemed to take as much pleasure in telling her stories as her listeners appeared to enjoy them.

Over the years, I came to realize Joan's stories were often tall tales of her skating travels. Interesting the first time you heard them, more interesting the second, and even more so the third. Each time through, the story would get larger, more grandiose, the characters more comical, and the conclusions more outrageously funny.

Sometimes, if you had already heard an earlier version of the story, and later heard it retold on its tenth or eleventh time out, with her embellishments, it might be a completely different story this time around. You could be getting the remixed version!

I learned firsthand how Joan's stories would begin—and later proliferate—earlier that summer at a non-qualifying competition. I was judging a pre-preliminary event of tiny little girls. Near the end of a group of about fourteen skaters, a six-year-old little girl skated in a cute little tie-dyed dress. She fell on an easy jump early in her program, and then just sat there crying. Soon, the referee coaxed her to skate over to him, where he asked if she was okay.

"I'm hungry," she responded.

Her simple, heartfelt answer caught the referee and all the judges off-guard, and its hilarity was in its surprise. Of course, this was the last thing that the referee or any of us judges expected to hear, and it incited an outburst of laughter.

In reality, her honesty was not such an unusual response. Her event had been held late in the morning, almost noon. She had probably gotten to the rink before sunrise and her coach likely didn't want her to skate on a full stomach during her freeskate, a common concern. Who wants to see a food baby poking out of tie-dye?

However, she was hungry, and at that moment, that was all she cared about.

Back in the judges' room, the story got retold, and all the other judges got a good laugh out of it, including Joan Burns who heard it secondhand for the first time.

Now, fast forward to Belmont, and Joan is retelling the story with a few new details: Ms. Burns is now a judge on the panel and has personally heard the "I'm hungry" punch line firsthand. The parents of the little girl are now hippies from Berkeley. "Why else would they have dressed their daughter in tie-dye?" she asked her listeners. A few new details that added a bit of character to the story, no harm done.

A subsequent version had a poor, dirty-kneed child skating with ratty dreadlocks in addition to her tie-dyed outfit and feather-roach clipped hair, the coach lived with the parents on a hippie commune, and the referee called in Child Protective Services! Okay, so I exaggerate, but you get the point. What started with a hint of truth became a very fascinating and hilarious tall tale! Joan is a master storyteller, and because of it, became the queen of the judges' hospitality room with the other judges hanging on her every word.

Because of Joan Burns, and several other characters equally as fascinating, I was finding my charge to spend more time with the judges much easier and enjoyable. I left Belmont feeling like I had made a few inroads into the judges' circles by mere association. I still wasn't saying much, but sometimes being a good listener is more important, and Joan Burns loved a good listener.

Though weary of being told to spend more time with the judges, I was beginning to heed the advice. The next month, I went to Spokane, Washington to trial-judge at the next level of judging, hoping to secure my next appointment.

All week, in an effort to gain further respect, I repeated to myself the recommendation that had been drilled into me before: "Don't fraternize with the coaches and skaters!" This advice served me well until the end of the week, after tiring of socializing with the same group of people. I felt like I should spend a little time with some old friends.

As I walked from the judges' seating area on my way back to the judges' room, an old skating pal of mine, Tom Wood*, stopped me and asked me to join him later for a drink. I knew by now that I should spend this last night of the competition with the judges at the hospitality room back at the hotel, but, to be honest, that was the last place I wanted to be for my final night in Spokane.

I told Tom (in a whisper) that I could meet him after my review meeting, which would take about an hour.

"Is that too late?" I asked.

"Not at all," he casually replied. "I'll just hang out until then. Try to find me when you get done."

Convinced I'd never find him, instead I gave him the key to my room. "Meet me at my room in an hour. If I'm late, just let yourself in and watch TV until I get there."

He agreed, and off I went to discuss and debate the placements and markings of several Senior Ladies, three of whom had just qualified for the National Championships. This was my first trial-judging experience at the Sectional level, and as I said, I was determined to make a good impression.

As it turned out, the meeting ran over and even though I raced back to my room at the first opportunity, I was already a half hour late. Knowing that Tom would still likely be waiting, I didn't bother to pick up a new key at the front desk, and instead headed straight for my room.

When I knocked on the door, I was met by an unexpected voice from a young woman. "Who's there?" the voice said.

"It's me. Jon. Who's this?" I asked back.

"Chrissy*," she said as she opened the door. Chrissy was Tom's 19-year-old sister and former ice-dance partner. Greeting her, I walked into the room and saw Tom with a beer in his hand, sitting in a chair on the other

---

* Not their real names.

side of the room facing the beds. The television was on, and the volume up too loud, but Tom was not watching it. He was having a conversation with a teenage girl who was lying on her stomach atop one of the beds watching pay-per-view porn. As I walked further into the room, I recognized the young girl as skater Tonya Harding.

I looked at Tom inquisitively, and hollered, "What the hell?" To which Tom smiled and replied, "Chill, dude, it's no big deal."

"No big deal?" I exclaimed. "You have your sister and her underage friend in my room watching porn? What are you thinking?"

"Hey, it's only Tonya. She's cool," he replied, still smiling.

I flipped off the TV, turned to "only Tonya," and said, as composed and controlled as I could, "I'm sorry; you are going to have to leave."

Then I turned to Chrissy. "Chrissy, it's great to see you, but the two of you are going to have to go."

From behind me, a now little Linda Blair hissed and ordered, "I'm not going anywhere! Turn that TV back on, I was watching that!" When I spun back around to her, I could see that Tonya was now sitting up on the bed, preparing for a fight.

I focused back on Chrissy. "Please, get her out of here. *Now!*" I said, this time in my sternest I-mean-it voice.

Tonya was not done.

"Who the hell do you think you are?" roared Tonya.

Then Tom piped up and calmly informed me, "Jon, really, it's no big deal. Tonya has seen a lot worse than this. It's nothing new."

Without even addressing Tom, I grabbed Tonya by the wrist and said, "Let's go!"

Suddenly, a mouth like none I had ever heard before, at least not on a little girl, unleashed and went into overdrive. As she tried to struggle from my grip, the expletives that naturally rolled off her little tongue could take the shine off paint. The struggling and cursing continued until well after I had her firmly planted outside my door. She cussed like a burly longshoreman who had smashed a thumb under a wooden shipping crate. Tonya was strong too. She was a trained athlete and, despite her age and height, she almost outmaneuvered me!

Chrissy joined Tonya outside my room and did her best to calm her down, "Cool it, Tonya! Jeez, you'll wake up the whole hotel!"

Nevertheless, I could still hear my name, mixed with profanities, seething from Tonya as she and Chrissy made their way down the hallway as they went to look for something else to do. Pity the person at their next encounter.

Frazzled, I went back in the room and asked Tom to hand me a beer. I pushed the rewind and replay button in my head. What had just happened?

My first realization was that the local organizing committee for this competition might believe I had been watching "Breast Blanket Bongo" if they happened to review my hotel bill. Would a night of "T and A" ruin my judging career, before it even started? It was somehow lost on me that an underage youngster had been watching pornography in my room with adults drinking alcohol. No, instead of being concerned about contributing to the delinquency of a minor, I was worried that the other judges would think I was a pervert!

"Well, at least it was straight porn," I consoled myself, and chugged down my beer.

AT THE END of the fall quarter, I had enough credits to graduate with a degree in Finance, though I would need to finish a few prerequisites. I signed up with an on-campus recruiter to interview for jobs that would start either at the beginning of the summer or late in the fall. Because I was only taking one class at the time, I took a job as a night auditor at the Sheraton Hotel.

This job made it very difficult to take any time off to judge skating competitions. Who would cover for me in my absence? The weekend auditor could help me out occasionally, perhaps a day here or a day there, but I was used to performing high-bar gymnastics with my work schedule to take off all the time necessary to travel around the skating circuit.

Without giving it another thought, I quickly made my way into a front-desk position. The Sheraton had multiple front-desk workers, so covering my shifts would be a snap. I had also moved into a larger apartment, and Greg had moved in with me. We were now officially "roommates" and, in my mind, boyfriends. But not in Greg's. Greg was still dating girls and encouraged me to do the same.

One of the front desk managers, Lisa Denooth*, showed some interest in me, so I began dating her. This only lasted a few weeks, as again, once we got to the point where I could no longer safely hang out at first base, I called it off. Of course, working together after the "breakup" was no picnic, but I had made my bed so I had to lie in it.

Fortunately, the on-campus recruiter landed me a job with NW Transport, a regional trucking outfit based out of Denver. I would be entering the "management training program" in their Salt Lake City terminal, with the understanding that after one year, I could transfer to another terminal in their expanding West Coast operation as an assistant manager.

Each terminal had several assistant managers. One for the dock, supervising the Teamsters loading and unloading the trucks, one for dispatch, one for billing, and one for administration and so on. Because of this arrangement, I spent my time with NW working alongside the employees in every department. I even loaded and unloaded freight from trucks, alongside some of the butchest men you will ever meet. I even convinced the manager of the dock to hire Greg, at night, to assist as a "casual" laborer, when they needed extra hands during busy times.

So, there I was, a former figure-skater, working alongside my gay lover, unloading diesel trucks in what can only be classified as the most conservative city in America! Looking back, it was quite an experience, and I enjoyed myself enormously. Of course, when working the administrative side of the business, I made fast and furious friends with the women who largely filled these positions. But I was still a fish out of water, so I took the GMAT, scored well, and began applying to business schools.

Now, working in a typical American job, where two weeks' vacation was the norm, it's a wonder I managed to judge any skating competitions that year, but I did, and here's how. First, all of my vacation days were spent at skating competitions. Second, some of the rotations were at night (billing and the dock rotation), so, because of that,

---

* Not her real name.

I arranged to take on double shifts in exchange for an additional day off here and there.

During the winter of 1988, Ida Tateoka arranged once again for me to "practice-judge" the National Championships in Denver. I hadn't made an official application to trial-judge, as I had not yet been approved at the requisite level in which to do that. Nonetheless, Ida used her powerful influence to persuade U.S. Figure Skating to allow me to attend the freeskating events, along with a credential to trial-judge. However, my marks and performance would not count toward my appointment.

I arrived late in the week, was given a credential, and was allowed to sit alongside the trial judges for the Senior freeskating events and the Pair events. I was also not invited to attend the performance-review sessions afterwards. Of course, I did not know this at the time, but merely judging the events, with no review afterward, did me absolutely no good, and not because the experience didn't "count" toward advancement, but because nothing is learned by a trial-judging experience if there is no feedback.

As an example, that year in the Pairs event, Katy Keely and Joey Mero placed fourth, missing a spot on the World team. However, on my judging sheet, I had placed them third. Clearly, in my mind, they were better than the brother/sister team of Seybold and Seybold. Because I wasn't allowed to attend the event review meeting, I might have never learned why. Fortunately, Ida was available later to talk to me about it, and she agreed that Keely and Mero should have been placed in third. We discussed our reasons why, but it would have been more helpful, at least in my development as a judge, to hear the reasons as to why the Seybolds were placed higher.

Thankfully, the headquarters for NW Transport were in Denver. As part of my juggling for days off to attend the Championships, I arranged a few meetings with the NW higher-ups in Denver on the Friday during the Championships, so I wasn't required to take any days off work. In my constant attempt to be at as many figure-skating competitions as possible, without abusing my vacation and/or sick days, at least the Denver Nationals practice experience had not used a single valuable day off.

Because word spread quickly around the terminal that I was involved in figure-skating, when the Calgary Olympics rolled around in early 1988, I became the resident expert.

Everyone wanted to know who was going to win. "What is that Debi Thomas like?" they would ask, especially after she appeared on the cover of *Time* magazine in a solid gold outfit. I didn't really know her. She won her Junior Regional title in Fresno the year I won my Novice title, and I remember her getting 5.0 marks, a very high score for the Junior level. This prompted the crowd to go crazy. But I didn't actually "know" her. This didn't stop me from rendering my opinion that she was a shoo-in for the gold. The rest of the competition wasn't even close!

When the tiny, yet stunning Jill Watson, with her equally good-looking partner Peter Oppegard won their bronze medal in Pairs, interest in the Olympics and figure-skating took off. Soon, they were all talking about the "Brians," Boitano from the U.S. and Orser from Canada.

"Brian Boitano, what is he really like?" Again, I had no idea. However, the "Battle of the Brians" kept me from being too optimistic about his chances, though I thought he probably would win.

"It will be very close, but Boitano will win," I remember predicting.

Sure enough, he won! Now of course, my celebrity status on the docks of NW was getting off on a good footing. My prediction that Debi would win was soon taken as gospel. I even think some of the laborers might have gambled on my prediction, betting their money either illegally, or at the sports book in Wendover, Nevada, a popular two-hour-drive gambling destination with this crowd.

When she didn't win, it was a huge embarrassment for me. "I thought you said she was a sure thing," they kidded, or ribbed, or angrily shouted, depending on how much money they lost on their bets.

"She didn't skate. It's a sport. I can't help that she didn't land her jumps," I would counter.

"A sport? Now that's a good one!" chuckling as they walked away.

The Calgary Games in 1988, Russians' Ekaterina Gordeeva and Alexander Grinkov, regarded by many as the best Pair team ever, struck gold, the seventh consecutive Olympic Pair gold medal for Russia.

From Plain to Plaid

HORTLY AFTER THE 1988 Calgary Olympics, I learned I had
been accepted into business school at the University of Washington in Seattle, and was also placed on the waiting list at the
University of North Carolina. I actually preferred North Carolina to
Washington, as that selection would have finally gotten me out of the
Pacific Coast Region where the judges were all so hostile toward my
hope for advancement.

North Carolina was not exactly a hotbed for figure-skating. But the
change in location would have also meant a change in the major players
that would determine the fate of my judging. Over the years, I met many
others similarly obsessed with figure skating, who made important life's
decisions based on how it would affect their "skating lives."

Throughout the spring and summer, I remained hopeful that North
Carolina would come through. I also ran into Victoria once again, and
began making amends for our lousy breakup. We went out drinking a
couple times, realized we still got along nicely, and soon put together
a wonderfully platonic friendship. In the meantime, I was also still
involved with Greg, though we had already been preparing for the
inevitable breakup.

The closer we moved to making our breakup final, it seemed the closer we became emotionally. I had begun to realize that our relationship was more than simply an experiment in bisexuality. Greg was also beginning to come to that realization. While it was enlightening to me, Greg's military position pushed him deeper into denying his sexuality, making him even more careful about hiding our relationship. Strangely, the closer we got, the greater the divide between us.

Sometime during the midsummer, I gave my two-weeks notice at NW. They were not happy with me after having invested a year of training in me, only to have me packing it in. They were just about to offer me a position in their Fontana terminal, and my departure left them with an unplanned opening.

Fontana was considered a prime assignment, so my fellow trainees, who otherwise were being stuck in places like Pueblo, Colorado or Twin Falls, Idaho, were more than happy to hear of my departure, as it opened up a cherry spot for one of them. The hardest part about leaving was that I had to say my good-byes to all my newfound friends, most of them women, unsurprisingly.

I also gave a thirty-day notice to my landlord, saying that I would be vacating the apartment. This upset Greg. He was still living with me and was planning to stay in the apartment under my lease. We lived in a studio apartment, and for the sake of appearances, kept two single beds to avoid drawing suspicion to our relationship, and once I was out of the picture, it would have worked out great for him and our dog, Bailey. The problem was that I had been paying all the rent: Greg had never chipped in a dime. I knew he couldn't afford the place on his own, and I sure didn't want to be responsible for his rent.

When I told Greg I had given notice, I mentioned that the landlord was willing to allow him sign a new lease for one year after running a credit check. He went ballistic! He started foaming at the mouth and yelling at me, blaming me for various issues I had never heard anything about, acting like a spoiled child throwing a tantrum. In retrospect, I realize that he was reacting more to the heightened, emotional powder keg created by our "planned breakup."

As the argument heated up, I pushed into uncharted waters. Were we in fact a gay couple, and if we weren't, why were we arguing like this?

I suggested there must be deeper emotions at play here, knowing that these kinds of disagreements didn't normally escalate to such a heated level "between friends."

In Greg's frustration of hearing from me what he was not ready to accept, he picked up my precious cactus-inspired planter, my "A" from pottery class, and hurled it in my general direction across the room! I watched in horror as my most valued possession flew through the air, hit the wall, and shattered into tiny pieces, spilling its dirt and plant across one of the beds. Then there was dead silence.

He suddenly realized what he had done and started crying about it. He came toward me to hug me, repeating, "I'm so sorry! I love you so much!" like a broken record.

I didn't say anything. I simply left. I finally realized how unhealthy this relationship was for me even though I was still very much in love with him.

I drove to a truck-rental center and rented a U-Haul. My plan was to pack immediately and leave Greg. He could figure his own plans out during his 30 days of free rent.

Along the way, I picked-up my friend Sherri and filled her in on what was going on. In a minor way, I had my first coming-out experience with her. It was "minor" because though she had never said anything, Sherri already "knew," so coming out to Sherri was really not coming out at all.

When I returned to my apartment with Sherri and a U-Haul, I realized that it wouldn't sit well with Greg, so I asked Sherri to wait in the truck. As I went inside, Greg was already working himself into a rage. So I left again, fearing that another UFO might find its way toward my head. As I backed out of the driveway, I could see all my clothes and furniture flying out the door and into the back yard of the adjoining apartment.

We later returned to find that Bailey, "Rage," and his belongings had vacated.

At that point, I considered staying, but figured that'd be the first place he'd look, so with Sherrie's help, we pulled what was left of my clothes and dishes out of the roses and flowerbeds and packed the U-Haul without further incident.

It was time for a lot of changes. The next day, I planned lunch with Victoria. I picked her up and without so much as a bag of sandwiches, drove her to a park near the Capitol and I finally came out to her. Just like that.

I told Victoria just about everything. How scared I was, how I didn't really like the gay people I knew, how I didn't have a single gay friend, how I had never been to a "gay bar" or even wanted to go, but that I was, in fact, gay and I needed to start dealing with it.

Victoria was completely understanding and supportive. She told me she knew tons of gay men. She taught aerobics at one of Salt Lake City's better fitness clubs, and many of her fellow male aerobics instructors, along with nearly every male who attended her classes, happened to be gay, and offered to introduce me to a few. I declined her offer, telling her I was not ready for it. I said I would let her know when I was ready, and she could introduce people to me then.

At one point, she even scolded me for being so negative about being gay. My impressions of homosexuality were ideas I had collected from years of secretive figure-skating, backward Mormon theology, and from having spent the previous two years with a guy buried deeper in denial than I was. All the negative stereotypes I had learned were reinforced by Greg, strange as that now seems.

Later that day, Vic called me up to see how I was doing, and asked if I was up for going out to La Frontera later, our favorite Mexican restaurant on Salt Lake's west side, and then on to the Dead Goat afterward for a pitcher or two of beer. The prospect of drowning my sorrows in alcohol was too appealing to pass-up, so I accepted the offer.

We were seated at a four-top and just about to order, when someone Victoria knew squealed from across the room, wildly waving his arms. "Hey, Victoria! It's Kevin! Over here! Oh, my gosh!"

Vic waved back, "Hey! Kevin Dana!"

Kevin was a bottle-blond with pompadour bangs, as physically fit as any football stud, while still as delicate as an aerobics instructor. He talked with a giggle that he seemed especially proud of, because he couldn't have cared less who heard what he had to say, and every person within a mile could.

As he approached the table, I could see him butch up his demeanor a bit from his terrorizing greeting, and his voice finally lowered several octaves and decibels. "Hey, Vic!" followed by "You haven't 'introduced' me to your friend!" and, turning to me, he said, "Hi, I'm Kevin."

"Kevin, this is my friend, Jon Jackson." Victoria quickly jumped in, just as I said hello and introduced myself.

Kevin then blurted out, "Well, nice to meet you, Jon Jackson." Turning to Vic, he continued, "Yeah, Dale and I thought we would come down here for a bite to eat. But, I don't know, we may not stay. The wait for a table is like 45 minutes, or something crazy like that."

As if on cue, Vic's response was "Oh, please, Kevin, join us! There's room at our table." I couldn't help but wonder if this was planned from the beginning.

Then Kevin started waving his arms around again, summoning this Dale from the waiting area.

That was how I met my first openly gay friends in Salt Lake City. Though at first I was mortified, it wasn't so terribly painful. Both Kevin and Dale were great conversationalists, covering every topic from film, music, fashion, and politics. I had never met anyone that seemed to know everything about everything. No matter what issue was supposed, Kevin and Dale seemed to have access to current information.

At the end of dinner, Kevin and Dale announced they were going out to the Sun, one of Salt Lake's largest gay bars, and asked if we wanted to go. The Sun was the same place Charles Kennedy's secret heavy had followed Ian to, blowing the story about his wedding.

My introduction to Salt Lake City's gay culture began that night. I found out that there was nothing seedy about the Sun at all. It was just like any other smoky bar I had been to, except it was filled primarily with men dancing to better music. There were also a few drag queens and a couple of gals who I learned were called "fag hags." Fag hags—such an unfortunate name for some of the greatest people in the world.

Kevin and Dale seemed to be very popular and knew a number of Salt Lake City's openly gay men. After hanging out with them a few weeks, it wasn't long before I was also being invited to a number of cocktail parties, dinners, and outings down to the Sun.

I recognized some of the guys I met, mostly from my days at the Maxim, though occasionally I would also meet someone from college, or high school, and think "You too, huh?" It's amazing what I found out when I finally opened that big, scary closet door.

I also found myself very comfortably in the middle of Kevin's entourage, a gay gaggle of several others dubbed "The Esprit Club," so-named after a line of women's clothing fashions of the time by another group of very pretentious friends who found out they had been nicknamed the "Polo Club."

The Esprit Club evolved over a few years and included mostly driven and ambitious gay men who were good-looking and stylish by nature. Most were raised in the Mormon Church. Most wanted something better for themselves, and we watched or participated as the gay rights movement evolved around us during the next few years.

After a few weeks of getting to know my newfound friends, it was time to bid Salt Lake City good-bye and head to Seattle to start business school. But now I didn't want to leave. I had just met a great group of people, and was not looking forward to "coming out" again when I got to Seattle.

So I called on my dad.

On more than one occasion, my dad had dropped the name of his old dorm mate from business school, who was now a high-ranking professor in the Finance Department at the University of Utah. I asked my dad if he could call his old friend and see about getting me into the U's MBA program at the last minute.

My GMAT score was far better than their admission average, and my GPA well within range, but I had not even bothered to apply there, even as a backup in case I not been admitted elsewhere.

I told my dad my decision to stay in Utah was financially motivated. I was going to be paying for my graduate school education on my own, and the thought of a huge debt after graduation was weighing on my mind. In-state tuition at the U was a fraction of the out-of-state tuition at UW. It was an easy sale really, which, with my Dad, was always easy when we were talking his language: dollars and sense.

My dad placed the call; I filled out the form and got in, nothing much to it really.

I was not yet comfortable outside the proverbial closet, so at work and at school, I kept that door shut. That all changed when I met my second boyfriend, a former co-worker of Kevin Dana's, Jay Cook. That relationship was the catalyst that prompted me to come out to my family and friends.

∞

IN THE EARLY part of the winter semester, the Dean selected me to be his intern on a special project with the Governor of Utah. That meant with the stipend I would receive, I could quit my night job and focus more time on my school work.

Soon after receiving the internship, I was off to Baltimore to trial-judge the National Championships.

I arrived in Baltimore early in the week because I had been approved to trial-judge the figure events there. I wasn't able to stay the entire week, however, as my internship required that I be back in Utah on Thursday.

Nationals begin on Sunday and conclude the following Saturday. Even though I would be missing a substantial part of the experience, Ida still encouraged me to attend. She even allowed me to sleep on the floor of her hotel room so I could save money, because it was important to her that I trial-judge the figures, and even more important that I attend the event-review meetings that I missed in Denver.

On my first day there, I met a good-looking-for-his-age gentleman, the aforementioned Slick Hardwood, a man whose reputation had preceded him. His charm and charisma were apparent from the moment we met, and surely he wasn't pouring it on for a young gay man from Salt Lake. Rather, it was so inherent in his nature that it wasn't something he turned on for women and off for men. It was just him. Good-looking, charming, charismatic Slick Hardwood. All of the stories I had heard now made perfect sense.

On my last night in Baltimore, I trial-judged the Pair event, and also met, for the first time, Gale Tanger, an attractive, tall, slim blonde from Milwaukee. She was an International judge, and very influential. She was in charge of the event-review meeting after the short program for the Pair event. Having missed the Denver opportunity, I wanted to take full advantage of this meeting, speaking my mind, asking

questions, and I made a positive, lasting impression in the mind of
Gale Tanger.

I went back to work in Salt Lake the next morning, and missed what
was largely considered one of the biggest judging travesties in the United
States up to that time. The brother/sister team of Seybold and Seybold
had been favored to win, but skated terribly. The judges, up to their old
tricks, placed them in second place to keep them on the World Team,
rather than the fourth or below they deserved. There was outrage from
the fans, skaters and even some judges. Somehow, every judge who "held
up" the Seybolds ended up on a fast track to nowhere, and the trial judges
who judged it accurately were all promptly promoted.

The trouble was, I had not been there to judge it accurately (or inac-
curately for that matter); I was back working and studying in Salt Lake.
But when it came time to make an application for my appointment in
the fall, for what I believe was merely a Junior competition appointment,
Ida included in my application my "practice scores" from the Denver
nationals. Remember, at those championships, I marked Keely and
Mero over the Seybolds. Now couple that with the impressions I left
with Gale Tanger.

When you put those two facts together, it equaled quick approval
for my appointment. The funny thing is, the facts were twisted, who
knows by whom, and it is now commonly believed that I was one of
the trial judges who got it right in Baltimore, even though I wasn't even
there! And in the skating world, once something becomes accepted as
fact, it's impossible to correct. To this day, I understand there are judges
who would swear on their mother's grave that I was at the competition
in Baltimore, and that I judged the Seybolds correctly.

This would prove to be a good lesson to me. Sometimes fighting
"accepted beliefs," no matter how false or invalid, is an impossible, head-
against-the-wall-hitting experience, and is better left undisturbed.
There is nothing you can do to the change the minds of figure-skating's
establishment once they have made up their collective minds.

Back in Salt Lake, busy trying to impress the dean, some hambone at
the Medical Center declared to have discovered "cold fusion." Suddenly
the governor, and everyone else of importance in the state, including the
dean of the MBA school, were sliding down rainbows, fast-chasing this

nonexistent pot of gold. While I still received my stipend, the projects I was working on were deader than the end of the cold fusion street. By the end of my internship, as history now tells us, the tests on the cold fusion were faulty, and it simply did not exist, at least not in the aquarium tanks of a few humiliated researchers.

During this "downtime" of having little to do, I ran into my old friend Todd Leishman from high-school debate and my internship in D.C. He was finishing his first year of law school, and loved it. He also had just received a summer clerkship at one of Salt Lake's more prestigious law firms, and the salary he was going to get blew me away. According to him, the salaries were even higher after graduation.

I couldn't believe it. I was interviewing for a bunch of boring jobs that paid nothing in the range of Todd's "clerkship." Todd further informed me that it was easier work than what we had done in D.C. Fewer hours, lots of lunches with partners, and weekend getaways with the other clerks, all part of being wined and dined to come to work at their firm after graduation. Wined and dined? I liked the sound of this.

"Just how does one get into law school?" I soon asked.

A few months later, after acing the LSAT, I found myself admitted to law school. You should have seen the look on my dad's face when I told him.

"A lawyer? A lawyer!?!" To him, the lawyers were the enemy of business. I imagine the news was even harder for him to take than finding out his son was gay!

Needing a summer job after graduating from business school, I called another friend, Alvin, who got me a job waiting tables with him at the Old Spaghetti Factory in Salt Lake's Trolley Square.

I had already incurred a small amount of debt in student loans to get me through MBA school, but it paled in comparison to the sizable debt looming ahead to get through law school. I had made the decision not to work at all during my first semester of law school. According to Todd, all my job offers would be based on my placement in the class from that semester. I was determined to break my bad study habits and hit the 100 percent attendance level.

∞

MY FIRST SEMESTER of law school, somehow, I managed to get to class and study. I actually studied. I scored a GPA placing me in the top five students of my class. Just as Todd promised, this landed me multiple job offers at outrageous salaries, for a summer clerkship.

I was traveling very little for skating, for the first time in a while, having focused my attention wholly on my first-semester grades. I did judge on one occasion.

As a mid-level judge, I was invited to judge my first Sectional championships in San Diego. At those championships, I met Steve Winkler, a judge who would transform my skating career.

Steve, a self-invited blueblood country-clubber from Seattle, had a successful dental practice on Washington's Olympic Peninsula. Though much older than me, Steve was also on the rise in the judging ranks.

It wasn't long before he too asked me why I wasn't spending much time in the judges' hospitality suite at the hotel, or in the judges' dining room between events. I thought I was making an extra effort to do so, but apparently it was not enough. I told him I'd do better and, to his delight, finished the week getting to know him better.

He was very complimentary to me and my school studies, even commenting that I was just the image skating was looking for.

"Too bad you're from Salt Lake City," he said all week, but backpedaled when I pressed for the meaning of his statement. He obviously thought of me as some rube from Utah. He had heard of Ida using her influence on my behalf, and was expecting something quite different than he found. "You're actually quite a good judge," was another one of his backhanded compliments.

I couldn't speak to his motivation, but Steve actually phoned me after that trip, and kept a lengthy conversation going. He was preparing me for the upcoming National Championships in Salt Lake City, where I would be juggling my schoolwork while attempting to trial-judge and, this time, attend all events and all the event-review meetings. Steve seemed sincere in his desire to help me out.

At those championships, Steve introduced me to Ron Pfenning and Bob Horen, two other very influential and very out-of-the-closet U.S. Figure Skating officials. Ron Pfenning was a heavyset gentleman with a commanding presence. I could hardly believe he was gay. Bob Horen was equally "straight-acting."

Nevertheless, they were gay, and not at all closeted about it. According to Steve, it was acceptable in figure-skating to be gay, just so long as one was not flamboyant about it. Just as he was giving me this lecture, I spotted Joe Inman, and ran over to say hello. Well, this greeting steamed Steve.

"How do you know Joe Inman?" he later pressed.

According to Steve, Joe was exactly the kind of gay judge who was going nowhere fast in the skating world. "Can't you see how flamboyant he is?" Steve argued. "He has a very big mouth, and that means very big trouble. Birds of a feather flock together, and if I were you, I wouldn't be seen with that old hen!"

The comments continued for some time, and again later. Of course, later in the week, when Steve needed Joe to help him out with the manipulation of the Ladies' event, he could not count on Joe to help his scheme: Steve Winkler did not like Utah's Holly Cook, a local vying for a spot on the World Team. She was a master at figures and an expert jumper. Problem was, she had a reputation for not being such a great "presentation mark" skater. The presentation mark is half the score, the other being the technical mark. Presentation involves a number of things, mostly centered around music and its interpretation.

Holly's reputation for having poor presentation was completely undeserved, but as I mentioned before, once something became "accepted" in the skating world, there was no changing this "fact."

Well, Steve felt that this "fact" warranted keeping her off the World Team. Steve explained to me how one could calculate exactly which place Holly needed to finish in order to drop out of the top three. She not only needed to place below a specific spot, but Nancy Kerrigan needed to beat her by two places.

Holly was a former dance partner of mine (1979 Big Sky Preliminary Dance Silver medalists!), and a very good friend. I wanted her more than anyone else to be named to the World Team, so I lobbied Steve hard on her behalf. His comments in reply were typical of his elitist approach to judging.

"She orders Thousand Island dressing, for God's sake, Jon," he snipped.

That was just one of his completely irrelevant indictments supporting his reasoning to keep Holly off the team. I made a mental note to stop ordering Thousand Island dressing, but continued my lobbying efforts.

When the marks came up, it appeared to me to be an attempt by Steve to manipulate her into the "correct" place, propping up the marks for Nancy. In the end, Joe Inman, along with the other judges on the panel, judged it fairly, and Holly went on to win the final figure-eight ever skated at a World Championships, a loop, and brought home the bronze medal, with Jill Trenary taking silver. After those World Championships, the figure-eights were eliminated from competition.

When I later pointed out to Steve how the U.S. would have been shorted a bronze medal if Holly had not gone to Worlds, he pointed out correctly that I was wrong. Kristi Yamaguchi finished fourth, and had Holly not been there, Kristi would have received the bronze. This turned out, however, to be the highlight of Holly Cook's career. She would have been robbed, along with her entire family for the sacrifices they had made on her behalf.

This incident took place at the end of the week, a week after Steve had spent showing me some other ropes.

He came with me to the practices, analyzed the skaters, and explained to me the manner in which to put the skaters into groups based on what we saw at the practice. This method of judging is quite common, and begins to set in the minds of the judges just how the event will come out. It's very self-fulfilling, and this is how it works:

Based on the practices, of which one is encouraged to get to as many as possible, a judge begins to set a ranking of how the skaters will likely come out. Skaters are assigned to A, B, C, and D groups, based on how well they perform, and the difficulty they are executing, in practice. As the week progresses, and more practices allow for further analyzing, pluses and minuses are added. Between practices, while in the judges' hospitality rooms, and at the cocktail parties held during the week, this "grouping" is discussed, with a general consensus reached even before any of the skaters has taken officially to the ice. This is commonly known as "chatter."

Of course, when the actual skating takes place, the judge must judge what is skated, and these groups just give a general guideline to help the judge get through the event. At least that was the argument made by Steve. It seemed to smack of prejudging in every sense, and gave plenty of opportunity for powerful judges to lobby less powerful judges to push up or push down a certain skater.

Well, I stuck to the system as a trial judge, and miraculously, I was able to put the skaters in the order they came up. By talking with Steve, and by listening to other trial judges, I had a good idea how the event would come out, and was only off when I varied from the predetermined groupings. Let me say that again: I was only off when I varied from the predetermined groupings. What happened to judging the events as they are skated? It became apparent to me how a majority of the judges had ended up with the Seybolds in second place the prior year, and similar mistakes were sure to happen with nearly every judge participating in this farce.

In my opinion, judges should be banned from attending *any* practice. They should see the skaters for the first time when they officially come to skate, with no predetermined idea of how the skater might or might not perform.

Many of the judges are insecure in their abilities, and, by double-checking with other judges prior to the performance, they obtain confidence in the judging of the event, and, by scoring similarly to the other judges, give the appearance that they know what they are doing. The system fosters bad judging, trains potentially good judges to pre-set their minds a certain way, and has a great deal of influence on the final placement, and careers, of the skaters.

But, hey, it got me through the week, and it got me noticed as a judge who seemed to know what he was doing, except on those occasions where I really did know what I was doing and went outside the predetermined groupings. Since those incidences were rare, it was apparently forgivable.

Following the National Championships, Steve and I spoke by phone for hours at a time, three or four nights a week, with him filling me in on the gossip and goings-on in the big-league judging circles, including the latest dalliances of very married and very influential judges.

Eventually, he invited me to spend my spring break with him in Ixtapa, Mexico. After a very, very long fall semester of devoting myself to studying and juggling the skating with my studies in the winter, a break to Mexico sounded fantastic. Still, I was reluctant. It just didn't feel right, accepting a free trip from someone superior to me in the skating world, particularly from a man practically twice my age who was single and gay. It had "come-on" written all over it. So initially I turned him down.

Soon after Steve's initial invitation, I learned that I had landed a plumb clerkship assignment with Kimball, Parr, Waddoups, and Gee, a top downtown law firm. It was the most sought-after firm that spring; I landed one of only three spots. I shared the good news with Steve during one of what were now becoming frequent phone conversations. He congratulated me, as you might expect, and then, again, he offered:

"Let me take you to Mexico during Spring Break to celebrate. It will be my way of congratulating you," he promised. He countered my continued hesitation with the assurance that he was inviting me "just as a friend."

"All your studying paid off, Jon. Don't you deserve to reward yourself?" Just who was rewarding whom? Better judgments rarely win in the end. I finally agreed to go.

Upon our arrival, it was clear to me that this was going to be a first-class week. The Camino Real Hotel was the southernmost establishment of the Ixtapa resorts, separated from the tourist hubbub by a good half mile. The rooms were spacious and luxurious, the bathrooms spa-like and covered floor-to-ceiling in beautiful white marble.

This was one of the finest hotels in all of Ixtapa, a quaint Mexican resort area, just a few minutes north of the small fishing town of Zihuatanejo and settled on the shores of the Pacific. In this beautiful oasis, Saltillo tiles covered the floors and spilled out onto private balconies. Our views of the beaches, and of the ocean, were accentuated by the positioning of the hotel, built high on a cliff above the exclusive cove below.

When we arrived at the hotel, I expected a room of my own to be waiting for me. Steve had made our arrangements, but after returning from the check-in counter, he informed me that the hotel was full. We'd be sharing a room. Walking into the room, I noticed that the two beds had been pushed together as if to make one large, king-sized bed. "Oh well," I thought. "At least half of it is still my own bed."

How lucky for me that Steve wanted company on his little getaway vacation, and even more fortunate that it was on his dime. He, after all, had assured me that I would not have to pay for a thing if I agreed to go along with him as his personal, platonic guest.

We had arrived late in the day, so we made our way to the hotel bar for a drink before dinner. Steve ordered a gin and tonic, and I ordered a strawberry daiquiri. Back then, I usually only drank beer, but this was a vacation. Besides, Steve was buying.

Then Steve exclaimed, "A strawberry daiquiri! Are you kidding?" as the waitress darted for the bar to fetch our drinks.

I sheepishly thought to myself, "Damn, maybe I should have gotten a beer. It was his bar tab after all. That was probably rude of me to order such an expensive drink."

"Oh, I'll only have one," I said, trying to cover. "Then I'll switch to beer."

"Beer? You drink beer?" Steve muttered in further disbelief, looking away and to the floor with an exaggerated look of disbelief and a pained look of humor on his face. I have now seen this look a hundred different times, and know it to be his partly condescending, partly kidding manner, combined with a huge dose of exaggeration. But here, I was seeing it for the first time.

"Yeah, mostly I drink beer." I respond defensively, "It's cheap and I like it."

"Good Gawd!" he exclaimed, vainly dragging out the pronunciation of the Lord's name. "Well then, it's time for your first lesson. I can see I'm going to have to teach you how to drink."

Upon delivering the daiquiri, the waitress frantically began writing down Steve's next order. He said without taking a breath, "Another gin and tonic, a martini, a vodka tonic, scotch on the rocks, and a white wine." Then, addressing me, he said, "Jon, what kind of white wine do you like?"

"What kind do they have?" I asked.

Steve let out a loud guffaw, and then looked at the waitress and smirked. "Bring us a Chardonnay," he said.

"Okay, Jon," he said, beginning the lesson. "First, there are only a few acceptable cocktails you can drink before dinner." He continued, "Taste all of the ones I just ordered, find one you like, and stick to it—and by sticking to it, I mean for the rest of your life. Every cocktail party, every dinner, order the same thing. You should be known by what you drink. My drink is a gin and tonic," Steve informed me.

"I hate gin," I said. "The last time I drank gin was with some buddies on the golf course at school. Unfortunately, after the golf ended, the gin didn't. I've never been sicker in my life, and I'll never touch gin again!"

Without missing a beat, Steve replied, "Well then, you've already narrowed the field, and the drinks have yet to arrive!"

When the drinks were placed between us, I took a sip out of each glass just as Steve had told me to do. Watching my facial expressions as I tried each drink, he declared, "You'll never pass that one off. Next!"

After I tasted them all, Scotch on the rocks became my drink of choice. It was light and heavy all at the same time, and I could feel it take its calming, relaxing effect almost immediately. When he saw that I liked a drink I didn't wince through, his lessons continued.

"Once dinner begins, you may not order another cocktail. Finish the drink you have, and then move on to wine. Obviously, you will also need to learn about wines." Steve continued with the basics. He was so impressive and worldly with all the things he knew. I had no idea that good etiquette required so much study. Still, I hung on his every word. I was tired of feeling backward and inexperienced. Steve's little lessons made me feel slightly less naïve and a lot more in control of my future.

Though I had only known him for a couple of months, I admired Steve, and I felt like we were developing a solid friendship. Yet, while he was muscular, handsome, and already a successful dentist, the 15-year age gap positioned him more as a father figure than a potential suitor.

By the time dinner rolled around, my head was full of new information on cocktail etiquette and wine lists, and I was feeling more than a bit tipsy. Just before we left the bar, Steve pulled from his pocket a little plastic packet. He smiled and waved the little packet in the air and asked, "Have you ever tried Valium?" I said I hadn't. I didn't even know what it was.

His smile grew bigger, revealing his perfectly straight, white dental work, and he said, "It's called a Marilyn, after Marilyn Monroe. You take a Valium with your cocktails. You can buy it over-the-counter at the pharmacies here in Mexico."

"Can I try it?" I replied. "What is it going to do?"

"It's a muscle relaxer. Dentists give it to their patients to help them relax during treatments." Steve went on to explain that he and some of his friends used the Valium to calm themselves while judging high-profile events. I could not believe what he was telling me.

"Oh, Jon, don't be so uptight!" he said. "You won't understand the pressure you are under until you are actually sitting in the hot seat, as a National judge yourself, if you ever get there. You don't know the pressure. It's very intense." He leaned toward me but allowed his eyes to drift as though imagining himself performing in a major stage production, and then continued, "The bright lights, the television cameras, the audience-packed arenas, and all the stress of picking the National Champion and the World Team. It's just too much! The Valium helps. Besides, it didn't hurt in getting me promotions."

And just as matter-of-factly as that, Steve went on to explain the political side of judging, "The Game" as he and many others called it. Steve told me that if I learned to play the game, a national judging appointment would be mine, sooner rather than later, with possible International and World appointments too.

We stumbled back to our room a little while later, giggling and believing everything the other said was the funniest thing we'd ever heard. We got ready for bed, but as I lay down to fall asleep that night, though still a bit Valium-clouded, my mind was racing with all sorts of information. I had some good thoughts, some bad, but all of it troubling. What was I to make of all this? In a state of mind that would make Jacqueline Susann proud, I was having trouble keeping it all from churning my stomach.

Just as I began to grapple with some of these thoughts, Steve suddenly rolled over from his bed. He went straight for a kiss, his tongue missing my mouth by a fraction. As I collectively mustered all my remaining strength to push away his muscled frame, he fell onto the floor beside the bed.

I could not help but mutter, "There goes my National appointment."

The next morning, he apologized, blamed the pills, and got right down to business. Before the week was over, the makeover blueprint that would transform a new judge from the sticks into an international "superstar" was laid out before me. We spent our days at the beach, in lengthy discussions, the evenings having cocktails and playing back-gammon. All during this time, Steve was coaching me in the tricks of the trade, creating my "image," and teaching me how to "play the game." We discussed everything from my hairstyle and wardrobe to judging demeanor and cocktail etiquette, all of which, according to Steve, needed his immediate attention.

In the years that followed, Steve would take to calling me "Grasshop-per," in reference to the television drama *Kung Fu*, in which the older and wiser Shaolin priest, Master Kan, mentors the up-and-coming martial arts master.

UPON MY RETURN to Salt Lake City, I learned that my homosexu-ality, which I did not attempt to hide in law school, was "leaked" to my potential employer. While Kimball, Parr (as it was called) was a well-respected firm, what I had not known when I accepted their clerkship offer was that they were also known for being very conservative. And in conservative Salt Lake, a very conservative law firm was perhaps not the best place for a gay man hoping to make his profession.

Not knowing what to do, I sought out a professor on staff who was respected by the students as a "listener." Terry Kogan was young for a law professor, his wife Linda was also on staff as a professor, and they both had reputations for interacting frequently with students. Because of his reputation, I decided to speak to him about the problem, even though I had never met him.

His advice was sage: Simply ignore the rumor and do your work. Your sexuality should make no difference, he argued. "And if it does, you will find out during the summer, which is better than finding out after accepting a job offer." Further, in his opinion, if word were to get around the legal community that any firm discriminates based on sexual orientation, they will be toast when it comes to recruiting again.

He was curious: "How did this 'rumor' find its way to Kimball, Parr?" I assumed that because Salt Lake's legal community was very small, that it would not be difficult for someone to find out as a matter of course. I did not suspect anything underhanded about the rumor; besides, it was true!

"Where are you ranked in your class?" he continued.

"About fifth, I think, but I'm not sure," I replied.

The grades of each student were confidential, and the rankings were not made public until graduation, when it is necessary to bestow the "Order of the Coif" on the top graduates. But in the competitive environment that was the Utah Law School, in a matter of days of grades being published, the "gunners" had the list calculated from about one to 10.

"Fifth? And you got one of the three spots at the best law firm in Salt Lake?" He continued probing, "Who is above you that Kimball, Parr passed over?" When I told him, he simply said, "Might you have learned something about the character of the two individuals who didn't get the job?" And in true law school/Socratic method, I learned just how competitive the legal community was, and how vindictive some people can be, especially when they perceive a weakness.

The trouble for them was that I no longer perceived my sexuality as a weakness. I took Professor Kogan's advice, and had one hell of a summer with the great lawyers of Kimball, Parr. At the end of the summer, they offered me a job, to begin two years hence, after graduation. Further, so confident were they that I would accept this offer, they encouraged me to spend my next summer clerking with another firm to make a sound comparison.

Rather than save the money I earned that summer to help pay my expenses, I spent it all on clothes. I became obsessed with suits, ties, and shoes. I had started the summer with two nice suits, one that I had purchased as an MBA as my "interview" suit, and another purchased new for clerkship. I had maybe a handful of ties, and one pair of black dress shoes. I finished the summer with several suits, about thirty ties, and five pairs of very nice shoes. This buying spree again took place under the direction of Steve Winkler, who sent me tear-outs from men's fashion magazines and mailers he received from the likes of Versace and Armani.

Most of the clothing was purchased to be worn in the winter (the figure-skating season) and was more comfortably worn at an ice rink than in the parking lot or the halls of a law firm during a sweltering Salt Lake summer. But I wasn't buying these clothes for the office. These clothes were purchased for the Nationals in Minneapolis, where I would unveil my new image.

In the fall, feeling very secure at school, I once again traveled extensively (more than I should have) for skating. First up, the Northwest Regional Championships in Spokane, Washington. Steve was also judging, and was absolutely mortified when he saw me at the judges' dinner.

"Jeans!" he nearly shouted.

I was wearing a very expensive pair of Girbaud Jeans, very fashionable in Salt Lake at that time, with a pair of brown loafers, a button-down white shirt, great colorful tie, and a plain looking, but nice, blue blazer.

"Have you not listened to a word I've been saying?" he hissed.

"What's wrong with jeans? These are a nice pair. I thought I looked good." I answered, red-faced.

"Never, never, never, wear jeans. Not to the judges' dinner, not on the judges' stand, not in the hospitality suite. Never, never," Steve insisted.

"But I like jeans, and they can look nice," I countered, my pride a bit crumbled. I really did believe I looked nice. In fact, I had carefully planned this outfit for this very purpose.

"Grasshopper, you must listen to me. Trust me! Never again wear jeans. You look like you're ready to dig a ditch. Save them for the airplane, wear them at home, but not at the competition. Jeans are not the image we are creating here," he warned one last time.

And with that, I made my way through cocktail hour and dinner, very self-conscious in the ditch-digging digs I dug.

$$\infty$$

AFTER RETURNING FROM Spokane, I spent my fall break traveling across the United States, visiting potential law firms for my second-year summer clerkship. I was sought after for my grades, and I was finding that my MBA looked impressive alongside them.

I interviewed with firms in San Diego, Los Angeles, San Francisco, Portland, and Seattle on the West Coast, Denver and Chicago in the Midwest, and New York City in the East. Eventually I selected Brobeck, Phleger, and Harrison, an established, large California firm. I would be clerking at the office of its headquarters in San Francisco. So much for getting out of the Central Pacific Region!

With the interview process out of the way, and my clerkship lined up for the summer, I traveled to Omaha to judge the Midwestern Sectional Championships at the Ak-Sar-Ben arena. (That's Nebraska cleverly and ironically spelled backward, for those of you not lucky enough to have been to this fine city.)

I wasn't worried much about my image in Omaha. I would be judging with the crowd that I was most comfortable with, the down-to-earth midwesterners. Many of my Colorado judging friends were there, and I enjoyed meeting others, many from Texas, Oklahoma, Minnesota, Michigan, all over the place really. The referee, Caroline Haman, was a delight to judge for, and a formidable bridge player as well.

Nebraska is *very* cold in the winter months. I spent nearly all of my time socializing and playing bridge with the judges. Not only was there nothing else to do, but I sincerely enjoyed the company of this crowd. Not that these judges don't on occasion make similar mistakes in "pre-judging."

In the Junior Men's event, Damon Allen, a skater out of Colorado, had a superb performance. It was obvious to me that he out-skated the pack, so I placed him first. The other judges didn't see it that way. When I queried some of them, their responses were similar, essentially: "Yes, he skated well today, but he is usually inconsistent."

What does "usually" have to do with his placement on *that* day?

In figure-skating, it has a lot to do with it. The judges go onto the stand with preconceived ideas, and the skating they see tends to fit into their preconceived notions, though they are all very well-meaning individuals.

I should tell you, there are only a few devious and calculating judges in the ranks of the hundreds of judges in the midwest. I know that the panel of judges meant well, but what effect was it having on the skater who clearly went out and claimed his place that day?

Fourth place is what it meant, and it nearly cost him a trip to the Nationals, by the skin of his teeth. I can only imagine where he would have ended up had he blown the short program.

Damon would go on to the National Championships in Minneapolis, skating as well during the practices as he did at Midwesterns. He would end up claiming the National title, this in front of judges who only knew him from his excellent practices, and not from a history of blowing it. The preconceived notions for Damon in the minds of the National judges were polar opposite to those in the minds of the Midwestern judges. And what a difference in the outcome.

Speaking of Minneapolis, the walk from the Marriott hotel to the Target Center was a mere three blocks, yet in the dead of a Minneapolis winter, there is nothing "mere" about it. The below freezing weather, together with the windchill and ice-covered streets, can make a city block feel like a country mile. For this reason, most of downtown Minneapolis is entirely indoors, with buildings connected by underground passageways and climate-controlled bridges. Sort of like a human hamster Habitrail or a giant Ant Farm. While the Marriott Hotel, host of the 1991 U.S. National Championships, is connected to downtown, it was not connected to the Target Center.

Sure, the local organizing committee had provided chartered buses for the coaches, judges and competitors, but not being one to wait in lines, I opted to walk. I raced from the hotel doors to the credential entrance at the Target center to keep from freezing solid, dressed head to toe in an Armani outfit. Or perhaps "underdressed." Having no overcoat, I froze my butt off the entire week. Fashion before function, I would later console myself.

Inside the Target Center, with dress rehearsals over, I would soon be on stage and would begin playing the game. At this event, my quest would be working on making an impression. According to plan, I was to be noticed—noticed at the practices, the parties, and the events.

Yes, there were still those damn trial-judging event-review meetings to deal with, but that was the *last* place I wanted to be noticed, according to Steve. I was always very scholarly about these meetings, treating them like oral exams. I knew the rules, the latest rule changes, the deductions, the illegal movements, everything possible to know about figure-skating. I gave every event my complete focus, including the practices. The marks I gave were well thought-out, and I knew I could back them up with the rulebook. I was well trained (at least in my mind) and determined to show the higher-ups that I knew my stuff.

"Not so fast!" instructed Steve. "If you are talking in the event-review meetings, you're talking too much! Leave that room unnoticed. Get noticed somewhere else!"

Up until Minneapolis, I was doing exactly the opposite. Rather, I looked forward to the event-review meetings and the opportunity to show the evaluators, usually World and International judges, just what I could do. Not this time. My clothes would be loud, but my voice would be silent.

Upon my arrival in Minneapolis, I unpacked immediately, and then began to iron my shirts—a ritual I continue to this day. The number of different shirts I wore during the week, all perfectly pressed, did not go unnoticed. Steve's plan was working.

After I finished unpacking, I jumped in the shower and then headed to the trial judges' meeting (in an outfit selected specifically for this purpose). At the meeting, the referee reviewed the rules and the expectations for the week, and handed out our trial-judging assignments. I listened intently but made no comment.

With that meeting out of the way, I was back to the room for my first costume change, into more formal attire for the evening's judges' dinner, the first in a week filled with cocktail parties and hospitality suites.

The party-going judges chattered nightly about skaters, and openly determined placements with cocktails in hand and biases in mind. Steve spent time with me hammering home the A, B, C, and D grouping method of pre-judging that he had taught me in Salt Lake. More and more, I was realizing the downside of this common practice. This method, which is terribly unjust to the skaters, pegs them to a group, and an ultimate placement, that they seemingly cannot rise above regardless of how well they perform during the actual competition.

Often, hints and conversations between judges of who's on top and who's on bottom are discussed and determined well before the skaters ever actually compete. Many times, the conversations aren't even traded in hushed tones. I once sat a National Championship practice session, in an unofficial capacity, and overheard one judge sitting behind me ask another, "Well, did you learn anything new?" The other judge simply answered, "Nothing we didn't already know."

In the Junior Men's event, I made a huge "mistake" by going against the predetermined groupings. John Baldwin, an A–/B+ skater from California, had done well in the short. But in the long program, he opened with a horribly executed triple lutz, bent over, with his head nearly touching the ice. The rest of the program was equally dreadful. So I placed him where he deserved, down in 9th or 10th place. The marks came up—and, with them, my lunch. Well, almost. The judges kept him in the same predetermined grouping, with the exception of Shirley Sherman, a judge from the midwest. She was correct, and so was I; but, based on the other judges' marks, it looked like we were extremely out of line.

I prepared for the judges' event-review meeting, where I knew I would be questioned about my marks.

A buffoon of an East Coast judge with black shoe-polish hair fired the first comment about Baldwin's skating. He stated that he had placed Baldwin high because, even though he didn't complete many jumps, by hanging on to the triple lutz, he proved that he had "big jumps" and should be at the top of the pack.

And before I was even asked a question, the buttinski debater in me caused me to blurt out, "Don't you mean that the triple lutz proved that he could *not* do the big jumps?"

The subdued laughter that followed was exactly the response I was hoping for, but it did me little good. I received a lecture from Steve as soon as he heard about my outburst.

"Never speak unless spoken to in a judges' review meeting. Let your marks and image speak for themselves," he said very firmly. But I had to justify why I had marked him low, so I countered, and he shut me down, saying, "I warned you about not breaking the groups, and see what happened? Now, are you going to listen to me about not speaking in the event-review meetings or not?" Point taken. After that, as best I could, I kept my counsel. The appointments I was seeking soon followed.

∞

BACK IN SCHOOL, I was taking a class in Trust and Estates from Professor Terry Kogan, and a family law class from the dean, Lee Teitlebaum. Both professors were masters of the classroom environment, and made their topics equally fascinating. I discovered that I actually wanted to attend their classes, and I found myself in each of their offices after class like a little nerd, trying to learn more. Previously, my impeccable attendance was forced and I had never visited a professor. I ended up getting the American Jurisprudence award for both classes, having written the best essay in each.

I didn't judge much that summer. San Francisco is a great place to be wined and dined, and that is pretty much my experience with the Brobeck law firm. I found a studio apartment in the back of some random guy's garage, with the outrageous rent of $600 per month (I was paying $157.50 per month back in Salt Lake, sharing a 3-bedroom house with five people). I didn't have much time for skating, but I did get out to Stockton for one weekend to judge. It was fairly uneventful, and uncomfortable, back judging again with judges who didn't much care for me, though now I had gained rank on most of them, having received my Senior Competition appointment.

I spent my mornings socializing with many of the lawyers, lunch with partners, afternoons working, and evenings at various social outings. I was getting pretty good at socializing with people of all ages, so I was not the least bit intimidated, as some of the clerks were, by the older, powerful senior and management level attorneys.

But I was still unsure how the gay card would play in a prestigious law firm. Yes, I know, San Francisco is the gayest city in world. But figure-skating is the gayest sport in America, and being gay was not so easy there.

I decided to find out first-hand if it would be an issue. The firm had a directory of its 400-plus lawyers, with the names of their spouses. I reasoned, if this firm is accepting of alternate lifestyles, wouldn't at least one or two lawyers list a spouse of the same sex?

I began my search at the beginning of the directory, and became more and more uneasy as the pages remaining became fewer and fewer. Finally, I found it. Richard Paul. A senior associate, and his spouse had a male name. I was so excited that I went directly to his office, down a few floors from mine.

I knocked, introduced myself, and asked if I could come in. "Sure," he responded which in and of itself was not unusual. The lawyers and clerks were encouraged to spend time getting to know each other, and with 400 of them to meet, it wasn't going to happen unless I went out and introduced myself.

Once in his office, he was taken aback by my request that he shut the door. "Is this serious?" he queried.

"I hope not," I said. I then explained to him that I had been going through the directory and noticed that his spouse's name was male, and by that, was he gay, and if so, what was it like being openly gay at work.

After a very loud chuckle, he said being openly gay was not a problem at Brobeck, and then added, "It's safe to open the door!" A double entendre directed at both his office door and the one to my closet. Richard would be one of my confidants that summer. He had a brilliant mind and an affable sense of humor. He would later move on to a high-level position within the Clinton administration.

Most of the work I was assigned was fairly straightforward and interesting. They were, after all, trying to recruit us. It was not likely that we would end up with our heads buried in the library. No, they would save that work for us when we returned, if we returned, as first-year associates.

Thanks to a creative argument I came up with that won a case on appeal, I landed a job offer upon graduation. I had fallen in love with San Francisco, and I enjoyed the work environment much more than at Kimball, Parr, who had encouraged me to make a comparison, and in doing so had helped me find my right place.

One other unusual event took place that summer. I received a call from my professor and default guidance counselor, Terry Kogan. He explained to me that he was in the midst of a divorce prompted by his coming out of the closet as a gay man. We spent many nights that summer on the phone, as Terry dealt with the same issues I had dealt with three summers before. It solidified a lasting friendship. Now comfortable with my job offer from Brobeck, I formed the Gay and Lesbian Law Alliance back at the law school. Terry Kogan was the faculty adviser.

THAT FALL, I learned that I would not be required to trial-judge the National Championships in Orlando. I had met the minimum requirements for a National appointment, and Ida assured me that I would be approved when she submitted the papers. She was planning to submit them in May of 1993, eighteen months hence, two years after receiving my Senior Competition appointment, the delay being in response to some people feeling I was moving along too quickly.

When fall break rolled around, I used up all my accumulated air miles to take my boyfriend Jay to Maui. We both immediately fell in love with the island. It was a break both from skating and from law school. I had been so busy that, other than seeing each other in the evenings, we weren't spending a great deal of time together. It was in Maui that we discussed my job options, Salt Lake versus San Francisco, and ultimately we agreed to move together to San Francisco.

I decided I would go the National Championships even though I wasn't trial-judging. I was starting to enjoy the cocktail parties and the socializing at the practices—and besides, it was an Olympic year. The Olympic Team would be chosen at those National Championships. I roomed with another up-and-comer former-skater judge, Rob Rosenbluth, a travel agent from the East Coast, about my same age, who had not only already received his National appointment, but had judged the championships the previous year in Minneapolis.

The Men's short program had Mark Mitchell acing out the more experienced Paul Wylie. Only the first- and second-placed men would be sent to the Olympics. Christopher Bowman finished first, Mark second, Paul in fourth. Mark earned a few first placements ahead of Christopher.

Mark had clearly outskated Paul, and quite possibly Christopher. Steve Winkler, I was relieved to find out, went with Mark.

Later that evening, at one of the cocktail parties, I congratulated Steve for having Mark in the right place. Steve responded by saying it was not right. Mark was placed too high, Steve's marks for him were too generous.

Evidently a very big wig with the International Skating Union (ISU) had cornered Steve about his marking. The ISU guru was very influential in determining who would be "next" for international appointments, or so Steve believed. According to Steve, Mr. ISU calmly and carefully pointed out that Paul's jumps were higher, and he had better interpretation of his music. The conversation ended with Steve agreeing that it would be better for the U.S. to send Paul to the Olympics than to send Mark, or at least this is what was relayed to me by Steve.

Who knows what else was said? But, for the record books, the majority of the judges, with Steve acting as the fifth and decisive vote, put Paul higher than Mark in the freeskate, denying Mark Mitchell his deserved placement. Mark had clearly outskated Paul in the freeskate, even more so than he did in the short program. It was yet another judging travesty in figure-skating, and it put a damper on my desire to be a judge.

It was February of 1992, and I would not judge anything of significance again until the summer of 1993. Nearly a year and a half. A very large span of time, during which I did a great deal of soul-searching, focusing my energies on my career rather than on this unjust "hobby."

Ironically, Paul would go on to the Olympics and win the title that would define his career. He won a medal, but ended up with the wrong one, a silver that should have been gold. He had clearly outskated Victor Petrenko, the Russian favorite going in. In the minds of the pre-programmed judges, Paul finished second to Petrenko's inferior freeskate.

Had it not been for Steve Winkler, and few other judges, Paul would not have even been there in the first place to compete. At the Olympics thanks only to questionable judging, Paul now found himself short-ended by similar shenanigans.

And what medal might Mark Mitchell have brought back to the U.S.? His family, his coach, his entire support system, and the hours of training devoted to chasing his dream, will never have the answer to that question.

At the 1992 Olympics, not long after the fall of the Soviet Union, Russians Natalia Mishkutenok and Artur Dimitriev, won the Pair gold medal. With the Soviet Union shattered, would this eighth consecutive medal prove to be the last?

A Shooting Star

GRADUATION FROM LAW school was a little bittersweet. I absolutely loved being in school, and really missed it the moment the cap hit the grass. I'd been pursuing various degrees for nearly a decade and suddenly felt a little lost. To clear my head, I decided to cash in some frequent flier miles I'd accumulated, while skating and interviewing, and took Jay on a trip to Europe. It was my graduation gift to myself, as well as to Jay for putting up with all my traveling and studying.

We first flew to Switzerland, arriving in Zurich, and immediately fell in love with all things Swiss. Even the airport seemed to have Old World charm. I thought traveling the states, with an occasional trip to Mexico, had put me in the jet set; it was soon apparent that I had a lot to learn about world travel.

Wanting to see the whole of Europe, but realizing we never could, we meandered down to Italy, hitting Rome, Florence, and Milan, before we found our way to the French Riviera. Those amazing old cities really stimulated an interest for European travel. When we arrived back in Salt Lake and started preparing for our move to San Francisco, I was already looking forward to my next trip to Europe.

Just as Jay and I settled into a rather expensive place in San Francisco, I learned that a few of the lawyers I was anxious to work with were moving to Brobeck's newly opened Palo Alto office, nearly an hour's drive south of San Francisco. I made a few inquiries, and soon secured a spot there as well. Jay and I stayed in San Francisco long enough for me to take the bar exam, then packed up again and moved to Mountain View, a suburb south of Palo Alto.

The judging fiasco at the Orlando Nationals had left a bad taste in my mouth, so I decided to focus on other things for a while. Not much was going on in my skating life, and at that point it was something I could live without. Ida, however, was still planning to submit my National-level appointment application the following May, but she heard otherwise from a chorus of Midwestern judges. "May? Why the delay?" Though Ida was reluctant, she submitted the papers in the fall; the Board of Directors for U.S. Figure Skating approved my National appointment that October. I was now qualified to judge the National Championships; but, uncharacteristically, I was not looking forward to it.

I'd had it with Steve Winkler and skating. I lost touch with him for the most part. No more late-night phone calls. No more skating gossip. I had lost interest in both him and his tomfoolery. The National Championships were held in Phoenix that year, which is one of my favorite places, but they came and went without my even blinking so much as an eye. I don't even recall watching them on television.

I was working hard at the law firm, already putting in too many hours, including weekends. Initially, I was assigned to the securities litigation group, but found myself working a great deal for the intellectual property litigation group as well. I was learning a valuable trade from some of the most skilled lawyers in California.

During that first year, working at Brobeck, it struck me as odd that the partners generally arrived before the associates, and many of them worked well into the evening. The myth in law school was that as an associate, the hours were long, the work hard and tedious, but after six or seven years of putting in your time, elevation to partnerhood puts you on Easy Street. Boy, was that ever a lie! The partners, though making a great living, still work very, very hard for it.

Initially, I pursued the litigation groups because of my experience in debate, and those groups included the lawyers with whom I most enjoyed working. However, I was far better suited for corporate work, and I soon realized that I had chosen a poor career path. Both in pursuing a large firm, and once there, not pursuing corporate work.

I realized it was time to start looking around. My plan was to spend a good two years with Brobeck, then head to a corporation as general counsel. In doing some early research, I ran into a sole practitioner whose specialty was tax law, with a growing corporate practice. He also happened to be gay. He needed an associate to help him with what was becoming an overwhelming workload. I was reluctant to leave Brobeck so soon. I was carrying a hefty student loan debt, and I needed to make sure I kept up on my payments. Eventually, though, I left Brobeck and joined him at his law practice, near San Francisco's civic center.

It was 1993, and Jay and I packed up our things once again. We managed to purchase a house in the then-depressed San Francisco housing market, not far from my office. I was throwing myself into work when I received a call from Steve Winkler. I didn't tell him what a creep I thought he was, and he went on to tell me that I had been selected to judge the Olympic Festival that summer in San Antonio. He congratulated me too, and since he would be judging as well, encouraged me to accept. Reluctantly, I did.

I didn't take much time away from work. I recall leaving San Francisco on a Wednesday evening and returning home on Sunday, so it wasn't much trouble getting the time off. That one event, however, sucked me right back in to the whale's open mouth.

According to Steve, the fact that I had made myself "scarce" is what had prompted the invitation in the first place.

"Good strategy!" he said, as he congratulated me over dinner at one of San Antonio's finest restaurants.

"I hadn't really planned it that way, Steve, but it's nice to be invited again," I replied.

We were skipping the opening ceremonies which were held inside a huge brand-new domed sports complex in San Antonio. Though I had a nice time catching up, eating, drinking, and regrouping with Steve that night, I still regret missing the big indoor fireworks show that is said to have been simply fantastic.

After having one or two too many drinks, we hopped into a cab and went back to the dormitories of the university—the housing for the officials. The Olympic Festival brought together a number of sports. To make it an affordable event, the officials and athletes all stayed together in an Olympic-style village. At least that is what they were calling these abandoned-for-the-summer dorm rooms.

The loudest complaints about the housing were leveled by the skating officials. Personally, I was not too far removed from dorm life, so I didn't mind much. However, the other skating officials, including Steve, accustomed to their plush hotel rooms and hospitality suites, were crying like babies the entire time. On one level, I could understand their grievance. Nearly every other sporting official present was being paid for his or her time. One wouldn't expect the other paid sporting officials to care much about accommodations, as their wallets were filling-up nicely in the meantime.

Figure-skating is one of the last holdout sports to keep its officials "amateur" (in other words, free of charge). Figure-skating officials view the high-class perks that come with the "job" as payment for their services, and the resulting entitlement mentality, particularly among the elite-level officials, borders on greed. But then again, I understand where they are coming from. It's the very least the multi-million dollar figure-skating organization can do for them while taking their services. Should it surprise anyone that this greedy mentality exists in an environment where organizations worth 50 to 100 million dollars continue to exploit a volunteer workforce?

In any event, at my first practice session, I remembered why I loved this sport so much. A very young skater took to the ice, and I suddenly recognized the flow and easy movement of the Russian Protopopovs. Only this time it was a little Asian pre-adolescent by the name of Michelle Kwan. She was simply elegant, a word I would usually find difficult to use to describe a young girl.

Yet there she was. The quality of edge was effortless, her glide easy, she carried herself as if she were floating across the ice. And lucky for her, she could jump! She would not fully develop the artistic side of her skating for years to come, but the basics of what makes a skater great, the flow, easy movement, precision of edge and body carriage were already there. She had "it," in spades. To this day, other than Michelle Kwan and the Protopopovs, I've only seen "it" again in one other skater. I'm told that American Janet Lynn, a champion in the early seventies, had it, but I've only seen her skate on videotape. Seeing it performed live is another story. It astounds you.

San Antonio was Michelle's first televised competition at the Senior level. It was the beginning of a career and dominance in a sport that continues today. At the same time, during the course of her career, I was simultaneously pursuing my own. Ironically, I would end mine before she would end hers.

The 1994 National Championships were hosted by the city of Detroit. I wasn't able to attend, though I would have loved to. Nationals week was a favorite for me, but I was very focused on the work of my clients and the development of my legal career, so I just couldn't swing the time off.

1994 was also an Olympic year, which was unusual, because Olympic Games are usually held every four years. The International Olympic Committee (IOC) decided to separate the Summer Games from the Winter Games to better capitalize on its brand. To make this separation, the Winter Games, after their "normal" year in 1992, were held again only two years later, in 1994. Since that time, the Winter Olympics have been back on the four-year rotation, now staggered by two years with the Summer Olympics.

By not going to Detroit, I wound up missing the Olympic-qualifying National Championships, and that in itself was tough enough. Missing the biggest figure-skating incident of the century was even tougher.

∞

THE DETROIT NATIONALS are now infamous for the "whack heard round the world."

I first heard the news about poor Nancy Kerrigan being attacked at Nationals on the radio at my San Francisco law office. Knowing about the rivalry between Kerrigan and Tonya Harding, my thoughts immediately and perhaps unfairly jumped to the conclusion that Tonya was in on it.

It would turn out the scheme was hatched by Tonya's ex-husband, wacko Jeff Gillooly and her 300-pound Trekkie windbag bodyguard, Shawn Eckardt. Together they approached the hapless Shane Stant to carry out their dirty work. Three ne'er-do-wells, two of whom had ties to Tonya. Nancy would get the whack, but was she the real target?

In a world where our male skaters are supposed to be straight and our female skaters are supposed to be princesses, Tonya Harding, neither male nor princess, never had a chance. She was caught somewhere in between. Tonya didn't posses a single princess quality, and if she were never a princess, what were her chances of ever making Ice Queen? Instead of capitalizing on her assets, her physical prowess and the triple axel threat, U.S. Figure Skating chose instead to villainize her long before her unfortunate implication in the Nancy Kerrigan/Jeff Gillooly incident.

Numerous accounts of Tonya's childhood have it that when she was a little girl, her family didn't have the finances necessary to keep up with other skating families. She was known to show up at events having spent the night in her mother's late-model Ford Pinto. She would often have her mother park down the street or around the corner so the other kids wouldn't see her pull up in their makeshift "house." Her costumes were often homemade, most of the time not properly fitted, and usually overly revealing for a girl her age. Her parents were no strangers to the bottle, and Tonya was often the victim of verbal abuse and, some have said, even physical abuse from her mother under the influence.

As a small child, Tonya grew up in a trailer park outside of Portland, Oregon. Compared to the country-club lifestyle of figure-skating's ideal, this was completely unacceptable. Even less so by officials who fly first-class around the world, dine on caviar and escargot at four- and five-star hotels, and lie in wait to judge her further. It's a wonder that any judge could see her skate with their noses held so high, but somehow our judges managed.

It's no secret that Tonya could swear like a sailor. She smoked too much, drank too much, and got mixed up with all the wrong men. Thanks to her father's tutoring, she knew her way around a Hemi, and could probably split a cord of wood after lunch without breaking a sweat. She could huck a loogie to the other end of the rink and skate down fast enough to slide through it before it froze. Your Zamboni breaks down; call Tonya! Even when wasted, she could throw a Frisbee like a hubcap and heaven help you if you were her target. If you were going to date Tonya, make sure you have major dental, because you were likely to lose a few teeth before it was over. In other words, Tonya was an easy target for exploitation in the media.

Tonya was not tall, slim, or graceful. She was short, buxom, muscular, and athletic. Not unattractive by any means, her reputation as a foul-mouthed party girl always kept her in the minds of the judges in a class of her own, and unfortunately, it was a low class.

Still, with a host of personal disadvantages, once she mastered the triple axel, Tonya managed to win two National Championships along with a list of other titles, despite the growing odds against her. Tonya was one of only a few women ever to land that difficult jump in competition. Any good judge would have been hard-pressed to deny her a title based on her technical superiority alone, but that doesn't mean there weren't those who tried.

However, the bigger question here is: Why didn't U.S. Figure Skating spin her into gold? Russia has done it many times for their champions; where was U.S. Figure Skating? Oksana Baiul, abandoned by her parents (spin: orphaned), raised by her coach on the wrong side of the tracks (spin: where are Russia's right side of the tracks?), became a gold medalist despite landing nearly every one of her jumps on two feet. The whack to Nancy was not done so much by Tonya or her cohorts, it was done by the judges at the Olympic games who bought into the Russian propaganda and placed an overly feathered, overly dramatic Oksana in first. Where was the outrage from U.S. Figure Skating when that happened?

Russia is now working the same spin on current World Champion Irina Slutskaya. And it's working quite nicely. Irina, like Tonya, has great physical prowess. Yet she doesn't have the triple axel, and it's a decade later. Irina flails her arms in the rotation of her jumps. Tonya never did that. Irina breaks away from her program in preparation for her jumps, telegraphing to the world that she isn't paying any attention to the music. Tonya didn't pay much attention to the music either, but she didn't telegraph her jumps. Irina skates with her back hunched over to gain the outstanding speed she is known for. Tonya didn't hunch over. Her speed came naturally.

Yet Russia has spun Irina into a World Champion and contender for the Olympic gold medal. Russia does it through propaganda, and the judges eat it up. It does help that Irina is as cute as a button and nice as pie. She and Michelle Kwan are reportedly good friends.

Yet one needs only to look at the scores for presentation at the 2005 Worlds to see just how well this propaganda works. Irina ranked highest among all competitors in the presentation marks—the things she is downright terrible at. What about Sasha Cohen and her perfect carriage, in comparison to the hunched-over Irina? Irina's marks are higher. What about Michelle Kwan and her perfect edge quality and flow, in comparison to Irina's two-footed skating? Irina's marks are higher. What about Japan's Shizuka Arakawa, with her delicate interpretation of the ice in comparison to the pained and brutish expressions of Irina? Irina's marks are higher. And how about Italian Carolina Kostner and her effortless entry into jumps compared to the telegraphing of Irina? Irina's marks: unexplainably highest.

This after Irina was hospitalized last season with an enlarged heart, the cause of which cannot be explained. In the U.S., when one of our athletes learns of an enlarged heart (a basketball star, a football player, or the like), immediate suspicions are raised concerning drug use: steroids or illegal drugs, perhaps. But when a Russian athlete is diagnosed with a similar condition, they succeed in spinning it into a "poor little Irina" story, and the press and judges eat it up. Did we all forget that Yelena Berezhnaya was disqualified from the 2000 World Championships with a doping violation? That would be the death knell for a U.S. athlete. Not so for the soon-to-be 2002 Pair gold medalist.

The Russian propaganda machine goes to work early: The judges are convinced before the practices, then agree on the marks later at the cocktail parties, and then give Irina high marks for presentation, astounding every skating enthusiast who can see that this empress has no clothes. American judge Joe Inman, at the Salt Lake Olympics, seems to have bought into the Russian spin. Although he gave Kwan one tenth (one tenth!) of a point higher in presentation, he placed Irina ahead of Kwan.

Under skating's old scoring system, this one tenth would have made the difference between Michelle's bronze medal and a gold one.

The point here is that U.S. Figure Skating knows that this goes on. So why don't they take a skater like Tonya, who can outskate Oksana and Irina, even in a boxing ring, and spin the straw into gold? Tonya could not overcome the U.S. judges' distaste for her background. That's right: the U.S. judges' distaste. The European judges, the Eastern European judges and the Asian judges could all look past Tonya's personal life, but the U.S. judges simply could not.

It is my firm belief that the body that kept Tonya struggling the majority of her career, and that continues to keep her out of making a livelihood at what she does best—figure-skating—is most at fault. Could it be that seeing a little raggedy girl, who maybe drank too much, or who stomped her cigarette butts out with the edge of her blade before going out to perform, reminded many of her judges just how close to home they still were?

The judges who play games at the expense of athletes are a parasitic army of insecure barnacles, many of whom have gone out of their way to live exotic lifestyles, wearing fur where it doesn't belong, jewels without state dinners, and hors d'oeuvres and cocktails at fancy galas. Too many are fake and phony, from their monotone hair color to their plastic surgeon–pulled faces, and even their skating wardrobe–filled closets (mine notwithstanding). Somebody a little trashy, a little edgy, and on a little bit of a struggle, okay, a lot of all that, was too strong a dose of reality in a self-interested world of make-believe.

There was never any solid evidence that proved that Tonya had anything to do with her worthless ex-husband's attack on Nancy Kerrigan. Tonya said she didn't know anything about it. No other court of arbitration was involved to prove otherwise. Yet the bungling simpletons of U.S. Figure Skating blamed and convicted her anyway, making her the first person ever banned from the sport for life. They didn't care that there was no proof. All they cared about was that they finally had a way to get rid of the shabby little girl that didn't represent their ideal of figure-skating.

The attack on Nancy was a raid on the federation that was pushing her through the moat, over the drawbridge, and into the sparkling ice castle where a reigning princess belonged. The subsequent investigation was U.S. Figure Skating's way of getting rid of the ogre under the bridge.

I believe the attack on Nancy, which can never be justified, would never have happened if it hadn't been for the corruption of the skating federation and its phony judges. Violence wouldn't have been necessary, because if Tonya had been fairly treated all along, mastermind Gillooly, who amounted to nothing more than a deranged fan, wouldn't have found it necessary to level the playing field.

If Tonya could have stayed focused, she probably would have medaled at the 1994 Olympics. She was technically better. She had the skills to beat—or at least be on the podium with—Nancy Kerrigan. She didn't have the elegance of Nancy, or the propaganda of Oksana, but she was a better athlete, and she had a triple axel.

U.S. Figure Skating had the Lillehammer gold and silver medals in its pocket. Unfortunately, they forgot to check the integrity of the hem, and let one of them slide down their leg and into the hands of the Russians, rewarding them nicely for their nationalistic and honorable support of Oksana.

IN THE SPRING of 1994, after the Olympic dust had settled, I learned that I had been invited to judge my first National Championships, scheduled the following January in Providence, Rhode Island. This would be a huge milestone for me.

I spent the summer focusing on my client work, which kept me busy traveling up and down the West Coast, with an occasional trip to Chicago or New York.

When fall came around, I found myself in Portland, Oregon, judging the Pacific Coast Sectional Championships. Joe Driano, a respected judge and referee from the Seattle area, grabbed me out of the judges' dining room to go "hear a practice."

"Hear a practice?" I asked him.

"Come on. Just come and listen," he said.

As I approached the sideboards of the arena, a private practice was just beginning. A young Michelle Kwan was the skater left on the ice. There was no music playing, and the only sound in the arena would have been that of Michelle's skates against the ice as she practiced a few laps of stroking to adjust to the ice—that is, if she actually had made a sound, because there was no sound in the arena.

"Now listen as she skates." Joe said.

"Joe, I've heard it before. Twice," I responded.

"Jon, you couldn't have heard it. There is nothing to hear!" he countered. "Now listen!"

"Joe, that's what I'm telling you. I 'didn't' hear it when I watched her skate in San Antonio. And I 'didn't' hear it years ago when I watched the Protopopovs practice one night in Salt Lake City. I can hear it. It's what's not there that I'm listening to."

Stunned that I already had the information he wanted to share, Joe simply stared at me. "You've got it! You will make it very far in this sport. Do you know how many judges will never understand the importance and nuance of that silent edge?"

Sadly, I did know, and with that, he patted me on the back and we both watched in the silence-that-should-not-have-been as Michelle finished her warm-up.

Speaking of not knowing the nuances of judging figure-skating, Morry Stillwell, the president of U.S. Figure Skating, was also attending those championships. One night, in the hospitality suite, I ended up having a drink with Morry, Joe Driano, and the chairperson of the event. The chairperson started asking Morry some very difficult questions related to figure-skating's "ladies," gay men, and about their roles in the sport.

She raised the issue first from a feminist's point of view. She wanted to know how Morry Stillwell, a straight man like every other president before him, had been elected to govern what was predominantly a female sport. How did the men in figure-skating get through the women's liberation movement of the '60s and '70s and continue their lock on the leadership positions? Moreover, how was it that, some twenty-years later, they still retained their control?

Morry, even when soused, has never been a man at a loss for words, but the alcohol had removed his naturally misogynistic inhibitions, and he began to argue that the women in figure skating were largely housewives and had no place running a business like U.S. Figure Skating.

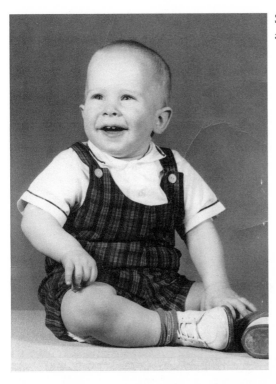

Smart dresser
at the age of one.

My family—1970—I'm 6 years old. LEFT TO RIGHT: Me, my mom
Sharol, my sister Tami, my dad Bruce, and my brother Eric.

My mom showing me how to perform in our hotel room, Great Falls, Montana.

Second Place Intermediate Men, Fresno California; 15 years old. First, Stephen Nelson; third, Michael Dianda.

One of my conservative navy blue costumes; 16 years old.

Ice dancing with
Barbara Howard;
20 years old.

With Victoria Banchero,
shortly after coming out;
24 years old.

Team leader and judge, Slovenia. Team doctor, Branden Overett, Lisa Nesuda, J. J. Mathews, Justin Dillon, me.

Team leader and judge in Ortisei, Italy. Johnny Weir, Sarah Wheat, Ryan Bradley, Sasha Cohen.

LEFT TO RIGHT: Ron Pfenning, me, Paolo Pizzocari (Italy), Walter Tiogo (Italy), Joe Inman.

A fancy dinner with Steve Winkler. LEFT TO RIGHT: Debbie Currie, Ann Greenthal, Steve Winkler, me, Debbie's husband, Bob Horen, Joe Inman, Mary Cook, Rob Rosenbluth.

Passing the world exam, Oberstdorf, Germany, 2000. Beth Crane (Canada), me, Katarina Henriksson (Sweden), Massimo Orlandini (Italy).

LEFT TO RIGHT: Will Smith, me, Rob Rosenbluth, Ron Pfenning.

At a gala banquet. LEFT TO RIGHT: Gale Tanger, Ann Greenthal, Michelle Kwan, Joe Inman, me.

Team leaders, Junior Worlds in Sofia, Bulgaria. Lorrie Parker and me.

Celebrating numerous medals at the 2000 Junior Worlds, Sofia, Bulgaria.
LEFT TO RIGHT: Benjamin Augusto, Lorrie Parker, Tanith Belbin, me.

Celebrating numerous medals at the 2000 Junior Worlds. Coaches and
parents. BACK: Susan Magalnick, Priscilla Hill, Patti Weir, Lorrie Parker,
me, Ann Greenthal. FRONT: Debbie Storey, Ann Eidson, Elizabeth
Coates, Tanya Lycasek.

2002 National Championships, Los Angeles. The panel of judges for the Ladies' event. LEFT TO RIGHT, BACK ROW: Peggy Graham, Anne Cammett, Steve Winkler, Jeff Wolf, Will Smith, me, Ron Pfenning, Joe Inman. FRONT ROW: Wendy Enzmann, Tamie Campbell, Kathy Slack, Kitty Delio.

With my coauthor, celebrating the conclusion of the California AidsRide, a fundraising bicycle trek from San Francisco to Los Angeles.

2002 Salt Lake City Winter Olympics. Sally Stapleford, and me.

Nantucket, away from the rink. Ron Pfenning, Don Rocchio, me.

World Skating Federation press conference, March 2003. LEFT TO RIGHT: Lorrie Kim, Sundeep Pandya, Britta Lindgren, me, Paul Wylie, Sonia Bianchetti, Barbara Silby, Kathy Casey, Ron Pfenning, Judith Furst-Tombor, Sally Stapleford, Howard Silby.

World Skating Federation secret meeting in Copenhagen. CLOCKWISE FROM FOREGROUND, LEFT: Judith Furst-Tombor, Barbara Silby, Haig Oundjian, Sonia Bianchetti, Don Mcknight, me, Ron Pfenning.

Angrily, but just a bit tipsy herself, "Ms. Chairperson" countered with all the politically correct arguments, which I need not mention here, since in this day and age everyone, except apparently Morry Stillwell, is familiar with the reasons why women are just as good as, if not better than, men at running a business. Those rational and reasoned arguments aside, women in the sport certainly would have a better understanding of the needs of its women athletes. This argument went nowhere with Morry. Ms. Chairperson didn't care, and Archie Bunker/Stillwell got a lecture on women's rights I'm sure he won't soon forget.

After letting him have it on his sexism toward women, she changed gears and moved on to homosexual men. Morry was extremely defensive about the topic, more so than on his backward views of women. In her opinion, many of the male skaters were probably gay, yet the sport's hierarchy continued to be dominated by straight men. She also believed that the judges were prejudiced against the gay skaters and gay coaches. She went on to ask him why U.S. Figure Skating had failed to address the AIDS epidemic on any level, listing several elite-level skaters, coaches, and judges who had died from the disease. She mentioned the publicized deaths of Rob McCall and Olympic gold medalist John Curry, as well as Rudy Galindo's coaches, Jim Hulick and Richard Inglesi. Already a long list, but I could have added the names of Ian Knight and Todd Kaufman, my former coach and unrequited crush respectively.

Morry Stillwell was struck dumb on the AIDS issue. It was clear that he hadn't even thought about it, other than to dismiss it, and with a few vodka martinis already in his bloodstream, he wasn't about to tackle the delicate topic.

As for homophobia in figure skating, Morry was much more to the point. "It simply doesn't exist," he claimed. "Nobody cares about that crap any more."

Ms. Chairperson wasn't buying it.

"Why then do gay skaters have to hide their sexuality, when straight skaters flaunt theirs?" She said, not letting him off the hook with his dismissive statements.

"You will have to ask them. I can't tell you why, and it's none of my business, and quite frankly, it's none of yours!" he spat.

Irritated, she turned to me and asked, "So, Jon, tell me what it's like being a gay judge in the homophobic sport of figure-skating."

Up until that question was directed at me, I was listening intently and silently cheering her on.

I answered her, "There's no question that homophobia has run rampant in skating. But among the ranks of the judges, it does seem to be disappearing," I responded, thinking back to a night in Minneapolis where the judges' hospitality room more resembled a gay bar than a stuffy judges' soirée, filled with so many openly gay judges. "I think figure-skating has to find a way to push that acceptance down into the ranks of the coaches and the skaters."

"But it's not the coaches and the skaters that are the problem," she argued back. "The judges must do more than just be accepting between each other. They need to reach out to the coaches and skaters and let them know it's okay to be gay."

At this point, Morry jumped back in. "No judge or official is ever going to talk to a young skater about being gay! It will never happen. They are too young!" He took the "we have to protect them" road of reasoning.

Ms. Chairperson was not giving up that easily. "Morry, I'm not talking about adolescent teenagers here. The elite level men are all adults, most in their twenties. What's wrong with a judge talking about it with them? It has to start somewhere," she reasoned.

"It's not the judges' problem. It's not a skater's problem. If we had more positive role models among the coaches, we wouldn't have this problem at all," Morry countered.

"Positive role models." That is where I first learned figure-skating's code word for straight male coaches. You see, it's simply a matter of having more straight male coaches. Then figure-skating would have more straight male skaters, or at least according to Morry's queer manner of thinking on the matter.

It's a funny dichotomy, gay men and figure-skating. It's clear in every fan's mind; it's clear in the minds of the skaters; the coaches too. However, homosexuality is not clear in the minds of figure-skating officialdom, particularly at the highest levels. They can't admit it to themselves and they refuse to see it.

In February of 1995, the National Championships opened with a grand affair for the judges held at the Rhode Island School of Design (RISD) Museum. The museum was set with various food stations, open bars, and live music, with the judges wandering from place to place throughout. It was an extravagant affair and something that would repeat itself many times thereafter. Nothing more than a gathering of figure-skating's hoi polloi, dressed to the nines with their pretense dripping from their upturned noses, with their middle and lower-middle class backgrounds well-hidden by the latest St. John knits and Armani couture.

Back at the skating arena, I judged the Pairs event. Jenni Meno and Todd Sand were the hands-down favorites, and likely to go on to medal at the World Championships.

In their short program, as the first marks came up, the one for technical merit, I heard a gasp escape from behind me as the judge questioned: "A 5.7?"

The marks were ever so obvious, previously agreed upon 5.8's, straight across the scoreboard, except for judge 3, which happened to be me. I sat in very uncomfortable silence, knowing that I would be questioned later about my lower mark, even though I still placed them first, as they clearly deserved to win.

After the event, without waiting for someone to approach me, I went straight to the gasping judge, Paula Naughton, someone who I knew well, and also knew to be the "monitor" for this particular pair.

I explained, "Paula, there was a deduction for Meno and Sand. In the short program, there can be no assisted lifts. They do a pull-through where Jenni leaves the ice in the footwork section." It was a mandatory deduction, and not one of the other judges caught it, nor had Paula.

She was immediately concerned that her gasp might have distracted me, and apologized. I assured her it hadn't affected my judging, and was glad I heard it; otherwise, I would not have known that she hadn't seen the deduction.

Once brought to her attention, she went to John Nicks, Meno and Sand's coach, to tell him about the deduction. She did not want them to arrive at Worlds, only to have a one-tenth deduction keep them off the podium, and rightly so. While one tenth would not make the difference at the U.S. Nationals that year, too often it can be the difference in medal placement at the Worlds or Olympics. As the monitor of this pair, she was obligated to get this information to them.

One of the favorite pastimes of the judges is to play the "monitor" for the skaters. The young skaters are charismatic, on their way to celebrity, and some judges simply love any chance they have to mingle with them. To play a role in their development makes a judge feel like a "star maker." On many occasions, the judges simply butt in where their input is not wanted or needed. Great coaches find a way of making the judges feel a part of the training, while keeping them and their opinions as far as possible from their skaters.

Paula Naughton was not one of these "star-making" judges. She played the role of monitor in exactly the way it was meant to be played. She relayed information only where necessary, steered completely away from interfering with the coach, and kept her comments to the skaters positive and encouraging. Later, when I was asked to monitor skaters, or even act as a team leader, I tried to mimic the behavior of Paula Naughton. She is well respected by the coaches and skaters alike, and I wanted to be just like her.

In perfect Naughton-like diplomacy, she relayed to Mr. Nicks that there was a move in the short program that could result in a deduction. It was an FYI. Many, if not most, monitors would have taken the "star-making" approach: "Bad news. We have to take out the assisted lift in the short. We don't want a deduction to keep them off the podium."

Instead, Paula's approach was to provide information, leaving the coach to make a choreographic decision ("one tenth, so what, we can live with that!" for example), the latter approach is to tell the coach—or, worse, the skaters themselves—what to do, while self-including the buttinski monitor in the process. Over time, the few that treat the coaches with respect gain the reciprocal respect of their skaters. The majority that do not, earn the disdain of the coaches and the skaters. The skaters learn fast who is interested in them, and who is just interested in hitching on to their rising star.

The worst of this bunch then spend the next season telling everyone who will listen "When Brian and I discussed his music . . ." or "Kristi took my advice to move her triple lutz, or she wouldn't have won Worlds . . ." or "I told them not to do it, and now look, they finished off the podium." The pattern is easy to mimic. "(Insert first name only famous skater) (insert advice given) (insert whether followed) (take credit or lay blame)." In fact, I think this formula is in the National judges' handbook.

DURING THE SUMMER, U.S. Figure Skating invited a number of young National judges to Chicago to participate in an intensive weekend of judges' education. I attended with other judges being considered for an eventual International appointment. Ron Pfenning, whom I had met a few years earlier, conducted the training. The small-group environment was a great way to get to know the other judges and Ron a lot better. It would be the beginning of my eventual lifelong friendship with Ron Pfenning.

It was a group of committed judges, all interested in the topic, assembled to focus their obsessions and sharpen their skills. How obsessive was this assembled group? One judge brought along his recently wedded spouse, so he could spend his honeymoon with her at an O'Hare Airport convention hotel. I'm sure that was a honeymoon his blushing bride will never forget!

One judge who was not at this special seminar was former champion Ken Shelly, who with his pair partner Jo Jo Starbuck, won many titles and the hearts of skating fans. Shelly too was in the accelerated judges' program for former skaters, as he should have been. But his age was working against him. The ISU requires that International judges be named by their federations prior to their forty-fifth birthday. Shelly was great skater, and an even better judge.

U.S. Figure Skating was aware of the age deadline for Ken Shelly.

They decided against appointing him as an International judge during the last year he was eligible, forever keeping him out of their exclusive club. Those making the decision already had their exclusive memberships, and they weren't about to let a well-credentialed skater come along and steal some of their spotlight. Shelly would have been the most accomplished former skater among the elite U.S. judges. This, U.S. Figure Skating would have none of.

LATER IN THE summer, I ran into Rudy Galindo on Castro Street in San Francisco. He was with his coaches, John Brancatto and Kevin Peeks. They excitedly told me all about Rudy's new training program and his music for the upcoming season. They were extremely enthusiastic about his prospects, particularly since Rudy would be skating in his home town of San Jose for the upcoming National championships. In the past, I had been enthusiastic for Rudy too. For some reason, this time their shared optimism didn't rub off on me. Rudy had had so many missed opportunities; I began to wonder if he would get any more.

In January, when Nationals did roll around, as usual, the judges were treated to a judges' dinner that surpassed all others. Joan Burns, the local big-wig, went out of her way to make this a memorable evening for her "friends" around the country.

The San Jose Athletic Club occupies one of the city's oldest and most distinguished buildings. Its ballroom, ornate with marble columns, banisters, and other details, is surrounded by an upper balcony that encircles the nearly 30-foot ceilings of the room. After hors d'oeuvres and cocktails were served in the lobby, the judges in their finery were ushered into the ballroom, replete with extravagantly set tables, and served one of the finest meals which the excellent chefs of the northern California region are famous for. After dessert, the judges were treated to a performance by three tenors, serenading them from the balconies above.

In contrast, Rudy Galindo likely ate a frozen TV dinner that night in the trailer he shared with his mother and brother.

I was assigned to the Ladies' event, so I didn't get a chance to catch any of the Men's practices, but I soon heard the chatter. Just as John and Kevin had predicted, everyone was talking about Rudy. The buzz in his favor could not have been more positive. When he skated his short program, I saw for myself his amazing improvement. He clearly outskated the competition, but when his marks came up, I knew that this year, like in the years before, he was again going to come up short.

Rudy had skated a perfect short program and clearly deserved to be in first. However, the judges saw it otherwise, and gave him second. The stadium filled with boos, with me joining their rancor. It was outrageous! He'd had first place stolen from him, and I thought that nothing could change his predetermined placement, no matter how well he skated in the long program.

I joined the cocktail chatter later that evening, expressing how strongly I felt that Rudy should have won. My unorthodox views were resonated by many others, but not by the judges on his panel—an expert group of judges, which is what made them the most dangerous. The more competent the judge, the better they are at justifying their placements, and the more likely they are to get away with what they intended.

One the day of the freeskate, in the final moments before the judges went to the stand, I asked a judge on the panel what he was going to do if Rudy were to skate as well as he did in the short.

"He won't," was his reply.

"But what if he does?" I persisted.

"He won't! I'm not even worried about that," the judge said confidently.

"Okay. Then tell me what the other judges are going to do," I said, thinking that he had already conferred with all of them.

"Jon, he is not going to do it. He won't be able to skate like that again. He is not going to be the National Champion. Not one of us is worried about that," was the judge's shocking reply.

I resigned myself to yet another skating rip-off and took my place in the stands. I knew the judges weren't going to let him take the National title. I'm not sure why, but it was clear they didn't believe he could or should or would.

When Rudy skated his program that day, it was as if he was saying to the judges, "Not worried about it, huh? Watch this!" He skated the program of his life, caught the judges *completely* off-guard, and won the title. The judges had *no* choice. They had to give it to him. Even that judge who "wasn't worried about it" marked him in first place.

Rudy Galindo, an openly gay Hispanic man, pulled off one of skating's greatest upsets, and he did so, I'm convinced, because the judges hadn't worried about it. If they had worried about him skating perfectly, they would have pre-planned their marks in such a way still to get away with giving him second. However, they hadn't given it any thought; because they didn't think they had to. So they were left with no choice but to fairly judge the event.

Rudy went on to medal at the World Championships as well. However, when the assignments were handed out for the next season's International competitions, Rudy was not invited to Skate America. Every other National Champion headlined the event, and had done so every previous year, but this year the U.S. officials were not going to allow the openly gay Rudy at their premier first-of-the-season event.

With the writing on the wall for Rudy, knowing he was not going to get another break from U.S. Figure Skating, he wisely turned pro and has made a celebrity name and small fortune by marketing himself primarily to skating's target audience: women and gay men. He does not apologize for his sexuality. He flaunts it and exaggerates it. His YMCA program as a political statement is a perfect example. His upbringing, his Latino roots, his sexuality, and his "up yours" message to figure skating's elite are all clear the moment he takes to the ice. Its genius is in its message and the manner in which he delivers it.

IN THE FALL of 1996, I traveled to Chicago to judge an event that would select the Junior World Team. In the Men's event, a young Ryan Jahnke skated a musical program, perfectly interpreted and presented to the audience, with only a few technical mistakes. It wasn't so much a difficult routine, but he was clearly the best "skater" of the group. While the other men were doing a lot more triple jumps, and at higher difficulty levels, they all missed multiple times. So, while Ryan clearly wasn't favored to do well, on that day, he outskated the others. With his remarkable knack for interpretation, his was the only program I would like to have watched a second time.

Another young judge, also open about his sexuality, was judging the event as well. We had trained together as trial judges, and often discussed the need to judge what is skated that day. And on that day, we both judged it as we saw it, placing Ryan in second. The rest of the panel had him with thirds and fourths, but their collective choices for second place were all over the map, so in the mysterious result calculation system, Ryan ended up in second, earning himself a spot on the Junior World Team. A spot, I might add, he earned with his performance *on that day*.

Later, while having dinner in the judges' room, I could not help but hear Gale Tanger, an International judge from Wisconsin, going off on the judges of the Men's event.

"What were they thinking, sending Ryan Jahnke to Junior Worlds? He can't jump!" she complained.

Gale was of the warped opinion that a Junior World Selections competition was just that. A selection. In her mind, it was the role of the judges to decide whom we thought were the best skaters to send on to Junior Worlds, not who skated the best. In Gale's view of things, we weren't to be judging what was actually skated, but what *might* be skated at Junior Worlds.

Tanger's way of thinking had clouded the consciousness of so many otherwise good judges at so many events that it was becoming an epidemic. It was getting so bad that oftentimes, before we sat down at the judges' stand, the referee would remind us that "You are choosing our World Team," or "You are choosing the skaters to represent our region at Sectionals," and so on. "The top four move on. Make sure that the top three (or top two) are the ones you feel can best represent us at the World Championships." Hard to imagine, so unfair, but so incredibly true.

What the referee was really saying was "don't forget to save a place for the skaters that have the best prospect for medaling at Worlds, even if they have a bad skate today."

If the referee were to say, "Judge only what is skated today, without regard for what might happen at Worlds next month," he would be doing a far better job of encouraging the skating to be judged fairly.

However, fairly judging is not something most in the sport are trained to or inclined to do. Better to let them take the stands with the comfort of their pre-planned determinations, and better preserve the chances for medaling at the next Championships.

I would make a similar "mistake," which was judging what I saw, a few months later at Skate America. It was my first event as an International Judge, something that had come quite rapidly after my National appointment. I judged two events as a National judge, judged them well, and suddenly I was the youngest of all the American International judges.

My inexperience demonstrated itself in the Pairs event. Stephanie Steigler and John Zimmerman, a relatively unknown American pair, skated amazingly well in the short program. So I gave them the marks. I was the substitute judge, so my marks did not appear on the overhead board, and it was a good thing. I had given them a well-earned mark in the neighborhood of 5.6.

The marks of the other judges came up, and they were mostly in the 4.8, 4.9 range. What on earth? The next pair, an overweight former Russian Olympian and his new partner, came out and skated dreadfully.

Now there is a 5.0 if I ever saw one, I thought to myself, turning in my marks to the Accountant seated next to me. Their marks went up, and by damn if they didn't have 5.4's to 5.6's!

I went to the practices, but not knowing any of these International judges, I hadn't heard the chatter. Apparently, these placements, for whatever reason, were determined beforehand, and I didn't know about it!

The long program was easy to judge, as it is always in Pairs. If a judge simply gives a Pair the same place they earned in the short, maybe flip 1 and 2, or 3 and 4, then the judge will be either exactly in agreement with the other judges, or within one place. My marks didn't count, so to save myself from the short-program disaster, I held my nose and did just that. Bingo!

On the Men's event, I was an official judge. In Singles, unlike Pairs, the placements, albeit still somewhat predetermined, vary much more from the "plan" with the manner in which the skaters actually "skate." So though nervous for the event, I judged just fine. By simply judging it the way I saw it, either I was in agreement with the final placement, or I had sound reasoning for what I had done.

After the event, as is tradition, the referee holds an event-review meeting with the judges on the panel to discuss and critique their placements. English is the official language of the ISU, and all International judges must theoretically be fluent in English to receive their appointments. For the most part, during practices and cocktail parties, the English of foreign judges is superb. When it comes to account for their actions, however, it suddenly disappears.

In the event-review meeting after the Men's event, led by American referee Joan Gruber, I would witness for the first time the dramatics and histrionics practiced by a red-haired French judge, Marie-Reine LeGougne, as she broke down in tears attempting to explain her poor judging of the event. It was all Gruber could do to keep the meeting moving along. I survived my first event-review meeting because of the kindness of Joan Gruber and the hysteria of Marie-Reine.

I ATTENDED THE National Championships later that year in Nashville, not as a judge but as an acronym: a JET. JET stands for Judges' Education and Training Committee. I was selected by this committee to train the trial judges who attended, to run the event-review meetings after the events, and to evaluate the prospective judges for their national appointments. I was assigned to work the week again alongside Joan Gruber and another World judge who I greatly respected, Susan Johnson.

Both women were a dream to be assigned to work with. While I could relate better to the trial judges, whom I was closer in age with, Joan and Susan conversely had a vast amount of experience between them, and would be able to handle any situation that might present itself. The three of us shared a common mindset in that our roles were primarily educational. The other group of judges JETting that year had the opposite mindset, determined to make evaluations, weeding out those judges who either didn't fit in or didn't "get it." That group was led by my friend at the time, the ever so long-winded Joe Inman. The trial judges loved coming to the Gruber, Johnson, Jackson set of JETS, if only to get out of the windstorm that often surrounds Joe Inman.

Susan, Joan, and I focused on the rules. We were determined that the trial judges in our charge would leave the Nationals with an understanding of the four objective components of the first mark (speed, difficulty, variety, and sureness), in addition to the seven equally objective components of the second mark (variation of speed, carriage and style, originality, composition of the program, expression in time to the music, easy movement and flow, and, for Pairs, unison). I coined the almost-acronym "SCOPE of the EU" to help me remember these essential components whenever I took the judges' stand, and I shared it with the trial judges.

However, in the end, I would learn more from Susan and Joan, and from the experience itself, than the trial judges could have ever learned from me. If one ever wants to master a subject, they teach it. It's amazing how much I had glossed over until I actually had to teach it myself. The person who learned the most that week of Nationals was me, and I became a much better judge from the experience.

SOME TIME DURING that year, I began traveling for business to London. On my second or third trip to London, the European Championships were being held in Paris, so I invited Jay to meet me there for a small holiday after completing my business in London. One night, we met up with a French ice dance judge I had met at Skate America, Gilles Vandenbroeck.

During the events, he invited me into the hospitality area reserved for the judges in the arena. Once there, he spotted Marie-Reine across the room. "Let me introduce you to Marie-Reine; she is a Singles and Pairs judge from France," Gilles offered.

"I've already met her. I judged with her at Skate America," I replied.

"Well, that's what I thought, but I mentioned to her that you were here, and she said she didn't know who you were. Let's walk over and say hello." He proceeded to take me over to Marie-Reine, who was then introduced to me for the second time.

As she dismissively looked away, I said, "We've actually met. We judged the Men together at Skate America."

She turned, squinted as she looked at me, pursed her lips, and said, "I'm sorry, I don't remember you." She then rudely left us standing there, without even excusing herself. Gilles nearly spit out his drink, as he found the whole exchange hilarious. "Well, now you know the real Marie-Reine. If you can't give her a promotion or advance her career, she has no interest. Don't feel bad; she treats everyone that way. Most of us here are invisible to her, and apparently you are too!"

IN THE SPRING, I was assigned to both judge and team-lead an event in Slovenia, a small country that was part of the former Yugoslavia. It was the first time the U.S. would send a team to this emerging country. I was excited to attend, not so much for the judging experience or for the travel, but because I was for the first time a Team Leader.

Why was I so looking forward to team-leading? For too many years, I resented that I had to socialize only with the judges and officials. Too often, early in my career, I got myself into trouble by socializing with the skaters and coaches. As team leader, it would be my "job" to socialize with them.

The Alps of Slovenia border on Italy and Austria. Both countries are a mere 10 minutes from the mountain lodge in which we were housed. Quite surprising to me, in this former Eastern bloc country, a great number of people spoke English. The Slovenians are a hospitable group, and very proud of their beautiful country.

The skaters who attended the event, I remain fond of to this day, and so too the coaches.

At one of the national or international events I attended, one of the coaches, when we were socializing together in the stands of the rink, suddenly said to me:

"You probably heard the rumors about me when I was a skater."

I responded that I hadn't. "Well, they're not true. Just so you know."

I thanked her for telling me, but assured her I had never heard any rumors about her.

"Well, allegedly, when I was a teenager, skating internationally . . ." she proceeded to spread the rumor about herself, all the while assuring me that none of it was true. Apparently, while in Germany, she and Slick Hardwood had played "hide the bratwurst." None of it was true. She can assure you.

> While Tonya and Nancy battled it out in Lillehammer in 1994—what turned out to be the most widely watched Olympic event ever—Russians Ekaterina Gordeeva and Sergei Grinkov won their second gold medal, the ninth consecutive Olympic Pair gold medal for a Russian pair.

Golden Boy

AN OFFENSIVE ODOR filled a cheese shop in France, but this musty, moldy pungency was one smell that beckoned me to come back for another whiff. It's as if my nose said, "Did it really stink that badly? I'd better go back in and take another sniff to be sure." Once over the initial shock of the reeking aroma, I started to like, in a way, its nasty stink. It's a lot like the way I liked having my braces tightened as a teenager. My gums ached for days afterwards, but just enough so it actually hurt kind of good; at least that's what it was like for me.

While judging a Junior International event in St. Gervais, a small mountain resort in the southeastern corner of France, I passed by one of those "eau de toilet" cheese shops each day as I walked from the judges' hotel to the ice rink. A Coca-Cola Light sign (European Diet Coke) was in the window, luring me into the stinky cheese shop my first morning there. Initially, the smell was appalling. In fact, had I not been addicted to Diet Coke, I would probably have plugged my nose and left the cheese shop immediately. But the smell started to grow on me. Eventually I came to enjoy my morning stops (and sometimes a second stop later in the afternoon) to the shop to sniff the cheese and pick up my small, warm Diet Coke.

In many ways, that aromatic cheese shop in St. Gervais was comparable to my hobby of judging figure-skating. Initially, when I started learning about the politics—"the game"—witnessing the injustices, it was like the cheese, quite disgusting to the senses. But eventually, I came to enjoy the camaraderie that went along with the politics, the cocktail parties and judges' special dinners were amazing, and the judging irregularities became somehow excusable. I actually enjoyed the stink.

In St. Gervais, I received a national bias demerit from the competition referee for placing Natalie Vlandis and Jered Guzman in first place in the short program. Vlandis and Guzman were an attractive blonde/brunette team out of southern California, with amazingly good pair technique.

The referee was a chain-smoking frau from the former East Germany, with a bad up-do poodle-style wig, who reprimanded me. She looked like a character out of a Sad Sack comic strip. Vlandis and Guzman clearly deserved first, so I didn't feel bad about "overmarking" them.

Timothy Goebel and Matt Savoie made my job easier during the Men's event, earning first and second places respectively. The talent displayed by these two men clearly outshone the competition, and judging them was like a walk through the park after dealing with that German referee.

I was also serving a dual role as an assistant team leader, where, again, hanging out with the coaches and skaters was mandatory. They were all "down the hill," in less accommodating accommodations, but I didn't mind the walk back to my hotel after spending time with them. I'd rather spend time with the athletes and coaches any day.

At the end of the week, I learned that two male Canadian skaters were "playing cards" in a room with two female American skaters. Normally, this might alarm most team leaders, who are, after all, chaperones. Though the danger signals were going off in my head, I spotted Jered Guzman, gifted with a streetwise, straightforward attitude in addition to his pair moves. He had a bad-boy reputation with the judges, but I never let "reputations" get in the way of my friendships.

I asked him about the two Canadian male skaters and the situation with the girls upstairs, "Is there anything I should be worried about?" I had an idea that both of these boys might be gay, and Jered confirmed this, with a chuckle and a wink.

"There's *absolutely* nothing to be worried about," he said. So instead of causing a scene, and disrupting the "hair and makeup" socializing upstairs, I let it be.

Before long, I had earned a reputation among the skaters as a Team Leader that let the skaters be themselves. I didn't let their reputations get to me, and I allowed them to have their fun. Yet I still kept them out of trouble and got them to their events. On the surface, I gave the appearance of calm, while frantically working behind the scenes to make sure the events were taken care of. This reputation made me a favorite with the skaters, and soon they saw me as someone they could trust.

LATER IN THE season, I traveled to Philadelphia to judge the National Championships. The judges' dinner was held at an interactive museum, the Franklin Institute. It was a grand party, as usual, but a lot of it is somewhat hazy now. It had been a long flight to Philadelphia, and I was more than happy to "belly up" at the bar after getting past the fashion police, Steve Winkler and Joe Inman.

"Jon, is your coat part of the new Armani line? Steve asked, pointing to my sport coat.

"I don't think so," I answered, "Seems like I got it at a Boss something or rather."

"Oh, please! I know Armani when I see it!" shouted Steve, already having had too much gin and tonic.

"Yes, Jon, don't even act like you don't know who you're wearing. It's so unbecoming!" was Joe's input.

"Here, I'll show you," said Steve, as he reached for my lapel and began searching for a tag inside.

Before I knew it, Steve and Joe both had their noses inside my coat, snooping around, pulling on the neck, lifting the tails, looking for an

Armani tag to prove their fashion expertise. I would swear I suddenly got a whiff of the distinct smell of mothballs, no . . . cedar woodchips, no, both, coming from the two of them. Could it be that these two fashion experts were actually wearing last season?

After what seemed like a thorough inspection just short of a cavity search, Steve finally spotted the small Hugo Boss label sewn on the inside seam, then made a big deal about how Boss had knocked off the same designs of Armani, because it was unmistakably an Armani coat. It was just a plain blue sport coat! I knew damn well I got it at a Hugo Boss store, and now it was worth every dime to see those two fashion mavens falling all over themselves only to disprove their own point. They went on, of course. "Oh, did you see the new Versace line? Armani's black label?" Yadda, yadda, Prada.

On another night, there was an "elite" dinner held that was organized by Steve at Le Beq Fin, one of Philly's finest French restaurants.

Steve was becoming known for his annual exclusive-guest-list dinners, where only the most stylish judges were invited to attend. The powerful and not-so-stylish were rarely invited. His dinners were more about making a scene in public than about earning points with skating's influential. It was as if he believed he'd wind up on the society pages of *Vanity Fair*. Steve knows how to "dine" better than anyone else. His restaurant choice was outrageously expensive, but again worth every nickel to be included in his group of fashionable favorites, all dressed in their Gucci, Pucci, and Prada!

In the Ladies' event, Michelle Kwan avenged her previous year's loss to Tara Lipinski at the World Championships by winning the title with a program that brought tears to the eyes of two very different judges: Joe Inman and Steve Winkler. They were now becoming good friends, and I had to chuckle as I remembered Steve's egg-laying words of wisdom about Joe Inman just a few years earlier.

THE OLYMPIC WINTER Games were skated a world away. Japan's time zone required that I stay up until the wee hours of the morning, frequently checking the Internet as the results came in. I couldn't believe my eyes when I saw the Ladies' result. Lipinski over Kwan. Even though Lipinski had won the World title one year earlier, this was considered an upset.

I assumed Kwan, the favorite, had fallen. When I saw her skate on television the next day, and she didn't fall, I immediately decided the judging was suspect. "Tara could not possibly skate well enough to beat the program I just saw Michelle perform," I thought to myself. Then Tara came out and did just that. She outskated even herself in what can only be described aptly as solid gold. Sometimes, the judges do get it right.

LATER THAT SPRING, I walked into the gardens of the Olympic museum in Lausanne, Switzerland for the first time. It was the site of the Junior Grand Prix final, and I was both a team leader and a judge.

The host hotel was the Mövenpick, built right alongside the waters of Lake Geneva. Inside the Mövenpick bar, I learned about some of the tricky maneuvering that went on in ice dance. Kathleen Flaherty was the ice-dance judge for the U.S., and I watched as she was worked over during the cocktail hour. One judge in particular, a married male judge, was putting the full-court press on her, flirting with her and flattering her at every step. He was out to get her vote for his nation's dance team. Fortunately, Kathleen was wise to his not-so-subtle moves.

Later, he even put the moves on me, pressing his harder-than-it-should-have-been crotch against me as I sat at the bar, and then he invited me up to his room later for some "grappa." Grappa? Is that what the married men call it?

I judged the men's event, and really enjoyed myself. Tim Goebel once again made it easy for me, incredibly landing a quad salchow—the first ever performed in competition. He won because of it, despite the attempts of a few judges who "trashed" his presentation mark.

After the event, a few concerned coaches asked me whether I would ask the referee to confirm Tim's completion of the quad.

"Why bother? Of course it was completed. Clean as a whistle. He did it right in front of me," I stated in response to the request.

"Well, the Europeans might not want an American to hold the title of having completed the first quad salchow. They may dismiss it as having been cheated. Do you mind asking, just to be sure?" the coaches pressed.

I didn't exactly want to have that much interaction with this particular referee. She was Sally Stapleford, chair of the ISU Figure Skating Technical Committee. Steve Winkler had assured me, in advance of my going to Switzerland, that she was a very nice woman; in fact, he was actually friends with her. Nevertheless, I had heard from several other judges that she was a stern English taskmaster who didn't care much for Americans.

In the event-review meeting, after the discussion was nearing its end, I asked the question of whether Tim would get credit in the record books for his quad.

"Don't be silly, of course he will! Honestly. What kind of question is that? He did it, didn't he?" she plainly responded in the Queen's English.

The question made me feel both stupid and relieved at the same time. Of course he did it. Sally obviously couldn't have cared less that he was an American. He did it, and that was that.

The Skater's Gala at the end of the event was held at a fine seafood restaurant on a dock that jutted into Lake Geneva. It was a wonderful buffet. It included all the pomp and circumstance that befitted the crowning of the Junior Grand Prix title. After the party, the judges went back to the bar at the Mövenpick and continued their after-hours merrymaking.

As team leader, I was troubled by the last placement of an exceptionally talented young dance team, Jamie Silverstein and Justin Pekarek. I also suspected some game-playing and vote-trading by certain judges, as I had witnessed those manipulation attempts on the American judge.

To put my mind at rest, I approached Courtney Jones, the upperclass, very uptight and light-loafered British referee of the event, who was also a member of the powerful ISU Ice Dance Technical Committee. I asked him why the American team had finished so poorly. Normally, I would have avoided him at all costs, but I had already had more than a few drinks and now lacked any inhibition, and apparently so did he.

Courtney went on to explain to me that "Ice Dance is really just a form of lovemaking on the ice. The couple that performs the act most sensually to the music selected, the higher their placement." "The American team," he reasoned, "was simply not mature enough to make the recreation of the sex act believable." Unbelievable!

IN THE SPRING of 1999, I traveled to Ortisei, Italy in the Italian Alps, near the Austrian border. I was acting as a team leader and a judge, relishing again the opportunity to interact with the skaters and coaches. How things had changed since the time I trial-judged in the Central Pacific Region. I could still hear an echo in my ears, "Judges are not to fraternize with the skaters!"

The team included four amazing up-and-coming skaters, Sarah Wheat, Sasha Cohen, Johnny Weir, and Ryan Bradley. Sarah Wheat had a smile that could melt a glacier, and she quickly found a place in my heart, as did Ryan, Sasha, and Johnny.

The intrinsic talent in this group could not have been better, as later years would demonstrate. Nevertheless, Sasha Cohen missed her double axel in the short program, but still wound up first, that being a testament to how impressive her presentation was, even as a junior. Admittedly, I did not have her first in the short. I couldn't overlook the fall. In the freeskate, she was spot on, the clear winner, and I was thrilled to place her first.

Johnny Weir, like me, had started skating very late in life, so he really took me by surprise. Unlike me, he had already made the most of his few short years in the sport. His natural talent seemed endless, given what he had accomplished in such a short time.

The Italians, as always, were very pleasant and accommodating hosts, throwing an incredible gala for the skaters and judges at the end of the event, replete with delicious pastas and sauces of the region. The hospitality could not have been more superior for the skaters, judges, and officials alike. It remains one of my favorite skating locales.

IN THE FALL, I was assigned to judge the Nebelhorn Trophy in Oberstdorf, Germany. Oberstdorf is another place that holds a special place in the hearts of figure-skating officials. It is very much a choice German resort town. It's a ski resort in the winter, with hiking and relaxation in the summer. It is also the location of the annual meeting of the ISU big-wigs, and home to the "World Exam," a very stressful test given to International judges to qualify them to a level allowing them to judge an Olympic Games.

I really enjoyed myself in Oberstdorf, and was reminded once more why I had gotten so heavily involved in figure-skating's underbelly. It was really fun! The judges' dinner was simply fantastic. I wore a smart Versace navy blazer with a tan racing stripe down the back. At the dinner, I again ran into Sally Stapleford, who was there to administer the World Exam. I was still a little suspicious of her, though she was completely disarming and friendly. I was shaking in my boots when she commented on the uniqueness of my jacket. Only then did I realize that Versace was a bit much for a lazy, pampered, end-of-the-summer trip to the German Alps.

Ron Pfenning was also there, as a member of the ISU technical committee, to help administer the exam. Ron and I were good friends by now, though there was usually very little time to talk to him.

Taffy Holiday was the American judge seeking her World-level appointment. She was also a close friend, and, because of her nervousness, I was concerned that she might not pass the exam. It was not that she wasn't capable. In fact, she is one of the better U.S. judges. However, the end-of-day reports from her were not looking good. She was anxiously working herself into a frenzy, and I was afraid that it would affect her performance on the exam. I did my best to reassure her, but it didn't really seem to calm her down.

When I managed to get a minute with Ron, I asked him how Taffy was doing. He said that he thought she would be fine, but that he and Alexander Lakernik, the Russian member of the technical committee, were having a tough time convincing "the ladies" on the technical committee: Sally, Britta Lindgren (Sweden), and Walburga Grimm (Germany). So he, like Taffy, was worried, albeit for reasons much more political.

In the end, Taffy passed the exam, with Ron, Lakernik, and Britta voting in her favor, Sally and Walburga were for some reason against her. Ron secured Britta's vote by agreeing to vote for one of two Swedes sitting for the exam, both of whom had also worked themselves into a nervous whirl similar to Taffy's.

I didn't like hearing how Steve's good friend Sally had voted against my good friend Taffy. Even though Sally had been very pleasant to me, I made another note to myself to watch out for her.

Around that same time, a division was forming on the Technical Committee. The three women on the committee, Sally, Walburga, and Britta, were often times a odds with the two men, Ron and Lakernik. The political rift among the technical committee filtered down into the judge's rank with many choosing sides.

I sided with my good freind Ron Pfenning, and why wouldn't I? I did now know any of the other members of the committee beyond mere acquaintance, and Ron and I were good friends. I respected his knowledge, integrity, and ethics. If someone was at odds with Ron, I simply assumed that they were not in the right.

Steve Winkler chose to side with Sally. He and his good hen, Joe Inman, were traveling to London each summer for Sally's birthday. They had become very good friends. Steve didn't like that I was choosing ground on the opposite side of the fence. (Interestingly, these political lines and friendships fell apart after the events following the Olympic Pair scandal.)

From then on, I was boxed into Steve's "do not trust" category. My rapid advancement up the social climbing ladder of officiating put me near or equal to his rung of accomplishments. Steve often joked that he would "hunt me down and shoot me" if I got a World Referee appointment before he did, and I began to realize there was more truth to his words than not.

IN JANUARY OF 2000, Cleveland, Ohio played host to the National Championships. I was assigned to attend as a referee, the Men's event being my prime assignment, though I wound up merely an assistant on the event to New York's opinionated and athlete-unfriendly Lucy Brennan. She was, however, a huge fan of any skater who represented the Skating Club of New York, and dominated the practice chatter among the judges on their behalf. If you were not one of Lucy's chosen favorites, watch out! She was also not fond of a particular judge from the West—me.

I was assigned initially as the referee of the event, with Lucy as my assistant. Lucy, however, refused to be an assistant, much less for me, and pulled a tantrum and a few strings to get our two assignments switched. I should have thrown a fit of my own, but ultimately it didn't matter that much to me. The two referees sit center stage on the judges' stands, literally the best seats in the house. I was simply thrilled to get the assignment.

Timothy Goebel and Michael Weiss were battling it out for the title. Tim landed three quads during his program, which was not only remarkable at that time; it would still be considered a stellar achievement today. Michael Weiss, ever the polished skater, poured on his charismatic charm and style, and skated a near-perfect program. It came down to a contest between Tim's difficulty and Michael's presentation, and it was a very narrow margin. On my scorecard, and on Lucy's, Tim had won, but the referee's marks don't count. They simply run the event and monitor the judges. The judges went with Michael.

Tim felt as though he had been robbed of the National title that year. The following Nationals, he avenged the loss, but then felt as though he didn't deserve it. Michael should have won that one. Figure-skating can produce conflicting results, even at the highest levels. Sometimes a skater wins and doesn't deserve it, and sometimes he deserves it in spades and comes up short.

The rivalry between Tim and Michael was a golden marketing opportunity for U.S. Figure Skating. In them, they had two National titleholders, both World medalists, heading into an Olympic Games. Add Todd Eldredge, World Champion, who had recently come back into the mix, and it was a recipe for major success. How much media coverage did this potentially explosive battle of the boys get? Absolutely none. Yet another opportunity lost.

Tim and Mike's rivalry continues to this day. Timothy Goebel is a marketer's dream. He's blond, good-looking, with a boy-next-door smile. Michael Weiss, also good-looking, is a fitness-focused beefcake, with dark hair and a wry smile. Yet, strangely, U.S. Figure continues to ignore the potential story "legs" of their rivalry.

Fast-forward to the present day, and the competition rivalry between the men is even more complicated. Now, the infinitely talented Johnny Weir (two-time National Champion) and never-without-a-smile Evan Lysacek (World bronze medalist) join Timothy and Michael in the fight for first. Four equally accomplished skaters duking it out for only three spots on the 2006 Olympic Team. The field is even deeper with World team members Matt Savoie and Ryan Jahnke nipping at the heels of the four "favorites." The ability to market a suspense-filled Men's event has never been better. It's a marketing coup that should begin at Skate America and culminate in the battle for the National title. But U.S. Figure Skating will likely have ignored this enormous opportunity once again.

I FOUND MYSELF traveling to Oberstdorf, Germany—a year after my first taste of this beautiful Alpine town. It was my turn to take the World Exam. With my experience the year before, watching Taffy nearly stress herself out of her deserved appointment, I had an advantage over every applicant except one—the Swede who had failed the test the year before. She returned this time, calm as a cucumber, and skated through the exam. I took her cue, and successfully slid through myself.

In less than two years, I went from a National to an International judge, and in four short years, qualified myself to judge at the Olympic level. I was the youngest American World-level judge ever, and riding on a high that seemed endless at the time. I was traveling the world in high style and enjoying a sport I loved. Life for me could not have been any better.

ST. PETERSBURG, RUSSIA was the home of the former czars. The variable word czar, tsar, or tzar, pretty much summarized who the Russians treated the judges like at the 2000 Cup of Russia, one of the six ISU "Grand Prix" events held each fall.

I arrived in St. Petersburg a few days early, and decided to treat my new boyfriend, Sandy Miller, to a week of Russian extravagance. We lodged ourselves at the Grand Europa, one of St. Petersburg's finest hotels, and, while there, managed to catch two ballet performances at the Morinsky, more commonly known in the U.S. under its Soviet name, the Kirov.

When we were escorted to our seats for our first performance, of *Giselle*, it was apparent that we had lucked into an influential and entrepreneurial tour guide. Maya, a Ukrainian immigrant co-worker of Sandy's back in San Francisco, had given him the name of a friend of hers, who, she assured us, would act as our tour guide and help us find our way around the city.

When we asked the concierge at the Europa if we could buy tickets to the ballet, he indicated that it was usually sold out, but that on the black market, he might be able to get us tickets for about $100 each. Later in the day, while Maya's tour-guide friend, Mikal, showed us around the Winter Palace, we asked him about the ballet.

Mikal jumped on his cell phone, made a few calls, and then announced that he would pick us up later that evening in front of the hotel, take us to the Morinsky, get us in, and then have a van waiting to take us back to the hotel when it was over. However, he said, all this would cost us twenty-four U.S. bucks, total. For the cost of a couple burgers in the states, we were going to be seeing *Giselle* at the Kirov!

He had to be kidding. Still, with visions of nosebleed seats and obstructed views, we accepted the offer. In retrospect, it was unlike me not to try to barter for an even better price!

When we arrived at the theatre, we were met by a couple of thugs who looked at first like two Russian shot-putters, but who smiled and escorted us through a back door and up a dark stairway. They could have been leading us down a path to some damp gulag for all we knew, so "concerned" would be an understatement at that point.

However, within moments, we were walking down the center aisle and taken to our center seats in the fourth row. I was certain Kirov security would be rushing our row at any moment, and since the muscle had disappeared, we would be left to our own devices. I glanced over my left shoulder, and sitting within my peripheral vision about fifty yards away, in mediocre-at-best seats, was the U.S. Figure Skating president, Phyllis Howard, along with a delegation of Russian figure-skating officials.

Sandy nudged my arm, directing me to my right side, where, about three rows back, he claimed to have spotted Oksana Baiul. It wasn't actually Oksana, but a lookalike decked out in fur and feathers, sitting alongside her husband, Viktor Petrenko, the Olympic Gold medalist who had bested Paul Wylie.

We had scored tickets to the finest ballet in the world, and had better seats than an Olympic gold medalist. The performance was so good that first night that we returned again two nights later. Same bargain-basement price, same fourth-row seats.

But for twenty-four dollars! The average monthly income of the typical Russian family is about fifty dollars, a figure that is very difficult for an American to fathom, but true just the same.

It makes sense then that the judges from Russia, and other Eastern bloc countries, are willing to do whatever their federations request of them in order to continue traveling out of their countries to judge figure-skating. One day's worth of travel per diem is worth more than a month's salary. The honorarium given at Grand Prix events, three hundred dollars, is half a year's earnings. Put in that perspective, its easy to understand the motivation of former Eastern bloc judges to play the game. If they don't, they stay home.

But what of their Western counterparts? After years of practicing law, most of the time as a firm partner, I had already reached a position in life where I had traveled extensively on my own dime. It wasn't necessary for me to use figure-skating as a bridge to take me to faraway places; I was capable of doing that myself when I wanted to. I managed to get myself stellar seats at the Kirov without figure-skating's assistance, but could the same be said for others? Morry Stillwell was a guest in Russia and supplied with a private chauffer for him and his wife. He wasn't there as a judge. He wasn't there as a team leader. He was simply a guest of the Russian federation. A guest of the Russian federation, and had been on numerous occasions.

The competition began a few nights later, but not before the judges and officials were taken on a tour of several Russian palaces, the final stop being a huge formal luncheon in the ballroom of the Stroganoff Palace while a live string quartet played classical music. Beluga caviar from the Caspian Sea, chilled Russian reserve vodka, salted smoked salmon, and every other Russian specialty was prepared in Slavic proportions. Talk about killing the fatted calf! It was a feast unlike any I had experienced before.

In contrast, the skaters' gala at the end of the week was held in the basement lounge of the budget Pulkovskaya Hotel. It was adjacent to a resident stripper-and-hooker bar, with a few of the scantily clad women hired as entertainment for the night. There was plenty of vodka and plenty of good food. Nevertheless, it wasn't the Stroganoff Palace, there wasn't a string quartet, and the skaters weren't dining on caviar.

After returning home from what could have been my week of state dinners with the tsars, I was off to judge the Junior Grand Prix final in Scotland a few weeks later. Once again, the officials and judges were treated like visiting monarchs. The judges' dinner was held in a castle, high atop one of Scotland's rolling hills, with Wedgwood styled carvings etched into the ballroom walls. Though nowhere near as extravagant and opulent as the Russian affair, the Scots also know how to put on an incredible show.

At the dinner, I sat next to Elena Fomina, an attractive judge from Russia, who was assigned to judge the Men's division. During dessert, another Russian, Myra Oblasova, talked to me only a few seconds before focusing her attention on Elena, speaking completely in Russian. Though I could completely hear their unpleasant exchange, I couldn't understand a single word, except maybe "nyet!" It seemed to me that Elena was resisting whatever request was being put to her.

When Myra left, Elena let me know that she would now be judging the Ladies' event; Myra was taking the Men's event from her. When I asked why, Elena looked at me, shrugging her shoulders, saying only "Dance?" in a quizzical manner.

I can only guess what she meant by that. The Men's event shared a few common interests, country-wise, with the Dance event. Not so for the Ladies. If she was so inclined, in order for Myra to get placements for her Russian team from the other countries, she would need to promise something in return. With no common nationalistic interest on the Ladies, she couldn't make promises there. But if she was on the Men's event, if she wanted to, she could promise placements in that event, in exchange for placements in the Dance.

The result of the Men's event did not reflect the skating. Not even close. The three American boys, Parker Pennington, Evan Lysacek, and Ryan Bradley, were all screwed, while the Russian boys who skated nowhere near as well ended up second and third. The Russian dance team was second in the Dance event. It was becoming more and more clear why Myra needed to be on that Men's event.

At the dinner, I said hello to Courtney Jones, who was there as the referee of the Dance event. He was dressed impeccably, as usual. One thing I had always noticed about Courtney, and envied, was the way he tied his necktie. It was knotted to perfection, stiff and very formal, and perfect every time.

I decided to ask Courtney, the making-love-on-the-ice dance technical committee member, how he managed to knot his ties so perfectly. His reply stopped me in my tracks.

"Well Jon," he said, "it's all in the way you grasp the tie. I caress it, massaging it just so, and then carefully insert it through the knot, pulling it carefully to create a perfectly erect knot." Then he added, "Why don't you come to my room later and I'll show you just how I do it?"

What I percieved to be his not-so-subtle come-on was enough for me to avoid "Mr. Erect-tie" from then on.

IMPOVERISHED SOFIA, BULGARIA, is nearly halfway around the world from San Francisco, and as far away as I've ever traveled. It is essentially a second-world country. The roads are of poor quality, wild dogs roam the streets looking for food, and many of its residents live in terrible poverty. I wasn't looking forward to visiting this city. However, it was hosting the much-anticipated Junior World Championships.

I was assigned as Team Leader to the event, my assistant being the energetic Lorrie Parker from Kansas City, Kansas. Lorrie is part of a multi-pronged skating family: Her mother, uncle, aunts, cousins, and daughter are all involved in the sport. Friendly beyond the call of duty, she has no enemies and seems to know or talk to everyone she meets, and then remembers their names. Despite a beautiful smile and a twinkle in her eyes, Lorrie had a reputation for being a bit loud and a voracious partier. It seemed to me, going in, that I would be spending as much time keeping Lorrie out of trouble as I would be taking care of the coaches and athletes. Nothing could have been further from the truth. Once again, someone's reputation in skating had preceded him or her, and once it again it was completely wrong.

The athletes absolutely loved Lorrie. She relates to them on the level of an adult, and gives them encouragement that only a former skater and former skating mother could. Her enthusiasm is on the scale of a college cheerleader, which she just happened to be during a previous life.

Together, we made a great team. At the time, the team was winning medals left and right. By the end of the week, this particular Junior World Team racked up more hardware than any other team in U.S. Figure Skating history. It was an amazing show of talent, by an amazing group of kids: Johnny Weir won the gold and later won consecutive Senior National titles. Evan Lysacek took the silver and later collected it twice again and the World bronze medal. Ann Patrice McDonough was second that year, Junior World Champ the next. Tanith Belbin and Benjamin Agosto were Ice Dance silver medalists in Sofia, took gold the next year, reigning National Champions and reigning World silver medalists. Kristin Roth and Mike McPherson took bronze in the Pairs. The rest of the team was equally talented, most of whom I have stayed in contact with through the years. Watch for great ice dancing to come from Kendra Goodwin and Chris Obzansky, recently reunited after Obzansky's tour of duty as a missionary for the Mormon church. Lydia Manon, also an ice dancer, has a new partner in the dance event. And

Benjamin Miller, a single skater in Bulgaria, has turned his sights on dance. The U.S. Olympic Team in 2006 and 2010 should be chock-full of these exceptional skating talents.

At the end of the week, after a special night out at a Bulgarian disco for the skaters, Lorrie and I were up all night doing our best to keep the American skaters out of trouble. The Russian boys had taken a keen interest in a few of the American girls. Lorrie and I had to haul more than one of them out of the various parties scattered around the hotel in the private rooms of the mostly un-chaperoned "men."

One such incident occurred with a skater too drunk even to recognize who I was. I recognized her, though, and she was having way too much fun flirting with the Russian boys. As I grabbed her, I noticed two boys making out around the corner. I got her out of that particular hotel room post-haste. Did I see that right, two boys making out in a corner? One was a young Canadian skater who had hooked up with this other skater who I didn't take the time to identify, and were going at it surrounded by otherwise straight, drunk Russians, who couldn't have cared less. It was the year 2000, the turn of the century. This wasn't your grandfather's skating competition!

A few weeks later I hauled Sandy up to Vancouver to watch his first skating competition, the World Championships. He was a good sport, watching all of the events. He was bored silly watching the Ice Dance event. He just didn't understand all of the avant garde movements that were all the rage with the ice dancers that year. Maybe, if the ISU hadn't banned undignified moves and positions earlier in the year, the event might have held more interest for him.

Undignified moves and positions? Yes, the same ISU that encourages Courtney Jones's "love-making" on the ice, banned positions in which the Lady's crotch becomes the focus of the movement. (What about the man's? And the officials'?) Undignified moves and positions; ISU president Ottavio Cinquanta and his ISU kept themselves busy with the important issues of figure-skating. I would have loved to have been a fly on the wall witnessing the discussion when this rule was passed. It must have been a heated, controversial meeting. Most of those dirty old men probably needed a cigarette break after that one!

Lorrie joined me again a month or so later in Slovenia. I was again the referee and Lorrie was there to judge. Lorrie was working a marketing campaign, Russian-style, on the judges of my Novice Men's event. The American boy she was promoting was a master stylist, and Lorrie must have taken every opportunity to play this up. He finished second in the short program, but scored the highest presentation marks. In the discussions that took place afterward, putting a twist on Russian-style spin, Lorrie let the foreign judges convince *her* just how good the U.S. skater was in the presentation. "Really? Do you think so?" Pinky on chin, eyes to the ceiling.

In the freeskate, the American performed well enough. He missed a jump or two, as I recall, but he had remarkable presentation. A young Swiss, skating immediately after, nailed a number of well-executed triple jumps. He skated a perfect program, and was clearly the winner. Well, at least the assistant referee and I saw it that way. The Swiss judge, of course, did too. But Lorrie and her previously persuaded panelists all gave it to the American. They did it by giving him a wide lead in the presentation mark to make up for the loss of his edge in technical merit.

I'm still not sure how Lorrie did it, but I wish I knew. She accomplished her goal without ever trading a single placement, without ever making a promise, no quid-pro-quo. She couldn't have, there was no dance event, and Lorrie isn't even a dance judge! She accomplished it in the same way the Russians did for Oksana Baiul, and the way they tried to do it for Irina Slutskaya in 2002, and the same way they will try again in 2006. The American boy made Lorrie's job easier; he gave her a brilliant presentation to work with. Too bad Slutskaya can't give her Russian spin-masters such an easy job!

Its no wonder the skaters love Lorrie Parker. She will go out of her way to help any one of them, and has done so repeatedly. She is their clear choice as their Olympic Team Leader. Which means U.S. Figure Skating, who, like evil schoolmarms denying the kids their recess, will demonstrate their defiance of all athletes' wishes, will never put her in that position.

At that competition, Lorrie also saved my butt by helping me find my passport which I had lost when we made a quick trip in a rental car across the Italian border, without so much as stopping to say hello to the border guards. Its amazing we didn't get arrested. When we returned to Slovenia, my passport was missing. Searching in the dark, retracing our every step in Italy, we finally found it next to a pay phone I had been using.

On our last evening in Slovenia, I returned Lorrie's favor by smooth-talking the Casino security guards who were about to arrest her and a Canadian judge she was defending. The Canadian judge had taken a photo inside the Casino, something that was strictly prohibited. Too much alcohol, and having too much fun, we made a great team again on that great Slovenian adventure.

Soon it was the beginning of the Olympic season, building up to the Winter games in Salt Lake City. The season opened in late October with Skate America, held in Colorado Springs just weeks after the September 11 terrorist attacks on New York City and the Pentagon. My family was calling for me to end my skating escapades, fearful of all the travel I was doing. My mother practically pleaded with me to stop flying around the world. If I wasn't having such a good time, a phony amongst the phonies, I might have heeded her advice.

Skate America is the first of the Grand Prix Series, and despite the somber mood that still filled the air from the 9/11 attacks, this skate event would also end in controversy.

Pinned against the wall, I was doing my best to keep my composure. Christine Brennan, a reporter from *USA Today*, and Phil Hersh, from the *Chicago Tribune*, were there holding me to the fire. They had trapped me alongside Hideo Sugito, a World-level judge, who acted as referee of the event that finished earlier in the evening. Cocktails in hand, we did our best to answer the reporters' questions, reporters who had managed to penetrate the officials' hospitality suite at the Doubletree Hotel. Not that I minded.

A surprisingly lackluster performance earlier that evening by the popular Michelle Kwan was controversially awarded a gold medal ahead of a stellar performance by the then relatively unknown Sarah Hughes (who would later to go on to win the Olympic gold). In my role as the assistant referee of the presiding panel, I had seen this ruling differently than had the judges who ranked Michelle first. Though I personally adore Michelle, Mr. Sugito and I this time both placed the young upstart jumping sensation Sarah Hughes ahead of her.

I freely expressed my opinion to anyone who would listen, including my fellow judges and, to the surprise of many, the officially ignored yet detail-hungry press. Two members of the press corps had tracked me down and now cornered me in the hospitality suite.

The press corps in figure-skating has their own micro-culture. They are assigned a hotel separate from the judges and competitors. They are officially credentialed, and are given access to the event venues. They are designated an area in the arena where they can watch the events. They have a designated pressroom in the bowels of the arena, and access to the press conference rooms as well as the "free zone," an area just outside the kiss-and-cry booth where reporters can fire questions at athletes who are on their way back to the dressing room after receiving their scores. "So what the heck happened out there?" they might fire at a skater who had just botched a quad toe. "When you hit the ice and saw your gold medal dreams come crashing to an end, what was going through your mind?" So they have plenty of unrestricted emotional access to the athletes. But that is where the "access" ends.

The press and the officials do not mingle. There are no after-event press conferences for officials, where the judges might be held accountable for their scores. There is no "free zone" where the press might catch a judge fleeing the judging panel for the sanctity of the judges' room. The judges are warned repeatedly about the dangers of speaking to the press. It is understood, both on the record and off the record, that judges are not to speak to the press. If the press wants a comment from an official, they have to hunt them down. Fortunately, many reporters are very adept at doing just that. But even then, only the protection of being "off the record" would prompt some officials to speak.

Thus, while the press is "official" in that they are credentialed, they are completely ignored by the actual officials.

The Skate America event provides the earliest opportunity for skaters to premiere their new programs and the latest "triple cows" and "flying sows" mastered over the summer. It is also the first opportunity for the officials to establish their early rankings and ratings based on the banquet buzz and cocktail chatter of the daily, hourly, and nightly parties and socials. For the press, it's their first opportunity of the season to get a story—and, being an Olympic year, this was a chance to build readership going into the Winter Games. This Skate America event gave them a front-pager, and, oddly, a premonition of what ultimately would transpire in Salt Lake City.

Earlier that evening, I was given a heads-up that Brennan was looking for me. As I said, I had told anyone who would listen that I thought the judges got this one wrong, and apparently Brennan caught wind of it. I sought the advice of Ron Pfenning and Sally Stapleford for their perspective as ISU Technical committee members. They both encouraged me to speak to the press, and assured me that there was nothing in the rules against doing so. In fact, a referee's obligations might even require it. So on this night, Brennan and Hirsh got a story: Sarah had been robbed.

"Mr. Sugita, can you tell us why the judges placed Michelle over Sarah?" queried Brennan.

"No . . . no." replied Sugita.

"Why not?" countered Brennan.

"Ah . . . yes. Yes, because, . . . no," said Mr. Sugita. His English, which was generally pretty good, was failing him now.

"Mr. Jackson, help us out here, huh?" Hersh pleaded.

"Phil, please call me Jon, okay?" I said. "Mr. Sugita and I cannot comment on why the judges placed Michelle ahead of Sarah because we have no idea why they did that. Until we have our judges' review meeting in the morning, we won't know why they marked the skating the way they did." I stated this as succinctly and as carefully as I could.

"By saying 'you have no idea why they did that,' are you implying they were wrong to have done so?" Brennan followed up.

I replied, "Christine, all I'm saying is that we only have the judges' marks and their placements. I can confirm to you that both Mr. Sugita and I placed Sarah Hughes first. Neither of us can comment on the marks of the other judges until tomorrow morning." Again, choosing my words carefully.

The questions continued in a similar vein. An occasional question was asked of Sugita, and many times I directed the reporters to him, but he continued with his less-than-perfect-English act, so the questions found their way back to me.

As I answered Brennan and Hersh's questions, I could see Sally and Ron still talking on the other side of the room while stealing glances at me. When I looked over, Sally raised her glass to me, giving me a reassuring smile. When the firestorm subsided, I found my way over to Ron and Sally.

"Hey, old boy, can I get you another drink?" Sally asked. "So, how did it go? The reporters aren't so bad, are they?" Sally is a slight, attractive woman with a winning smile and personal demeanor. Yet she still seemed powerful and unapproachable to me, and I had heeded the warnings from other U.S. officials to stay out of her way. But the icy glaze I had imposed on the relationship, solely because of her reputation, was beginning to melt.

I went on to give them a rundown on what had transpired. I saw a very likeable side to Sally for the first time that evening. My willingness to veer from the expected norm at that event may have earned me Sally's respect. I left Skate America with the beginnings of a friendship with this very powerful woman. I didn't realize at the time how important that friendship would turn out to be.

After Skate America, I judged the Pacific Coast Championships, and then jetted off to Sweden to referee a Junior Grand Prix event. It was my first time out of the country as an official referee for an International event. While I felt good about my performance as referee at Skate America, I was a little anxious heading off to Sweden. Sally Stapleford and Britta Lindgren were also referees. That the chair (Sally) of the ISU Technical Committee and one of only four other members of that same committee (Britta) would be watching my every move, only seemed to heighten my nervous discomfort.

After I landed in the beautiful city of Copenhagen, the salty old queen of the sea, I took a short train ride across the sound of the Baltic Sea that separates Denmark from Sweden. I had arrived the day before the championships to situate myself in the time zone.

Lorrie Parker and Kathleen Flaherty were there as the American judges, so I knew I would be having a good time, even if I fell flat on my face as a referee. I had judged many times with Kathleen, both on the West Coast and abroad, and Lorrie and I were becoming fast friends. I managed to get through a very trying event of numerous ladies falling this way, that way, and every which way they could. One skater from Lithuania came out in a tie-dye dress, reminding me of Joan Burns's starving young hippie from the Berkeley commune.

I didn't mingle much with Britta or Sally, not that they didn't try. I was up to some of my old bad habits, preferring to hang out with the people I knew well, Lorrie, Kathleen, and the coaches and skaters, rather than the higher-ups I didn't really know that well, Sally and Britta.

When I returned from Sweden, I was only home a few weeks before I was on a flight to Chicago to assist Rob Rosenbluth refereeing the Junior National Championships. Then I went home to Salt Lake for Christmas, down to Las Vegas for New Year's Eve, and off to Los Angeles for the National Championships. Boy, this jet-set life was starting to get a bit hectic!

I judged the Ladies' event in Los Angeles. Four of the American women all held World-level credentials, Michelle Kwan, Sasha Cohen, Sarah Hughes, and Angela Nikodinov. Three other women were nipping at their heels: Jennifer Kirk, Junior World Champion, Ann Patrice McDonough, Junior World Champion, and Amber Corwin, a perennial threat.

It would turn out to be the highlight of my judging career, with the depth of the talent so deep and so enjoyable to watch. In the end, Michelle, Sasha, and Sarah earned their spots on the 2002 Olympic Team.

Two weeks later, having about as much time as needed to get to the dry cleaners, I was off to South Korea to judge the Four Continents Championships. It was just a few weeks before the Olympics, so most of our Olympians took a pass, sending the up-and-comers instead. In the Ladies' event, all eyes were on Ann Patrice McDonough. The chatter amongst the judges at practice and at cocktails was all about Ann Patrice. I tried in vain to remind them that Jennifer Kirk was also a skater to be reckoned with.

In the short program, I was the lone judge to place Jennifer Kirk first. She clearly skated the best that day, but the judges had their attention on Ann Patrice and two young Japanese skaters. Jennifer did manage to come in second, but she should have been first. By my placing Jennifer first, I provided the other judges the opportunity to approach me about my placement. It was also a perfect opportunity to prepare them for the freeskate, without the appearance of lobbying for my skater.

In the long program, it was clear. Lobbying or not, Jennifer Kirk came through while Ann Patrice skated poorly, falling out of the top three, with the Japanese girls coming in second and third. I have come to know Jennifer Kirk as a skater who comes through when it counts. She has had a few tough skates in her career, a death in the family, and a number of coaching changes, but I believe she has a wonderful professional career ahead of her.

In the Pair event, the Canadian judge, who I love dearly as a person, outrageously placed all three Canadian teams ahead of all three of the American teams. Talk about national bias! The result, however, was quite different. It went Canadian, American, Canadian, American, Canadian, and American. How did she get away with such blatant judging bias? The referee himself was also Canadian, and he never said a word about it in the event-review meeting. I was starting not to care too much for these Canadian judges and their referees, or for the games they seemed to be playing.

Because of figure-skating, in less than four years I had traveled internationally to Slovenia (twice), St. Gervais, Lausanne (twice), Gelsenkirchen (Germany), Nice (France), St. Petersburg, Scotland, Bulgaria, Oberstdorf (twice), Vancouver, and South Korea, not to mention my domestic travel to Nashville, Philadelphia, Cleveland, and Boston, in addition to the qualifying and non-qualifying competitions in Detroit, Kansas City, Denver, Indianapolis, and the like.

Joe Inman and Steve Winkler, fearful that a young upstart was on their tails, began calling me the "Golden Boy" behind my back. When they said it, I'm told their tone was ripe with sarcasm, disgust, and distrust. Or was it envy?

Russian Artur Dimitriev wins his second Olympic gold medal with new partner Oksana Kazakova, at the 1998 Nagano Olympics, bringing to ten the number of consecutive gold medals won in the Pairs event by Russia. The Russians are unstoppable.

Salt Lake City Winter Games

THE SALT LAKE City Winter Olympics of 2002 came with an opportunity to attend the figure-skating Pair event. The Pair event features difficult feats of derring-do such as death spirals, triple twists, and spectacular overhead lifts, but ultimately the event is won by the chemistry exhibited between the couples. The chemistry on this cold, damp Monday night in February would prove explosive. The Salt Lake City spectators, and the television viewers watching from around the world, were not expecting the heat displayed on the ice that night.

The Olympic Winter Games is the pinnacle event for a number of winter sports, and figure-skating has become the Olympics' premier event. The importance of the Olympics in figure-skating goes beyond even the level of a World Championship. And this "world championship" is held only once every four years. In fact, its significance is so unique that the title of World Champion should not be confused with the much more meaningful and prestigious title of an Olympic Gold Medalist.

At the Figure-Skating Pair event, I was provided a nosebleed seat in the Delta Center arena with two fellow Team USA members, Denise Thomas and Carolyn Kruse. Denise, Carolyn, and I were there helping the U.S. Figure Skating Team Leaders, with my focus being on the coaches.

On that night, my anticipation was for the expected skate-off between the Russian and Canadian Pair teams. The Canadians were a charming and attractive couple, sparkling Jamie Sale and her partner—both on and off the ice—the handsome David Pelletier. The Russians were the technically precise and classically styled—and equally attractive—team of Yelena Berezhnaya and Anton Sikharulidze.

For the first time in over 40 years of Olympic competition, a non-Russian Pairs team had a great chance to win a gold medal. The Russian dynasty in pair skating began at the 1964 Olympics in Innsbruck, and continued seemingly unstoppable, with an unprecedented string of ten consecutive Russian gold medals. However, it was possible that the Russian Pairs dominance would end that night in Salt Lake City. The defending World Champions were the Canadians, and this was their chance to end the four-decade Russian run.

Just before NBC would go live with their prime-time coverage of the day's biggest event, the pairs took to the ice for a 6-minute warm-up. While the skaters were loosening up, anticipation began to build in the arena. As each couple was introduced, the crowd went wild, especially when Jamie and David skated onto the ice. It was clear that the Canadians were the favorites, but the cheering for the Russians was almost equally loud. All the skaters were spinning and gliding in every direction, and it was difficult to keep an eye on any one particular skater.

Suddenly gasps erupted, followed by a sudden hush in the arena. Jamie Sale was down on the ice, David rushing over to help her. She was holding herself, but was she hurt? Somehow, there had been a collision between the two favorites; the Russian team, skating swiftly down the ice, had crashed into the Canadians maneuvering in a counter direction. In this unexpected crossing of paths, Anton had accidentally clipped Jamie.

Jamie was clearly shaken. But with David and Anton both helping, she pulled herself together, stood up, managed a smile, and threw her hand in the air as if to signal she was going to be okay. Anton skated back over to Yelena; Jamie began stroking around the rink, trying to regain her focus. At the end of the warm-up, as the skaters left the ice, foremost on my mind was whether Jamie could recover to skate well enough to win gold.

The last time a pair team had had a significant chance to end the Russian reign was in 1980, twenty-two years earlier. Tai Babilonia and Randy Gardner, the American team and defending World Champions, lost the opportunity to win gold at Lake Placid when Randy left the warm-up in pain, having injured his groin. As Randy left the ice, Tai was in tears, and the heartbreaking image was fixed forever in the minds of many Americans. My memory of that tragedy was no different, and at the moment, with Jamie Sale possibly injured, I recalled it perfectly.

The Russians would skate first. Taking to the ice with a warm Salt Lake City welcome, Anton and Yelena glided to their starting positions. Silence filled the arena. The music of the Meditation from *Thaïs* by Jules Massenet began to play, and the Russians began their effortless routine. An Auguste Rodin statue called *Eternal Embrace* had inspired their innovative and graceful choreography. Midway through what could otherwise be described as a perfect display of pair technique; Anton stumbled out of a double axel jump and made a poor recovery. In my mind, all hopes of continuing the "Russian dynasty" toppled at that moment.

Hold that thought. With Jamie still recovering backstage from her collision with Anton, would the Canadians even skate?

The "kiss and cry" area where Anton and Yelena awaited their scores on this night provided an excellent opportunity for television cameras to capture each skater's every bead of sweat while the world waited along with them. That night, the cameras captured perfectly the Russians' telling facial expressions.

What could be going through their minds? Anton was probably worrying about having to trade his skates in for cement shoes, as that would be preferred to facing Yelena once she unclenched her jaw and let him have it backstage. They knew that Anton's flub had left the door wide open, and their facial expressions let everyone else know it. A clean skate by the Canadians would win Yukon gold.

"Wow! They really blew it," I said to Denise Thomas, the congenial U.S. Figure Skating staff member sitting to my left. "It looks like they know they won't win."

"Whoa!" Denise replied. "I guess they didn't expect that. It's going to be all Canada!" Then she added. "I would hate to be Anton in a few minutes. Look at Yelena!"

Carolyn Kruse, sitting to the left of Denise and chuckling along with us, chimed in: "My gosh, she is going to kill him!"

We focused our attention back on the arena, as the Canadians took the ice. Jamie seemed to be all right as she skated around the rink "shaking it off." Silence again filled the arena as the Canadians took to their starting position. As the music from the movie *Love Story* began to air, they became individual characters, perfectly playing their roles from the famous Hollywood production. But could Jamie hold up in the jumps? Thirty seconds in, we knew the answer—side-by-side double axel–double toe-loop combinations, executed perfectly. The lifts and jumps that followed were executed equally as well.

After four-plus minutes, they completed a flawless performance! It was the best I had ever witnessed by a Pairs team—and at the Olympic Games, no less. Jamie and David skated effortlessly through the door the Russians had left open, hitting every jump, lift, and spin to perfection.

"It's over! It's their gold medal!" I exclaimed to Denise and Carolyn, as I joined the entire audience jumping to its feet.

However, as wide as that door was open, and as cleanly and beautifully as the Canadians had glided through, the door didn't lead where we'd all expected. As it turned out, the Canadians' fate was far more secure than Anton Sikharulidze's blade when he stumbled out of his double axel combination. How could a flawless performance lose to one that included both technical mistakes and a stumble on the ice?

Well, one need only recall the near-perfect performance of Nancy Kerrigan being bested, five judges to four, by Russia's Oksana Baiul, who sloppily landed most of her jumps on two feet, to know of Russia's history of winning gold even when they've been outskated. Another Russian, Viktor Petrenko, committed many mistakes in his 1992 Albertville gold medal performance over the unlikely, yet still better performance of American Paul Wylie. In the skating community, these incidences were discussed, even debated, but ultimately it was attributed to differences of opinion and differences in style, not to corruption. And now it would be seemingly the same story for the 2002 Pair Champions.

When the silver medal finish of the Canadians blinked onto the scoreboard, I was so stunned that my knees locked and I could not sit back down in my seat.

"Did I miss something?" I yelled to Denise over the roar of boos filling the arena.

The entirety of the shocked Delta Center crowd had been on its feet since the Canadians took the ice. It was Canada's night. It was their moment, and the crowd and the television viewing audience collectively roared in outrage.

A mass of energy was generated in the arena that night, during and immediately after the Canadian performance. That combustible energy exploded when sparked by the sheer force of five otherwise colorless judges: a Russian, a Pole, a Chinese, a Ukrainian, and the now infamous "Show me your gold, I'll show you mine" French judge, Marie-Reine LeGougne. The jig was up, and the show was over.

The less-than-perfect 5.8's and 5.9's that flashed in dim-witted bulbs on the Delta Center scoreboard for a perfect Canadian performance felt like a whack in the knees by a piece of leftover trailer-park lumber. What could possibly have gone so wrong? How could any judge not place the Canadians first? How could the deceitful judges—who had cast their votes in favor of the Russians—hear the hiss of the crowd and not know that their backroom design had been uncloaked for the whole world to see? I think that at that moment, the shamefaced knew that the world was on to them, and the bubbling of guilt began.

"I'm out of here," I said to Denise and Carolyn, as I clambered in front of the seats toward the aisle.

Still shocked, I stumbled aimlessly down the stadium stairway to the lower concourse and forced myself to watch the Chinese team, Xue Shen and Hongbo Zhao. As an insider, I knew that the Chinese team would not be considered to win the gold, even though their technical skills and style were such that they should have been contenders. The possibility simply did not exist in the minds of the judges who had already been preprogrammed at the sneaky-peak cocktail parties and back-room clambakes as to just who was in the running for what medals, and the Chinese would be lucky to mine brass.

The American team of the lovely Kyoko Ina and the hunky Alabaman

John Zimmerman skated so well that, in a fair world, they would have ranked higher than fifth. Some have speculated that to get the Chinese judge to vote for the Russians over the Canadians, a promise was made to secure the bronze for the Chinese team. China had never medaled in Olympic Pairs figure skating.

It certainly appears that some type of promise was made and kept. The Chinese team did not skate anywhere near as well as the American team, yet they won the bronze. And in the same five-to-four split that gave Russia the gold over Canada, the lower-ranked Russian team would finish in an outrageous fourth place, leaving the Americans in their architectonic fifth place spot.

If a deal had been made to put the Russians first, the Chinese vote had been secured by a promise of the bronze medal. Given the way the teams skated, this explanation seems likely.

It was all over. I felt a personal blow for my sport; the judging was dreadful, and the world knew it. My heart sank. I knew something was going to have to be done about this, but what? How do you change what judges have been doing for years? It's just not fair that all these athletes work so hard to get to this point in their careers, only to have it all taken from them by a group of conniving judges. And why, at this point, did this surprise me? Why was I so shocked that a few judges had slipped over the edge of the slippery slope of subjectivity?

With questions like these racing through my mind, my stomach began to growl. I had no obligations for the rest of the evening, so I decided to do what I always do when anxious: eat. Needing to calm my stomach with some food, I headed straight to Der Wienerschnitzel on State Street, an old favorite since undergraduate school, to take out all my frustrations on a deluxe cheeseburger and fries.

As I fretted at the drive-up window, waiting for my not-so-fast food to be prepared, I decided I would go to the officials' hotel and meet Ron Pfenning, who had officiated at the Pairs event that evening. If Ron could assure me that the judging result was simply a matter of questionable interpretation—that both the Russians and Canadians had skated equally well, and that this was simply a close call—then I would feel much better. Somehow, somewhere, I would find a rationale. I knew that often a spectator's armchair perspective from an arena seat, or from behind a bowl of pretzels at home, differed from that from the judges' stand, so I was hopeful that the judging oversight was merely a matter of opinion, and not one clouded by cold cash or blinded by barbiturates.

I grabbed my bag of calories and headed to the West Coast Hotel, still miserable but feeling hopeful about getting to the bottom of this mystery. I formulated a line of questioning for Ron, the answers to which might help me understand that what I had seen was merely a "difference of opinion." The nutritional grease would have to wait. I parked my car in the hotel parking lot and headed straight for the hotel lobby, where I could lie in wait for Ron.

Having positioned myself between the hotel lobby and the elevator bay, I paced about, anxiously waiting for Ron. Other officials walked in and passed me on their way to the elevators. One of those officials was the chair of the ISU Technical Committee, Sally Stapleford, the woman who had given me the "thumbs up" at my first "press conference" just a few months earlier.

We were still little more than friendly acquaintances, but she approached me and we talked a few minutes about the disappointing result of the Pair event. Sally's colleague, ISU technical committee member Britta Lindgren, as well as Britta's longtime companion and member of the ISU council John Hall, accompanied Sally that night. Britta excused herself to help the ailing Hall to his room, promising to return a few minutes later to meet Sally for a nightcap.

Sally stayed behind to discuss with me what she considered now as one of the greatest athletic injustices, or sport travesties, in the history of competitive sport judging. I had come looking for a rationale; instead, what I found was someone with whom to commiserate. I was thrilled to hear from an expert that she also saw things my way.

What came next can only be described as pandemonium. The French judge, in an explosive confession, laid out a sports conspiracy of Olympic proportion, and she did so right in front of me. Right there, in the side hallway of the West Coast Hotel.

Up until this moment, no one had wasted so much as a hushed syllable on "La Dame" Marie-Reine LeGougne, other than the usual discreet insider whispers of an alleged, never publicly confirmed, ongoing back-alley dalliance with a married and influential official within the ISU.

"It was a deal with the Russians," she screamed. I was blown away.

"Ice-dancing is ruining our sport!" she sobbed. "You have no idea! I must defend myself!" She continued: "You don't understand! I had to do this! Gold for gold! This was for my Dance team! You don't understand the pressure!" Over and over she repeated these rants. Sally, mindful of the rule against undignified positions and movements, saw fit to move this spectacle out of the public corridor. Britta Lindgren reappeared and joined Sally with LeGougne at the end of the hallway. Marie-Reine later claimed that no confession had taken place. Rather, she said, Sally Stapleford attacked her and attempted to coerce her into admitting that Didier Gailhaguet pressured her to vote for the Russians. That is not what my eyes saw, nor is it what my ears heard. I stood there in stunned silence, listening to Marie-Reine's repeated outbursts.

A few moments later, U.S. judge Janet Allen and Australian judge Wendy Langdon (neither of whom had judged the Pair event) appeared. They stared in disbelief at the animated goings-on across the hallway, and they looked at me inquisitively for information. So I simply said, "It's the French judge." Having caught the not-so-subtle message neatly contained in my otherwise meaningless reply, they nodded knowingly and moved away to the elevator bay, lest they find themselves ensnared in this sticky thicket.

These two women had duties of their own to worry about, namely the Men's upcoming long and short programs, and they had no desire to get caught up in the unrelated Pair event debacle. With the Pair event now clearly tarnished by cheating, it was reasonable to assume that more shams were planned for the other skate-offs. Perhaps they didn't realize this, but I did.

Just then, I saw another ISU technical committee member, Walburga Grimm, a less-than-casual acquaintance, come hobbling into the hot zone. She may not yet have seen me, but her good eye evidently caught sight of the makeup-streaked mug of tears, and felt it her duty to rush in for a closer look.

All the while, I felt like an eavesdropper. I was too far from the elevator to convincingly be waiting for it, and too far from the squawking henhouse to legitimately collect any eggs. Instead of standing there like a wooden Indian, I started toying with the idea of running into the lobby and out into the streets, to tell every person within earshot what the French judge had just admitted, but then I decided to be more systematic in my approach of spreading the word.

I went straight to the bar.

Walking in, I found Morry Stillwell, former U.S. Figure Skating president and ally of the Russian Skating Federation. The nightly news was showing on television above the table where Stillwell was drinking. The TV was loud enough for the whole bar to hear, and was airing a breaking story about the Pairs judging circus. Seeing the icebreaker, I approached Stillwell with a comment about the state of the skating sham. His reply suggested to me all I needed to know about where his loyalty, or lack of it, stood.

"You know, those were the best damn judges we have out there," he boasted. "If they thought the Russians should have won, then, by damn, that's the right result." He continued: "It certainly looked that way to me. I trust our judges were fair."

Perhaps after another round, even Stillwell himself would have bought that line of bull.

Suffice it to say, I chose not to share with Stillwell the French cave-in I had witnessed in the hallway just moments before.

When I left the bar, I slipped to the other side of the elevator bay where I could see Sally, Britta, and Walburga with Marie-Reine still carrying-on. Marie-Reine's body language suggested that she was still more than a little crazed, but I could not hear any additional revelations. I decided to continue waiting in the lobby for Ron.

But I still hadn't told anybody the big news. "Big news," because no judge had ever admitted to outright cheating. Sure, the rumor mill was full of similar accounts and speculation, and I was familiar with "the game," but the trading of gold medals? Shocking! I called some non-skating-related friends, and filled them in on the breaking scandal.

"Brian, you won't believe what I just heard!" I blurted into my cell phone to one friend. "The French judge just confessed! It was a bribed-up deal with the Russians, and you heard it here first."

And so it would continue to other friends who would soon get a lucky phone call. I suddenly cut one call short as lousy-seats-at-the-Kirov

Phyllis Howard, the reigning U.S. Figure Skating president, and her executive director John LeFevre, came waltzing into the hotel lobby.

Ms. Howard, it seemed to me, would be the most appropriate person to rectify a skating crime committed on U.S. soil on her watch. So I rushed over to the pair, said hello, and briefly related to them what I had just heard. She looked over her shoulder, as if checking for a reporter or a sinister spy listening in. Phyllis clearly realized the seriousness of the judging indiscretion, and invited me to her room so I could brief her in greater detail.

Before heading to Ms. Howard's room, I saw Ron enter the lobby. I could tell by his expression that he was very stressed and overwhelmed by the night's events, so I slipped him my cell number, and asked that he call me as soon as he had a free moment. I then went up to Ms. Howard's room to report on the French fess-up.

Ms. Howard and Mr. LeFevre appeared delighted to learn that the Russians would finally be caught with blood on their vodka-soaked hands.

"Are you sure she said the 'Russians'?" Phyllis quizzed.

"Yes, she was clear. 'It was a deal with the Russians. Gold for gold,'" I responded.

We sat and talked in further detail as I used Ms. Howard's computer to surf the Internet. I found that the public opinion was running 95 percent in favor of the Canadians. The chat-room crowd was calling for, if not demanding, an official investigation!

Just wait, I thought. *Just wait until they learn of the French confession! This will sort itself out much quicker than anyone possibly could have anticipated.*

"I can hardly wait to see the faces of David and Jamie when they are given the gold medal they deserve," I said aloud to Phyllis and John.

Marie-Reine LeGougne had admitted that the Games were fixed—plain and simple. It was an absolute crime. I knew it. She knew it. And now, three of the highest-ranked ISU officials in the world knew it (Sally Stapleford, Britta Lindgren, and Walburga Grimm), as well as the highest-ranking U.S. official (Phyllis Howard). As far as I was concerned, this was an open-and-shut case. A "slam-dunk," as they say.

Marie-Reine had admitted it, and there were witnesses! By morning, the story would be out, the usual suspects rounded up, and the Olympic title properly awarded. For once, a gold medal wrong would be a gold medal righted. With this loose-lipped French cat spilling out of the beanbag, the Russian ship was about to sink!

The Canadians, Jamie and David, had deserved to win that gold medal. This was an all-out misdeed done to them, their families, and their country; and, according to Marie-Reine's whistle-blowing, the Russians were in on it. LeGougne, in a moment of weakness, had already blown the lid off the scandal. For once, proof of the rumored backroom deals was out in the open. That figure-skating medals were being power-bartered and exchanged like baseball cards on a thug-controlled street corner would now be impossible to cover up.

However, naïveté can be so blinding. Unfortunately, I had completely underestimated the culture of corruption and collusion so deeply embedded in the figure-skating world, which would collectively leap into action to cover up the entire judging offense.

THE NEXT MORNING, Tuesday, I kept busy chauffeuring the coaches around, though my head was spinning and it was difficult to concentrate on what I was doing. I was also anxiously waiting for Ron Pfenning to call. We had met for drinks the night before, but he had refused to discuss the event or the judging fiasco, and would not let me tell him what had happened in the lobby. He knew something was amiss from the chaos he saw when he walked in, but he didn't want it to detract from the judges' meeting he was going to have to supervise the next morning.

When Ron finally called, he was not surprised at all when I relayed to him the events of the night before. Marie-Reine had made a similar confession in the judges' meeting, and then again to him privately after the meeting was over.

In our phone call, I asked him, "What do you think the ISU is going to do about all this?"

He responded, "I don't know, but I will be recommending LeGougne's marks be thrown out and the substitute judges' marks put in her place. It's the right and fair thing to do."

We later met for lunch, and I brought along my ISU rulebook. He was probably not expecting to be inundated with lawyerly tactics; he was trying to get away from the morass! I carefully walked through the rules with him, wanting an understanding of the effect of his decision: The rules were clear. The referee shall resolve all disputes regarding the event. The ISU would have no choice but to accept his decision. Ron was not so optimistic. "You don't know the ISU," he warned.

The next day, I found out all I really needed to know about the ISU. At a press conference that morning, ISU president Ottavio Cinquanta defended the previous night's judging of the Pairs event, and claimed that there was no scandal, that no judge had done anything wrong, and that the ISU would not review the decision.

I was outraged! I watched about 20 minutes of the press conference on television, and then had to leave to take Tim Goebel's coach, Frank Carroll, to the Salt Palace. Frank could tell I was upset, although I didn't tell him about the French confession. He believed my anger was levied at the ISU and Cinquanta, which I did express, and which was similar to that of the public and press. A "how could they not investigate?" anger, as opposed to the true anger I was feeling: "How could they cover up for the cheating French and Russians?"

I was on the brink of turning in my resignation, and told Frank, but he advised otherwise. He went on to explain to me what had happened to Linda Fratianne in the 1980 Olympics. According to Frank, she was robbed, plain and simple. He believed that Carlo Fassi, a respected coach world-wide, cut a deal with some judges to guarantee gold for Robin Cousins in the Men's event, and Linda was short-ended. Frank had been very angry and bitter for some time, and then he just had to let it go. He advised that I work through my anger. "Find your voice!" were his call-to-action words of advice. "Speak out until they throw you out. Quitting is the easy way out!"

I decided to do just that, but in my own way. I wanted to first know if this sport was capable of correcting this injustice itself. I wrote a long letter to Cinquanta, giving him the benefit of the doubt, that he might not have known about the French confession, and outlined everything I heard. I delivered copies of the letter to both Phyllis Howard and Claire Ferguson, the American representative on the ISU council, asking them both to deliver the letter to Cinquanta.

After that, Phyllis began calling me regularly. There was always some bush she'd beat around before finally landing on the point of her call. She'd start with, "So, are you ready if we medal in the Men?" indicating that she wanted me to organize and host a spontaneous party to celebrate any victory. Each of the calls finally concluded with an inquiry of whether or not I had gone to the press with what I had overheard, something I promised her I would not do until giving the ISU the chance to correct the situation.

A producer for the *Today Show* with Matt Lauer and Katie Couric called later in the afternoon. The young woman on the phone introduced herself, and informed me that they were looking for a judge to come on the show the next morning. Specifically, they wanted a judge who was outraged by the scandal, and they had heard that I was upset. Now, at this point, the *Today Show* had no idea of what I actually knew, only that I was outraged. (Frank had tipped them off.) I told her that it was not my style to speak out, but that I would take her phone number and be back in touch should I change my mind.

Later that evening, a friend of mine, National judge Ann Greenthal, hosted with me a party for the judges, officials, and coaches attending the Olympics. My former law professor and good friend Terry Kogan opened his home for us; my former girlfriend and now best friend Victoria catered the food. It was a fantastic, well-attended party, and a much-needed break from the stress of the previous days' events.

Already in hiding, Marie-Reine LeGougne and French Federation president Didier Gailhaguet did not attend, though they had been given invitations earlier in the week. Christine Brennan from *USA Today* stopped by, and I immediately knew that she suspected there was more going on than the press was privy to. She gave me her cell number and asked me to call her if I heard anything about the scandal that might be worth pursuing.

Sally Stapleford was also there. It was the first time I had seen her since I had left her with Marie-Reine, Britta, and Walburga in the side lobby Monday night. When she saw me, she immediately came over and wanted to know how much of Marie-Reine's little outburst I had heard. I told her I had heard "everything."

"Well, in your own words, what exactly is everything?" she pried, a bit nervously. Because she didn't really know me that well—we had had all of three or four encounters with each other before this all happened, the most significant of which took place at Skate America—she wasn't sharing a lot of information with me.

"Let's go upstairs," I suggested, not wanting anyone to overhear what I had to say. Once alone, I told her everything I had heard.

"Oh, Jon, you must put all this in writing. As a judge you have an obligation under the rules to report any wrongdoing," she appealed to me, not as a friend, or even a collaborating witness, but as an ISU official herself lecturing me on my responsibilities as a judge.

"I already have," I replied. "I sent Cinquanta a letter yesterday. I would think he would have called by now, but of course he hasn't. Now let's get back to the party!"

"Well done! Well done, old boy!" she said, patting me on the back as we made our way out of the room. Sally let me know that she also had written down everything to Cinquanta, and so had Britta and Walburga, but that Cinquanta didn't believe their eye-witness accounts.

The next day, I focused on the coaches' activities, getting them around and about. One of the coaches, Tamara Moskvina, cancelled her plans to leave Salt Lake City, instead staying to spin the story in favor of her Pair team, Berezhnaya and Sikharulidze.

I arranged another meeting with Phyllis Howard and John LeFevre. I came armed with my book of ISU regulations and urged them to file a formal protest on behalf of Kyoko Ina and John Zimmerman, the American pair who, with the vote-blocking, had finished fifth. I walked them through the rules, demonstrating to them the basis for the protest. In essence, U.S. Figure Skating would be filing for arbitration to force the ISU to follow its own rules, stand by the referee's decision to drop all of Marie-Reine's marks, and use the marks of the substitute judge.

John LeFevre, an attorney by profession, immediately understood my appeal to them, and, as I left the two of them, he seemed visibly excited about the prospects of U.S. Figure Skating stepping up to help out Kyoko and John. Phyllis was more subdued, and I had a gut feeling that she would do absolutely nothing.

One of the first times I ever saw Phyllis Howard was at the National Championships in Orlando, Florida. She had been brought down from Virginia to help clean up a local organizing mess.

I was on my way to dinner and had taken the elevator with three or four other officials from the East Coast, not one of whom I knew. On the way down, one of the women said to a man, "Do you know where this place is?"

He answered, "No, Phyllis made the arrangements, but I assume it's nearby."

"Oh, well; if Phyllis knows it, it's got to be good!" she gushed. "She said she'd be right down."

I remember wondering to myself, just who was this clairvoyant Phyllis who knows only good things. I had a feeling they might be talking about Phyllis Howard, but who knows, maybe they knew Phyllis Diller instead. Once in the lobby, I decided to wait and see.

I stood about six or seven feet from where this little group gathered, waiting for their leader. Just then, the elevator doors reopened and out stepped Phyllis Howard, dressed completely in black. She hurried toward her collection of co-diners, didn't make eye contact with any of them, and said, "Is everybody ready?" as she walked right past them toward the revolving door to the outside taxis. I realized that this was an obligatory "duty dinner," and these people meant nothing to her.

Phyllis is an imposing woman, in stature much taller than most. When she swept out of the lobby, I noticed her hair again, bouncing to the beat of her gait.

Back in Salt Lake, later in the day of after our meeting, Phyllis called me again and this time thanked me for taking the time to put the information I had together, and for meeting with them. Then she explained that there were "more important matters to attend to" than helping John and Kyoko. More important matters? Why did she think she was even there, if not to fight for fairness for her athletes? She wasn't judging, she wasn't cleaning the ice; she wasn't doing anything but going to parties and ceremonies. She was just there on the tab of U.S. Figure Skating, and not doing her job.

It was common knowledge that Phyllis Howard would be running for a seat on the ISU Council the following June. It was clear to me that she did not intend to rock the boat or do anything that might be construed as controversial, and risk her chances of election. She placed her own political ambitions over the interests of her athletes, and though I wanted to scream, I held my tongue.

Then the conversation concluded with her obsessive question of whether or not I had gone to the press. No, Phyllis. I hadn't.

In the evening, after dropping the coaches off at the Delta Center, I watched as Tim Goebel won the bronze medal for the United States. I quickly called the hotel to move forward on the celebration party I had "tentatively" planned, then raced back to make the final arrangements. It was a champagne and hors d'oeuvre reception, which Tim was obligated to attend before racing off to appear on the *Tonight Show* and on other NBC affiliates. The party, as one might expect, was for the U.S. officials to share in Tim's glory, mugging it up with him for pictures and camaraderie. I can imagine that a young man, surrounded by family, friends, and numerous athletes in the village, on the biggest night of his young life, would have preferred to be elsewhere. Nevertheless, he was a great sport about it, and as gracious and congenial as could be.

On Friday, Phyllis called me over to the West Coast Hotel, where I joined her in a meeting of various U.S. Figure Skating Executive Committee members, and Paul George, an official with the U.S. Olympic Committee (USOC). Phyllis wanted my opinion as to what the USOC could do to help resolve this situation. I responded, "Nothing. I need to see that 'Figure Skating' can take care of this mess itself. If the IOC or the USOC have to get involved to make things right, it will speak volumes about the corruption in figure-skating. The ISU needs to take care of this matter on its own."

That is exactly how I felt. The situation to me was crystal-clear. The resolution was more difficult, and I certainly understood that. Nevertheless, there had been corruption and it needed to be exposed and punished; that was not debatable. Any attempt to make it so would smack of a coverup.

How would they take the gold medal away from the Russian pair? I knew it would be difficult. However, isn't that what these same judges had just done to the Canadian pair? Of course. Those judges took something from the Canadians that rightfully belonged to them; only they used their marks and illicit deals to do it. It was Skate Canada who suggested that the Russians share the gold with the Canadians. Fine, I'm okay with that. Now let's get on to investigating the corruption!

In the afternoon, Cinquanta held yet another press conference, announcing that a second gold medal would be awarded to the Canadians. After disregarding the marks of LeGougne for the Russians, the IOC awarded a second gold medal, yet allowed her marks to stand for every other skater in the event! This not only made absolutely no sense, it completely ignored the recommendations of the referee. In his remarks, Cinquanta was emphatic that there was "no evidence" of any Russian involvement.

No evidence? He has to be kidding! I could no longer give him the benefit of the doubt.

I decided it was time I placed a call to Christine Brennan, and I nearly broke a fingernail doing it. Her cell phone rang and rang, but I couldn't reach her. Then I got her voicemail and left an urgent message for her to call me back. She didn't reach me until later in the evening when I was at the medals plaza, watching as Tim Goebel was given his bronze medal. I made arrangements to meet her back at her hotel, telling her only that it was urgent that I speak to her, and that I wanted to do so privately, without anyone knowing about it.

Covertly, we met in the lobby of her hotel. I gave her a general summary of what had happened. She wanted to know if this information was off the record. I said, "No, I am willing to back it." She asked that I keep the information to myself, to allow her the time to prepare a story for the Monday edition. I agreed to do so, giving her an exclusive story. We met a few more times over the weekend, repeatedly going over the details of exactly what had happened.

In the meantime, I made a courtesy call to Phyllis Howard to let her know that I was no longer remaining silent. I listened for the sound of popping champagne corks, or some other important matter, going on in the background. She thanked me for letting her know, then she hung up and got back to the very "important matter" of sitting on her ass. She didn't call me again for the rest of the week.

I later learned that Kyoko and John, accompanied by their team leader, Charlie Cyr, had also met with Phyllis and John a few days later to see if U.S. Figure Skating would fight for them. In the meeting, Phyllis warned them that it was a politically dangerous thing to do, and that if they pushed it, the Russians might not come to Skate America, damaging the event. Skate America, like the other five fall events in the ISU Grand Prix Circuit, relies heavily on attendance of the top International skaters to get good television ratings and to fill the stands. If the Russians were to boycott Skate America, U.S. Figure Skating stood to lose a great deal of money.

Heavy shit to lay on a couple of young athletes who only wanted what they deserved. John and Kyoko left, knowing that they did not have the support of the federation, or Phyllis Howard, if they decided to fight.

On Monday, February 18, 2003, *USA Today* broke the story of the exact details of what transpired that fateful evening at the West Coast Hotel, and finally, the Utah beehive had been kicked.

The ISU summoned me to a back room in the same hotel as part of its "investigation." I appeared before Gerhard Zimmerman (no relation to John, visually or genetically), a speed-skating member of the ISU Council, Gerhardt Bubnick, the ISU's legal counsel, and a court reporter. I provided my testimony in a darkened room with the blinds pulled tight. I was not there more than 15 minutes. Before leaving, I expressed my concern that the ISU was merely going through the motions of an investigation. I explained to them that it was clear that the Russians were involved, and it looked to me like a coverup. Zimmerman assured me that the investigation would be thorough, and that any Russian involvement was being explored.

In the afternoon, I went on a tour of the Olympic Village. Charlie Cyr and Paula Naughton escorted a number of officials and parents through the village, having obtained for us a temporary access pass to the grounds. On that tour, Lucy Brennan, the U.S. judge on the Pairs panel, asked me how my testimony had gone. I told her that I thought it had gone fine, and asked how it had gone for her. Her response stunned me. She indicated that she had answered most of the questions with "I don't recall." Surprised by that, I pushed her a bit.

"Lucy, it was just last week! How could you not recall?" Her reply was awkward. Something about everything going on, and such an uproar, and not remembering exactly what took place.

Immediately, I thought of an old saying. "If you are not part of the solution, you are part of the problem." Lucy had no interest in helping investigate the corruption. She took the politically easy way out. She didn't want to tell the truth, so she simply "didn't recall." Maybe she has a medical condition, but one of the biggest moments in figure skating history, probably one of the biggest moments in her life, and only seven days earlier, yet she couldn't recall it. Typical.

A day or so later, I heard Cinquanta rattling on again in a press conference about how there had been absolutely no evidence to indicate Russian involvement. I was outraged. I called up Gerhard Zimmerman in his hotel room. He agreed to come down to the lobby to meet me. Face to face, ironically in the same side lobby where Marie-Reine LeGougne had made her confession, I challenged him on Cinquanta's statements. How could he say there was "no evidence"? What do you call my letter to him? My testimony? The confession of Marie-Reine LeGougne? The quid-pro-quo? I made my argument orderly, understandably, calmly and clearly.

Zimmerman responded that, yes, I was correct. That he knew that, and I knew that, but Cinquanta did not. Zimmerman had not shared any of the findings of his investigation with Cinquanta. Cinquanta had not seen the evidence gathered, but I could be assured that the investigation had turned up the evidence needed for a complete investigation, and that it would be presented to the Council at the appropriate time: that being when they sat in judgment regarding any charges against individuals or countries. He seemed so assuring, that for some reason, I trusted him, and thanked him for his time.

The Olympics ended with some fine judging, though that didn't stop the Russians from filing a protest. American Sarah Hughes had the freeskate of her life, taking the judges by surprise, and bringing down the Delta Center house in the process. It was a clear win, though not all the judges saw it that way. One judge actually got away with marking Sarah fourth. Guess who?

Immediately, the Russians filed a protest, claiming that their truck-driving, arm-flailing Irina Slutskaya had been robbed. I wonder if the Russian Federation warned Irina that the Americans might not attend the Cup of Russia event if they filed the protest on her behalf. The protest was dismissed, however, by the referee of the event as having no merit. Why are the Russians so adamant in defending their athletes, the Canadians too, while the Americans are so reluctant?

I didn't stay around for the closing ceremonies. I was anxious to get out of town. After the last American coach had departed, I bolted back to San Francisco. I left Salt Lake with very mixed feelings about the Olympic Games, and most particularly about my sport. My stomach was tied in knots. Even so, I consoled myself, there is always someone worse off. How must Kyoko and John feel on their plane ride home? U.S. Figure Skating hid under the covers, in the interest of politics, and all when they needed them the most.

Just days before the Russian National Championships, in late December, 1999 World Figure Skating Champion Maria Butyrskaya was the victim of a car bombing, though she was unhurt. In 2002, just weeks before the Salt Lake Winter Olympic Games, the body of her boyfriend, Sergei Sterlyagov, was found shot dead in the woods. What had prompted these incredible attacks against this Russian figure skater Butyrskaya had suggested that she was tired of sharing her skating wealth with Russian mobsters.

Truth and Consequences

NAGANO IS A Japanese mountain town about four hours by car from Tokyo. In a lot of ways, it reminds me of a small European town, with its quaint downtown area, old architecture, rows of shops, and traditional parks and gardens. In the middle of the downtown area sits what most people would consider a first-class hotel. That hotel housed the officials for the 2002 World Championships. About twenty minutes away on the outskirts of town, the athletes stayed not surprisingly in a run-down, working-class hotel. What did they expect?

The 1998 Winter Olympics were also held in this same mountain town, and that history was not lost on the skaters and coaches. The Salt Lake Winter Olympics and its judging scandal were not lost on me. The Canadian and Russian pairs would not have a rematch here, both having decided to "turn pro," moving on with their professional careers.

Being the U.S. team leader for these championships kept me very busy doing my favorite job, working for the athletes. One problem that always seems to come up is room assignments; and, despite the importance of this competition, there was no exception to that rule. Kyoko Ina and John Zimmerman had asked in advance to have their own rooms, rather than sharing with other athletes, a request common for National Champions. Kyoko's room was assigned as hoped, but John's was not.

According to the organizing committee, U.S. Figure Skating had not requested a separate room for John, and now the hotel was sold out. John was at that time engaged to Italian skater Sylvia Fontana. It seemed to me, especially after the way the association had treated our two pair skaters at the Olympic Games, that the least they could have done here was to arrange private rooms.

I hustled up an interpreter and went straight to hotel management. The local organizing committee was not about to cough up a room, having already told me the hotel was sold out. According to the hotel management, there were plenty of Japanese-style rooms but no more Western-style rooms, the difference being a simple mat laid on the floor and having to sleep like a cat instead of on a properly mattressed bed. John, happy to have his privacy, licked his whiskers and pounced on the opportunity.

Over breakfast the next morning, I sat with John as he vented a bit over his frustration with U.S. Figure Skating. Mary Tyler Moore isn't the only one who can turn the world on with a smile; John can too, and absolutely light up a room. He's a very reserved, polite person. My friends at home always say, "Isn't he the good-looking one with the Farrah Fawcett hair?" referring to John's classic good looks and long retro '70s locks. He's one of the most sincere men I've met in figure-skating. Farrah hair, yes, but I wasn't getting a lot of smile today. John was troubled because he knew how much the U.S. had done for Kyoko and him financially, yet he also felt slighted. While the room mix-up was a minor offense to be sure, he didn't understand why U.S. Figure Skating was never there for him. It was at this point that he relayed to me what had happened to them in Salt Lake City.

From John's perspective, he and Kyoko were exhausted in Salt Lake from interviews, appearances, and American Express endorsements, all typical for being the highest-placing U.S. pair team, but also amplified by their unrewarded great freeskate and the disappointment of the judging scandal. As they saw it, the Russian and Canadian federations had stepped up for their teams, where the United States had not. After watching a few days of this neglect, John and Kyoko requested the aforementioned meeting with Phyllis Howard and John LeFevre. At this point in his story, John was literally close to tears as he relayed the disappointment he and Kyoko shared as they left the meeting, knowing that their own country was not behind them. If I hadn't already been outraged about the whole scandal, I certainly was now, more so by this outpouring of John's sincere heart.

THE ISU AS this point had planned, but had not yet announced, a disciplinary hearing for Marie-Reine and her French Federation president, Didier Gailhaguet, to be held in Lausanne the following month. The coaches and skaters remained focused on their business at hand; everyone else was talking about that upcoming unannounced hearing. It seemed that everyone there had two cents of advice for me. Without exception, their advice was *not* to attend the hearing as a witness.

"If you already made a statement, and reported what you knew, you do not have to go. No rule requires it." I heard that and similar observations from judges, retired judges, and spectators alike. It was almost as if there was an organized attempt to keep me from attending the hearing.

"You have so much going for you in figure-skating. You will be the next Olympic team leader; do you really want to jeopardize that?" was another attempt made for me to see reason. The rumor mill had been active for months, already naming me the next Olympic team leader. If it was true, it was probably the only job I really still wanted to do.

However, the question for me was much broader than giving up my dream job. Was I willing to ignore an injustice merely for the sake of my own personal political ambitions and figure-skating perks?

Having witnessed the manner in which Phyllis Howard acted at the Olympic Games, in my opinion putting the athletes' interest behind her own, my mind was already made up: The answer to that question was a resounding "No way!"

That same cop-out advice was repeated again in my latest summit with John LeFevre and Phyllis Howard, the first of many little get-togethers

I would be part of that week in Nagano. Ron Pfenning also attended these meetings.

The meetings started with a fresh argument of why Ron and I shouldn't attend the hearing, and finished with my argument that Ron and I needed a lawyer. John and Phyllis argued that every person in figure-skating who had spoken out in the past had somehow been punished by the ISU. Proving our point, I said, "That is exactly why we need a lawyer with us in Lausanne."

We also had to argue that neither Ron nor I were about to accept the protection of Tom James, U.S. Figure Skating's lawyer from Colorado Springs. I insisted on, and ultimately persuaded John and Phyllis to pay for, the services of a tough and competent San Francisco lawyer named Ben Kaplan.

UNDER NORMAL CONDITIONS, the job of a team leader is already stressful and hectic. With the added distraction of the nearly daily meetings across town with court jesters John and Phyllis, I was juggling a much larger load than should have been expected. To deal with the stress, I turned the situation on itself. My work for the coaches and athletes became my solace away from the ISU and U.S. Figure Skating stress. It was my downtime, my time to relax, and the time to remind myself of why I was involved in figure-skating in the first place.

Michelle Kwan was determined to make a better showing at Worlds than the outcome of her Olympics, and the Russians were determined to stop her. The campaigning for Slutskaya reached its peak during that week. Another separate campaign was brewing for the upcoming ISU elections, and Phyllis Howard was not the only person in attendance with a political agenda. Fabio Bianchetti, son of the much respected Italian and former Technical Committee Chair Sonia Bianchetti, was also there. He was politicking for a spot on the Technical Committee (the same spot LeGougne might have campaigned for a second time, having been turned away by an overwhelming vote against her the year before the Olympics).

These two campaigns, the one for Slutskaya to win the World title, and the campaign for Fabio Bianchetti, came together as one during the judging of the Ladies' event. Fabio made his allegiances clear when he gave Slutskaya the win over a near-perfect performance of Kwan, and he did so in the Presentation mark. The stringless marionette won the title over the poised positions and perfect edges of Kwan. Fabio was not the only judge to give it to Slutskaya, as the Russians flexed their muscle for all to see. The freeskate made it obvious that Kwan should have won. Slutskaya's win was an in-your-face flipping of the Soviet middle finger to anyone who questioned Russia's involvement in the Olympic Pair scandal.

Prior to the Ladies' freeskate, I was beginning to see a darker, different side to the ever-likable Pair coaching master and former KGB agent Tamara Moskvina. She was the coach for Ina and Zimmerman, but also the coach for Bereshnaya and Sikhalaridze. I watched in Salt Lake as she jumped into the spin campaign in defense of her Russian pair and ignored John and Kyoko. Though the thought had crossed my mind that she may have been in on the deal, she was such a likable character that I dismissed it. Her actions on behalf of her Russian pair, about to lose their gold medal, were the obligations of a coach, so I rationalized her behavior from that perspective. But I noted to myself that she didn't jump into a spin campaign on behalf of John and Kyoko. Maybe Phyllis wasn't the only woman at the Olympics who let them down.

In the short program in Nagano, Kyoko and John skated another amazing program, on par with their incredible and overlooked Olympic performance. Debbie Currie, my assistant team leader, and I were jumping up and down with excitement as Moskvina turned as if to head to the "kiss and cry." It appeared to me that as she turned, she shot a look of concern up into the stands, shrugging her shoulders as if to say, "What can I do?" She saw me catch her unspoken communication, and immediately pasted a big, phony smile on her face, grabbed Debbie and me in a congratulatory hug, and began the walk with us to the "kiss and cry" area. I turned to look up into the stands to see who Moskvina might have been apologizing to, and saw the very stern look of Valentin Piseev, the president of the Russian Federation. The unpleasant look on Piseev's face confirmed that the apology had not been accepted. Kyoko and John placed third, setting themselves up for a medal; but, more importantly, it put them in striking distance for gold.

In the long program, the favored Russian and Chinese teams really faltered. Kyoko and John could feasibly win with a solid freeskate, but it was not meant to be. They were within striking distance, but they missed a few of their elements. At the end of the program, Moskvina turned to Debbie and me, shrugged her shoulders, and insincerely mumbled, "What can you do?" At least there was no need to look up at Piseev again to apologize.

It was a bad night for all the pair teams, which worked to the favor of the American team, allowing Kyoko and John to retain their third placement. They brought home the bronze medal, not so much to the U.S., but specifically for their families who had supported them over the years.

On the Saturday morning of my week at Worlds, I went to a breakfast reception hosted by U.S. Figure Skating to promote the following year's World Championships to be held in Washington. Claire Ferguson, the U.S. member of the ISU Council, and I began talking about the upcoming disciplinary hearing in Lausanne. She, as would be expected, pointed out that it was unnecessary for me to attend. I indicated to her, much to her surprise, that both Ron and I were planning to be there anyway.

At some point, Ron happened by and joined the conversation. He and I both expressed our concern that the Russians were not being properly investigated, let alone charged. Ms. Ferguson was very defensive of them, and then became very defensive of Marie-Reine and Didier. Based on her understanding of the case, it was her opinion that a 3-year suspension would be appropriate, if not overly harsh. I asked Claire if she had seen the results of Gerhard Zimmerman's in-depth investigation, believing that she was basing her advance verdict on something legitimate. She said she had *not* seen any such report.

So I asked her, "Then how can you determine that three years is appropriate, when you haven't even heard the evidence?"

Claire's face was awash with anger, perhaps even hatred. The next thing I knew, she was "all up in my grill" for being too emotional over the situation. She told me that I was naïve and that all my friends in U.S. Figure Skating were just as guilty of similar injustices. Claire believed that what happened at the Salt Lake Olympics was merely "undue pressure" put on Marie-Reine by the French federation. She insisted that no corruption had influenced any of the judging in Salt Lake. In retrospect, it was clear that Claire wasn't merely telling tales out of school. She also wasn't just speaking for herself, but for the entire council. The crimes, verdicts, and punishments were already determined long before anybody appeared in Lausanne. Claire had let slip the secretly decided outcome a full month before the hearing.

Moments later, Cinquanta took the stage, greeting and welcoming the guests to the reception. He then unveiled his New Judging System (NJS), which he claimed was the solution to the ills of the sport. I found his presentation interesting. I find many of its goals appealing. But there were two things about it that troubled me then, and still trouble me now.

The first was that the perfect 6.0 was nowhere to be found. Figure-skating's only valuable brand was being tossed in the trash. The 6.0 is only thing about the sport that had even an ounce of respect, let alone recognition, from the outside sporting world. What kind of business-man makes a decision to trash its most valuable brand? A volunteer, and trained bookkeeper, Ottavio Cinquanta, that's who. The magical 6.0 was being replaced with meaningless numbers, like 112.63 or 134.65, numbers only an accountant could love.

The second problem is that the NJS didn't address the judging failures in Salt Lake City, nor the rampant culture of corruption that exists in figure-skating. In Salt Lake, the judges drove their SUV over the Canadian jay-walkers. It wasn't the SUV's fault; it was the judges driving it. But instead of changing the judges, Cinquanta changed the SUV. And now, with a new Ferrari sports coupe, with five marks making up the score for the presentation mark instead of just one, he has given the judges four new ways to drive recklessly over the athletes.

Shortly after Cinquanta's speech, I rushed back to the arena for the Ladies' event; but on the way, I could not get Claire's revealing words out of my head. I asked myself repeatedly, still dumbfounded by what I had heard, "Did I hear her correctly?"

A few weeks later, I found out that I had. Claire appeared on a local television news channel in Providence, Rhode Island, and repeated essentially the same thing she had said to me, and this was still before the hearings ever took place. She then went on to say that she believed that Marie-Reine had done what she thought in her heart was the correct thing to do. These outrageous statements, caught on camera, were an appalling and inappropriate conclusion to reach prior to having heard any of the evidence.

Shortly after the news story broke, Claire's 15 minutes were up and Ben Kaplan brought a motion to dismiss her from sitting on the panel that would finally hear the testimony and decide the fate of Marie-Reine and Didier. The motion was made to Cinquanta, the presiding ISU official, who not only ignored the request but also allowed the biased Claire to sit on the panel.

THE ICE DANCE event at the Nagano Worlds was by far the most controversial event at that competition. The judges awarded the bronze medal to the Israeli team of Galit Chait and Sergei Sakhnovskiy over the Lithuanian team of Margarita Drobiazko and Povilas Vanagas, who many believed had had the performance of the night. It was again very obviously a political deal—only this time, the skaters were outraged enough to do something about it.

Late in the evening, back at the athletes' hotel, the skaters organized. They prepared a petition challenging the result. The petition requested that the Ice Dance Technical Committee investigate the political deal. For the Ice Dancers, this event was their Salt Lake Pair scandal. So clear was the result, nearly every skater in the Ice Dance event signed the petition—except of course, the Israelis, as might be expected.

Later that evening, Galit's father Boris got wind of the petition. Boris is a very large mobster-looking figure, barrel-chested with mannerisms befitting the stereotype. When he heard about the petition, he went ballistic, stormed into a room of coaches, and allegedly made threats.

Later, in the wee hours of the morning, the American judge on the panel, one of the judges who had placed the Lithuanians ahead of the Israelis, received a phone call from a male who threatened to cut off her head.

The following Sunday, the technical committee held a seminar at the rink to introduce the dances for the upcoming year. It was at this seminar that the skaters presented their petition to Courtney Jones. In front of them all, Mr. Jones and his carefully hand-massaged necktie limply let it be known that he thought the petition was absurd, that there would be no investigation—neither upright nor erect—and then basically threw the petition in the garbage can!

So at the 2002 Nagano Worlds, over the Ice Dance competition and final placement of the participants, there were threats to kill people and threats to cut off the heads of judges. And despite all that, Courtney Jones, a member of Cinquanta's hand-picked minion-staff of Gucci loafer-lickers and much more literate yes-men, decided that there was no corruption and there would be no investigation.

Vanagas was outraged, quoted by the *San Diego Union-Tribune* as saying "It's just unfortunate that the system kills the competitive nature of the sport. . . . It seems like [Chait] and some of the ISU think they are 'The Godfather.'"

Boris Chait, a Russian Jew who emigrated to Israel and now lives in New Jersey, was quoted in the same article as saying "I'm still laughing at all the stuff they are saying. Mafia, bribery, threats—it's all nonsense."

But the best quote, captured by the staff reporter for the *Union-Tribune*, belonged to Morry Stillwell. "In my opinion, the results were exactly right." Stillwell deemed the athlete petition as "laughable."

In the end, from the official standpoint, nothing untoward marred the final results of the 2002 World Ice Dance Championships. The Israelis got to keep their first-ever medal. The protest petition from the athletes was essentially placed in the garbage, and Courtney Jones was back at his five-star hotel, with his head still intact.

The ISU, as usual, was going to sit back and do nothing but collect their honorariums and per-diems, together with any kickbacks they might stir up. The Olympic pair-judging investigation was evidently already one scandal too many for the ISU, and they were doing their best to get out of that one too! They certainly wanted to sweep both incidents collectively under a rug.

When I left Nagano, I had a sense that the corruption I had witnessed in Salt Lake was rampant throughout the sport, and completely out of control. The power-hungry people in charge would do or say anything to keep the status quo. I now looked forward to the Lausanne hearings, hoping that, somehow, Gerhardt Zimmerman's investigation would blast the Olympic scandal wide open. I thought the ISU would try to make it right.

∞

I ARRIVED IN Lausanne after a long flight out of San Francisco to attend and testify at the ISU's hearings that would determine the fates of Madame LeGougne and her cohort, Didier Gailhaguet, the president of the French Federation who allegedly coerced her into cheating. I was hopeful that once the hearing panel finally heard all the evidence, the Russian involvement of the gold-medal-for-gold-medal swap would actually be investigated.

Staring over Lake Geneva from a lakeside park bench behind one of the most awe-inspiring museums in the world, the Olympic Museum in Lausanne, my thoughts were muddled and I was still trying to find clarity and understanding over what I was doing there. I would soon give testimony that, seemingly, no one in the ISU wanted to hear, and that no one in U.S. Figure Skating wanted me to give. It was a difficult period leading up to the hearings, and the hearings themselves promised to be no different. It might have been easier to walk down to the lake, put rocks in my pockets, and go for a swim.

I tried to look out over the lake to see Evian, the city made famous for its bottled water, on the other side. This wasn't my first time next to this lake. I had visited Lausanne on two previous occasions, and had fallen in love with the gorgeous city and the wonderful people who lived here. Like a golden crown sitting high on the foothills that wash down into the north shore of Lake Geneva, it's a mix of stunning beauty and Old European charm. Its most precious jewel, in my opinion, is the Olympic Museum.

I planned to meet up later with ISU technical committee members Ron Pfenning, Sally Stapleford, Britta Lindgren, and Walburga Grimm. They were busy conducting skating business at the time, concluding one of their quarterly meetings, at the Mövenpick Hotel. After the meeting, they would move up the hill to join me and the other witnesses at Lausanne's Hotel de la Paix, where the ISU hearings were taking place.

Having made my way through this super-cool museum, a showpiece for sport complete with interactive video and highlights from previous Olympic Games, I decided to take in a stroll through the outdoor gardens. It was a beautiful Swiss day, clear and sunny—not at all cheesy. A walk through the gardens might have been just what I needed to put some perspective on the upcoming events.

The two architects of the museum, Mexican Pedro Ramirez Vasquez and Swiss Jean-Pierre Cahen, had ingeniously captured the spirit of the Olympics in the layout of the main building and its gardens. With beautiful water features meandering around the park or bubbling out of fountains, oversized sculptures of magnificently defined athletic bodies at play and in competition, walls and arches made of oversized granite slabs, and lawns that connect the museum above to Lake Geneva below, they had managed to capture the competitive spirit and energy of sport. This atmosphere was exactly what I needed.

Now, sitting lakeside, all of the emotions and doubt from the previous twelve weeks converged. How had I ended up here? Was figure-skating all that important? Had this sport dominated my life for too long? What were these people hiding? Why were they avoiding these easy questions about cheating, and were they actually easy questions? Tears began to well up in my eyes as I took in the awesome karmic energy of sport, releasing the stress of the anger that had built up inside me. Why was I fighting so hard for this? Why was it even a fight?

Still lost in thought, I headed over to the Mövenpick to meet my lawyer, Ben Kaplan. Ben had already met with Ron, Sally, Britta, and Walburga individually, to help them prepare for the hearing. His advice had always been invaluable; but that day, kindness, empathy, and understanding would be most important.

He was giving me last-minute advice, in a manner not unlike that advice given by my skating coaches just prior to my taking the ice for an important competition.

"Jon, just tell the truth. Don't hold anything back," he said, "Don't try to hide something, just get it out there. Keep your feet apart and on the ground. Do not fidget!"

Those were general instructions and words of advice that I used in my own career, and that I had heard before. The other witnesses found this advice helpful, likely having heard it for the first time. But for me it was merely a last-minute reminder, going into what might be the most important testimony I would ever give. The bond between Ben and me would make those words last in my mind. The confidence I felt from his mere presence got me through the testimony.

After my meeting with Ben, Ron, Sally, Britta, and Walburga joined us in Ben's room. The topic of dinner leaped into the conversation, probably on account of my audible, growling stomach. For dinner, Sally suggested that we invite along Benoit Lavoie, the Canadian judge from the Olympic Pair event judging panel, who was also there to testify.

Benoit and I had run into each other earlier at the baggage claim area upon our arrival at the Geneva airport. He said hello, but that was about the extent of our conversation there. Benoit is a charming, good-looking, and gregarious French-Canadian who is one of the friendliest judges in the sport. I had found his behavior at the airport baggage claim odd, and the company he was keeping even more suspect. While at the airport, Benoit had introduced me to Pam Coburn, the new executive director of Skate Canada, as well as another woman, Skate Canada's legal counsel. It was immediately clear to me that his lawyer did not find our idle chatter appropriate.

"Well, I guess I will see you later?" Benoit awkwardly blurted out, cutting short any further banter, unusual in itself for the otherwise talkative Benoit.

"How are you all getting to the Hotel de la Paix?" I asked, hoping to tag along with his group.

"Oh, we are staying at the Hotel Royal Savoy, not the Hotel de la Paix," Benoit replied, immediately realizing that he should not have revealed that information, based on the two flying daggers thrown by the women accompanying him.

"Well, okay." I said, "I'll see you at the hearings then. 'Bye." This conversation was very strange. Benoit was a friend of mine. It wasn't at all like him to be so dismissive. Still standing in awkward silence at one end of the baggage carousel, I could see the two women berating Benoit at the other end. Maybe they were only now beginning to understand the difficulty of their task in keeping the generally good-natured Benoit from fraternizing with the rest of us—if that was in fact their intent, and it certainly seemed to be.

After Sally suggested that we invite Benoit to dinner, I relayed to the group my strange encounter with him at the airport earlier that day. To which Sally replied, "Then it's settled. He must come to dinner with us, shouldn't he!" Then she looked up the number to the Hotel Royal Savoy, and dialed.

"I'm afraid we do not have a 'Lavoie' registered here," she was informed.

"Are you quite sure?" Sally persisted. "Perhaps it's been misspelled?" But according to the hotel operator, there was no Benoit, no Pam Coburn, no Canadian barrister, and no Canadian delegation at all.

"Well, maybe I misunderstood," I offered. Sally then insisted on calling the Hotel de la Paix, only to learn that Benoit was not staying there either.

"Jon, do you specifically remember him saying the Royal Savoy?" Sally quizzed.

I replied, "The whole situation was so strange. I may be mistaken, but I'm fairly sure I heard the Royal Savoy. But I know Pam Coburn was not pleased he had told me where they were staying."

"Well, okay. Britta and I will stop in at the Royal Savoy on our way to dinner," she said, without asking Britta if she was up for the walk. "We will find him."

When Sally and Britta finally did meet us for dinner, they were exhausted, disappointed, and empty-handed, with not so much as a slice of Canadian bacon. As I said, I get along with Benoit, so I was disappointed too. Sally reported no Benoit, no Pam Coburn, and no Canadians anywhere. Not at the Royal Savoy, not at the Hotel de la Paix. In fact, we didn't see them at all until the hearings began the next day.

When I saw Benoit in the lobby of the de la Paix just before his scheduled testimony, I walked up to him and mentioned we had looked for him to join us for dinner the previous night. "I thought you had said you were staying at the Royal Savoy," I said. His reply was even more mysterious. He said, "Yes, we are, but you would not have been able to find me, as we are staying under assumed names."

What? The Canadians were hiding out in Lausanne. What in the hell is going on here? It's their goddamned gold medal! It was their pair team that had been taken to the cleaners and nearly screwed out of their Olympic title! It was their feeble-minded, sheepish request to "share" the gold medal in the first place, and now they're at these hearings to correct the entire matter, and they're playing hide-and-seek? What did the Canadians believe they would gain by hiding out? Might they be working to curry favor with Ottavio Cinquanta while simultaneously meeting their obligation to be there on behalf of their athletes? Did the money they stood to make as key players in Cinquanta's New Judging System enter into it? The appearance of registering surreptitiously left me uneasy. The Canadians should have been in Lausanne with their heads held high, not hiding behind aliases and bushes!

THE HEARING WAS not uncommonly structured. It was held in the second-floor ballroom of the Hotel de la Paix. Cinquanta sat in front, looking like a godfather, but acting as the judge, along with his fellow henchmen council members as the jury, including Clair "give 'em three years" Ferguson. Gerhardt Bubnick questioned the witnesses and presented the case as a prosecutor would. Marie-Reine sat at one side of the witness table, with her diminutive lawyer. Didier Gailhaguet sat at the other side. While I was in the room answering questions, I felt as though Cinquanta congenially went out of his way to allow me to speak fully and freely. I walked out of the room feeling as though the court was more judicial than kangaroo. Other witnesses mentioned the same impression. Collectively, we were beginning to feel as though maybe, just maybe, the Council would take a tough stance with Marie-Reine and Didier, sending a message of "zero tolerance" to the skating-world judges.

Unfortunately, the council passed on this historic opportunity to put the judging games to an end. Instead, they suspended each "defendant" for a period of three years, with the added penalty of missing one Olympic Games. A very strange punishment, simply because the Olympic Games, to be held in four years, didn't jibe with the three-year ban. Cinquanta was having none of these two at his Olympic Games in Italy! While the rest of the skating world could be stuck with them again in three years, he was not going to risk the kind of negative publicity he had received in Salt Lake by having this duo turn up in Turin.

Clair Ferguson had clairvoyantly predicted the outcome all the way back in Nagano. How did she predict it with such accuracy? Might Cinquanta have predetermined it? Or perhaps she knew of a deal that he had already negotiated with Didier and Marie-Reine? After all the protesting they did proclaiming their innocence, they both lay down like sheep, and neither went forward with an appeal.

We received the news while sitting at dinner. This time, Benoit Lavoie accompanied our little "whistle-blowers" party. It was a cautiously celebratory dinner, tense yet optimistic. When the news came, the mood at the party sank like a body dropped in a lake. It was very disappointing. I remember looking at Benoit immediately after we heard the news. He simply lowered his head, looked into his lap, and shook his head. Benoit's body language was obvious. But was he disappointed in merely the outcome, or was his disappointment much greater, maybe with his Association?

His reaction was indeed puzzling, and it still haunts me.

Later that evening, Sally, Ron, and I went to the lobby bar to have a cocktail. Cinquanta was also in the bar with Gerhardt Bubnick, and we exchanged a few stilted pleasantries. However, on his way out, Cinquanta decided to lambaste Sally for not having taken a more active role in the creation of the New Judging System. It was a left-field angry comment, and completely off topic. Once Cinquanta left, Bubnick joined our group.

When Sally mentioned her disappointment in the outcome to Bubnick, he assured us all that it was in fact the harshest possible.

He said, "We were lucky to even have that hearing. As late as yesterday, Cinquanta was still trying to find a way to get out of it altogether."

Cinquanta was not going to give up on attempting to cover up the scandal, right to the bitter end. Then, once he realized that his resistance was futile, all his attention focused on the easily targeted French, still providing for the coverup of the Russian side of the deal to go completely unchallenged. For the Russians, he was successful: As usual, they got off scot-free.

I attended those hearings in Lausanne for my sport, for its processes, and for its athletes. The sport's leadership did not, and it was a difficult trip home.

Ever the optimist, I assumed there would be an outraged outpouring of criticism from the press, blogs, Web sites, chat rooms, and figure-skating's other officials—none of which happened to any significant degree. The fact that the Russian side of the deal, and really the only thing that could have motivated LeGougne to do what she did, had not been investigated at those hearings is something I'll never figure out.

I flew back to San Francisco, and shortly afterward attended U.S. Figure Skating's Governing Council meeting. At that meeting, they introduced Ron and me to the crowd standing in ovation. Our Association seemed proud of the manner in which we had stood up for what we believed was right. They came through for us when we needed legal counsel, by paying our attorney to accompany us to Switzerland. It was a high moment among many lows, and amplified for me even more when they selected me as chair of the prestigious International Committee.

The International Committee assigns the skaters to their events, participates in the selection of judges and team leaders, and has the most interaction with the elite coaches and skaters of any committee within the association. To be chair is to be having the best job in the association. My rocketing career was still moving forward, not deterred at all by standing firm by my principles. But it would not continue forward for long.

WEEKS LATER, THE ISU held its Bi-Annual Congress in Kyoto, Japan. Many of us were optimistic that the Congress would provide an opportunity to the member federations to express their dissatisfaction with the ISU for its handling of the French–Russian matter. Certainly, the outrage would cause a shakeup during the elections for new officers.

However, there was no outrage. The only outrage seemed to exist back home with me, yet again, as I learned of their disappointing election results. Ottavio Cinquanta ran unopposed. David Dore, a Canadian, unseated Katsu Hisanaga for vice-president of Figure Skating. Katsu had been one of the council members who fought a hard battle to keep the corruption investigation moving forward, as had Canadian Joyce Hisey, unseated in her position by the election of her compatriot David Dore, as no two members from the same country can serve on the council. In one fell swoop, David Dore, the most tenured and one of the highest-ranking officials in Canada, but who was mysteriously absent during the Pair freeskate at the Olympic Games, unseated the two council members who stood against the corruption. Rewind. One of the highest ranking officials in Canada, and mysteriously he was absent at what could have been the biggest moment in Skate Canada history, the Pair event at the 2002 Olympics. Why wasn't he in Salt Lake? What had David Dore known that the rest of us had not?

Phyllis Howard, having never rocked a boat she wasn't standing in, was elected to the council, though I didn't see this as progress. U.S. Figure Skating ran her in place of loose-lipped Claire Ferguson. Given the sacrifices athletes suffered at the doorstep of Phyllis's political campaign, how could I be happy? It was comforting that Claire was no longer in power, but as far as I was concerned, the replacement was much worse. Courtney Jones, the stiff-tied referee who dismissed and surreptitiously tore through the athlete's petition at the Nagano Worlds, was also elected to the council.

On the Technical Committee side of things, evildoers fared even better. Sally Stapleford was turned out as chair in favor of Russian Alexander Lakernik, the assistant referee on the Salt Lake Pair event debacle under Ron Pfenning. Alexander had, not surprisingly, gotten the Pair result dead wrong in Salt Lake, placing his Russian pair in first as if to give cover to the misdeeds he knew were transpiring amongst the judges. He was now running the committee.

Britta Lindgren, the Swedish member of the Technical Committee, who stood firm with Sally about the confession of Marie-Reine, lost an attempt to move up onto the council. Finally, the Ukrainian judge on the Pair event, Vladislov Pethukov, who also got his score wrong, being part of the five that gave the Russians the undeserved gold medal, was also elected to the technical committee. Two of its five members, Lakernik and Pethukov, were now former Soviet comrades, aligned at the hip for all intents and purposes, both having participated in the worst judging scandal in figure-skating history.

Italian Fabio Bianchetti, in reward for proving to the Russians that he would play ball by giving Michelle Kwan presentation marks lower than Slutskaya, was also elected to the technical committee, apparently by the same bloc that elected Pethukov.

The only good news that came out Kyoto was that Ron Pfenning won his reelection to the Technical Committee. His reelection was the only one out of the many who stood strong against the corruption.

Cinquanta also passed his revolutionary New Judging System, and did so in his typically corrupt fashion. He repeatedly assured the members that they were voting on merely a proposal, not a rule, in order to garner the votes for its passage. Once passed, he then promptly put it in the rulebook as a rule. The transcript of the elections has Cinquanta angrily repeating in a thick Italian accent, "This is not a rule, it is a proposal!" It's laughable, except that it's so tragic, to listen to an abbreviated hearing tape with only Cinquanta's "not a rule" proclamation some sixty-four times.

In adopting the Cinquanta's "proposal, not a rule," the Congress also unwittingly adopted anonymous judging, providing even more protection for injustice and something that remains in place to this day. Fourteen judges enter their marks, nine of which are "randomly" selected by the computer and counted toward an average. Never again would the skaters, the coaches, or the press know which judges determined the final placement. The ability to cheat athletes out of Olympic medals will now take place in complete secrecy.

I learned of the disastrous results of the Congress shortly before traveling to Colorado Springs to judge the Broadmoor Open, a well-attended summer competition held each year. The shenanigans in Kyoto were, of course, the main topic of every conversation. Many of us were relieved to learn that John LeFevre would be coming to the judges' dinner to give us a report on the ISU Congress. We were not expecting his confession regarding Phyllis Howard's election.

"We cut deals we would not otherwise have cut, with people we would not otherwise have cut them with," a slightly gin-infused LeFevre boomed across the assembled group of judges at a local country club. "But we got Phyllis elected!"

My table was stunned. We all looked over our half-eaten desserts with questioning glances. I asked Gale Tanger directly, "Did he just say we cut deals to get Phyllis Howard elected?" She confirmed that I had heard it correctly. Susan Johnson heard it too. Susan is a well-respected judge from Atlanta, and someone in the judging ranks whom I have always admired. She is also the repeat bridesmaid to the chair of the International Committee, my new position. Of all the people in the association, she is probably the most qualified, yet has never held the position. When I leapfrogged over her, I asked her to stay on once again as the vice-chair from the East Coast.

The next day, I was summoned to headquarters, John LeFevre's office specifically, for a telephone conference with Phyllis Howard. After conducting some business related to the International Committee, Phyllis asked that I not let anyone know that U.S. Figure Skating had paid for the lawyer who attended the Lausanne hearing. I reminded Phyllis that I had already told everyone at the Governing Council meeting that U.S. Figure Skating had done just that. She was not deterred. She was worried about the International community finding out. Would I please keep quiet about it? "I hear ya, Phyllis," is the only commitment I made.

Later in the day, in between events, Susan and I were discussing the dismal state of affairs. She tried to give me encouraging words; I think she sensed that I was ready to throw in the towel. "Jon, if you begin planning now, maybe during your lifetime you will start to see change. I know it won't happen during mine." A lifetime? I wasn't willing to spend one more year without some kind of change, let alone a lifetime. I immediately called Ron Pfenning.

"Ron, we have to do something," was the general message, but exactly what, neither he nor I had any idea. The following week, Joan Burns, the Paul Bunyan story-telling judge, was going to be celebrating her 70th birthday party in San Jose. We had both been invited, but originally neither of us had intended to make the trip. I now encouraged Ron to come out for the party from Hyannis, as an excuse to give us the opportunity to meet up and brainstorm.

Joan Burns's birthday party in San Jose would be the birthplace of the World Skating Federation (WSF), though, at the time, we didn't have a name for it, nor did it exist in idea form as it came to exist over time. Nevertheless, it was there that Ron and I hatched a plan to overthrow figure-skating's ISU elite and their entire organization.

Our idea was simple. Bring together an international group of like-minded individuals fed up with the ISU ingrained culture of corruption, establish a competing organization, and then appeal to the IOC and the individual member federations to replace the ISU's governance of figure skating.

While Ron and I began making initial confidential entreaties toward trusted individuals in the international skating community, a Russian mobster was arrested in Italy for allegedly having participated in the Olympic Pair fix. No, unfortunately Cinquanta wasn't arrested. Alimzhan Tokhtakhounov had bragged, in a phone call recorded by Italian police, to a gentleman identified only as "Chevalier," as to having contacted as many as six judges to help fix the Ice Dance competition. It was his hope that by fixing the event, it would help secure him a French visa so he could return to where he had once lived. Nobody squawked louder or came to his defense faster than the Russians.

Finally, we reveled; the Russian involvement will come out. Finally, the Russians will have to face the music. Finally, the ISU will have to do something. "Finally"? When was I going to get it?

The Russian Federation was the first to cry foul, saying that they had nothing to do with any mobsters. They even got Anton and Yelena mixed up in it again, with Anton threatening to sue all of American network television for showing their picture in connection with the man suspected of helping Russia fix the games.

"I saw our pictures appearing on the screen while they were talking about some kind of Russian mafia," Sikharulidze said on Russian television networks. "Together with people who are working with us, we are preparing to sue the television channels."

Perhaps Anton hadn't quite thought that one through yet.

Then he went on to say, "It's time for the Canadian and U.S. people to calm down and be happy with the [duplicate] gold medals they were given as a gift. These people must be happy with the gold medals they were awarded, I don't know what for."

Let me explain it to you, Anton. The French judge admitted she cheated on your behalf and you were indirectly caught up in it. She, along with four others, voted for you with a padded presentation mark. Unfortunately, you didn't win the gold because you skated better, you won because people cheated.

It's not like any Russian is ever going to say, "Yep, you got us! We're sorry. We've been cheating and now we're through!" The Russians will always deny their involvement in shady dealings and, instead, deflect all of it back on the West, or on to North American fairy tales.

The cheating mobster denied all the charges against him, even though there were wiretapped phone conversations that confirmed his involvement.

In France, Olympic Ice Dance champion Marina Anissina, a Russian émigré in France, acknowledged that she had talked "from time to time" with Tokhtakhounov. She and partner Gwendal Peirzerat won the event. She insisted that knowing him had nothing to do with her gold medal.

"Everything will go well now because the French, with their vote, have made them champions," Tokhtakhounov said, according to the transcript. "It happened, it happened. Even if the Canadians are 10 times better, the French with their vote have given them first place."

Other transcripts detail a conversation between Tokhtakhounov and a female ice dancer's mother. After the Olympics, the female ice dancer called Tokhtakhounov and thanked him for his help, but said that she could have won even without his help. While Anissina was the ice dancer who won the gold, the papers didn't identify her as the woman on the phone.

The ISU soon sent out a request to the federations to come forward with any new information. Did Cinquanta think that the federations might have had a few wiretaps too? Cinquanta was giving the appearance of reopening the investigation without having to actually do so.

Where is the IOC in all of this? The International Olympic Committee owes a fiduciary obligation to the world of sport to get involved when one of its own federations is misbehaving. In the bribe-filled hallways of the IOC, was not a wiretap-recorded phone call enough to prove to them that the ISU had failed in its investigation? Why was Dr. Jacques Rogge, the IOC president, continuing to ignore figure-skating's problems? Rogge has taken absolutely no responsibility for the IOC's inaction or for the ISU's failures.

Nonetheless, Ron and I were encouraged by this news out of Italy, the best news since the scandal first broke; we began preparations for an initial meeting of a core group of individuals to take place in Boston at the end of the month. It was there that we would map out the hoped downfall of the ISU. We didn't realize it then, but we had taken the first steps toward securing our own.

Xue Shen and Hongbo Zhao, a Chinese pair team, broke the Russian stronghold in Pairs, winning the gold medal at the World Championships in Nagano. The Russian dynasty, having hit a speed bump in Salt Lake, may finally have come to an end.

Legal Tricks and Maneuvers

POSSIBLY ONE OF the world's most beautiful cities, at least that I ever visited, was St. Petersburg, Russia. Certainly their collections of paintings and objets d'art are some of the most vast and varied of any city—or any country, for that matter. Sure, it might have been pillaged from other countries during the World Wars, or obtained unethically through the fabulous wealth of the tsars while the peasants starved; but, just the same, it was on display for all the people of Russia and those lucky enough to get a visa to see and appreciate it. I learned that I would never get to visit that city or that country again.

My lawyer and I were asked to meet with the FBI in lower Manhattan, a meeting that concluded with a warning never to go to Russia again. For that matter, they could not assure my safety if I traveled to any former Soviet Union country. "What about the former non-Soviet Eastern bloc countries?" I pressed. They said I was probably safe in those countries.

I had just finished telling them what went down, from my perspective, in Salt Lake City at the Olympic Games. We met with three FBI agents for well over an hour. Ron Pfenning had met with this same group of suits just before I did. These agents assured me that the Russian mob was involved. While they were confident in their investigation, they were not sharing any other details, other than to say that the Russian mafia was very dangerous and unpredictable. "Do not travel to Russia," they warned again.

After the FBI heard my statement, I traveled to Boston for the first meeting to discuss what would become the World Skating Federation. There were numerous questions without answers. "Where will we get the money to make this happen?" was one. "How much money will we need?" was another. "Will television even be interested?" "Which countries can we count on for support?" "When will the FBI close in on the ISU?" rang the chorus.

We met in Sally Stapleford's hotel room. Sally had flown to Boston from London for the sole purpose of this meeting. I was already in Massachusetts to judge the Cranberry Open on Cape Cod. Ron, who lives in Hyannis, a small town on the Cape, drove with me to Boston. Katsu Hisanaga made the trip from Japan, and Joyce Hisey came down from Canada. Jane Erkko, a former Finnish skating official, joined us by telephone.

We all knew and agreed that something drastic had to be done. Standing by, idly watching the sport of figure skating deteriorate further was an idea that did not sit well with any of us. Nevertheless, what exactly we should do was still open to discussion.

It was clear to all that working from within the ISU was not an option. The political environment had hardened in favor of the dishonest, its culture of corruption alive and thriving. A new organization was needed. It was also time to separate figure-skating from speed-skating. It simply didn't make sense to continue governing two very different sports as one. "Could we make an appeal to the IOC to intervene?" someone asked. "Possibly, but to do what?" someone answered. If we appealed to the IOC, what would we ask them to do?

Ultimately, it became clear that a separate organization would need to be established. A complete cleansing with a fresh start was necessary. So, as long as we were starting over, why not correct everything that was wrong with the governing of figure-skating? Why focus solely on the corruption in judging?

We decided to lay the foundation of our organization at the feet of the athletes. The organization existed for them in the first place, so it made sense to us that it should arise from their needs. We discussed various possibilities for an athlete representative in our group. American Olympic silver medalist Paul Wylie topped our list, but others were discussed. We needed someone who was willing to give a great deal of time, as well as his or her inside perspective. I said I would try to reach Paul.

We all agreed on a number of things during that first meeting in Boston, the first being that our actions had to remain completely confidential. We knew that if Cinquanta got wind of our activities, he would act to stop us before we had a chance to diligently pursue our plan. We also decided that if at any time we determined our plan would not work, that our secret would stay with us forever and that no one would ever know what we had started. However, we also recognized that there are no secrets in figure-skating. Somehow, anything and everything "confidential" spreads like wildfire over the skating grapevine. We all agreed to sign confidentiality agreements, and further decided that we would not discuss the idea with anyone unless they too signed such an agreement. We were all willing to work toward the common goal, but we needed to know that our actions would not be scrutinized until a full plan had been put together—and then maybe never, if such a plan proved unworkable.

One of the hurdles that would have ended our pursuit, and forced us to carry our secret to the grave, was the ability to raise money. If we weren't able to persuade some of skating's benefactors to help with the funds, then we knew we would not be able to go forward. The television networks were another possible impasse. If they refused to meet with us—or if, after meeting with us, they indicated no interest—then we would be stopped dead in our tracks.

We also knew that in order to loosen the grip the ISU had on the IOC, we would need factual evidence of the corruption that we knew existed. It was my idea that we would file a class-action lawsuit against the ISU on behalf of the ticketholders of the Olympic Games based on consumer fraud. By doing so, we would be given broad discovery powers that would allow us to expose the fraud in the ISU, not just at the Olympic Games, but rampant throughout its management and the judging of its events. Such a lawsuit would be very expensive, unless we could find a lawfirm willing to represent us on a *pro bono* basis, essentially providing us their services free of charge, or in exchange for a portion of any damage award that might be recovered. As an attorney, I was confident that finding such a group of lawyers was possible.

When we ended the meeting, our plan was simple and straightforward. First, we would need to put together a coalition of concerned and knowledgeable skating supporters from around the world. We discussed many possibilities and narrowed the list. It was important that the coalition not appear to be "North American" or even "Anglo-Saxon." All of Europe needed representation, as well as Asia and Oceana.

Next, we decided that we would meet again at Skate America in late October. That would give us a few months to get our budgets together, search out various individuals to bring on board, and begin a tentative outreach for money. We agreed that at Skate America, we would decide whether to move forward or kill the plan.

Finally, we would need to raise some funds immediately. We figured that we needed to raise at least $50,000 before Skate America as a test, to see how difficult the fundraising might be. We estimated that we would need an additional $200,000 to complete our work prior to making any public announcement of our plans, and another million or so after the announcement. We believed that if we could raise the two hundred and fifty thousand dollars in an environment of secrecy, that the million would come easier after the announcement. The immediate goal was raising the $50,000 so that we could move forward.

We divided the tasks among our small group, mine being the fundraising portion. We ended our meeting in high spirits, but also recognized the gray clouds of doubt. We arranged to keep in close touch. Joyce began to assemble as much financial information as she could about the ISU to share with us for planning purposes.

It was a grand plan, and it occupied much of my thoughts in the days that followed when I returned to Cape Cod to judge the Cranberry Open. Phyllis Howard made an appearance at the event, and cornered me to discuss her reelection for president of U.S. Figure Skating. At the time, she was the recently elected International Skating Union council member. Her dual roles presented an obvious conflict. Obvious to everyone except for her.

Phyllis was concerned that Morry Stilwell and his long-time skating friend Jack Curtis, an old curmudgeon who was always vocal in U.S. Figure Skating politics, were working against her reelection for president, perceiving a conflict of interest with her new role as an ISU council member.

I had at one time supported Phyllis, and I believe she was trying to firm up that support, knowing that the Olympics and its fallout had strained it. I used the opportunity to tell her that she had kowtowed to Cinquanta in the past, and that if she continued to do so, perhaps there was a conflict.

She then shared with me an exchange of correspondences that she believed proved she was standing up to Cinquanta. Earlier in the summer, to her credit, she had written a harsh letter to Cinquanta challenging him on the anonymity of the new judging system, among other things. She shared the correspondence with the press.

Outraged that the press received a copy of the correspondence, Cinquanta wrote back, attacking Phyllis for her dual roles, and outlined his belief that she had a conflict of interest, and lambasted her for publicly sharing his secret ISU business.

Phyllis responded, agreeing no longer to share her thoughts with the press if it related to ISU business, but held firm to her initial views expressed to them.

Phyllis believed that this demonstrated that she could juggle her two roles, and that she was standing firm and strong against Cinquanta. I saw it as just the opposite. The result was that she compromised the interests of the U.S. by agreeing not to share information with the press, one of the few methods that seemed to get Cinquanta to do anything. Further, Cinquanta had outlined just how difficult the conflicts were in being both president of a member federation and a member of the ISU Council. I couldn't have said it better myself, and English is my primary language.

I RETURNED TO my new home in Las Vegas with an already-taxed confidence in Phyllis only more deeply eroded, though somewhat more enthusiastic that perhaps it wouldn't matter. If our new organization was successful, Phyllis and Cinquanta might become inconsequential, so I focused my efforts on the fundraising.

The following week I was in Sun Valley, judging its end-of-summer competition. Lisa Webster, heir to the dictionary fortune and long-time benefactor to all things skating, was there attending. I approached her one afternoon and told her that there was something very important I needed to talk to her about, but also mentioned that I needed her to sign a confidentiality agreement in order to speak to her about it. She was adamant that she would not sign anything.

This put me in a tight spot. I was certain she would be supportive of our goals—but what if she wasn't? Could I trust her not to tell anyone? I knew she was very close with master story-teller Joan Burns, who was also attending the competition, and I knew Joan Burns couldn't keep her trap clapped if she knew a secret, but would Lisa tell her? The risk that Lisa might leak it to Joan led me to conclude that without the confidentiality agreement, I could not make my pitch to "deep pockets" Lisa Webster.

Her curiosity, though, almost got the best of her, and she pried for more information. If she signed it, just what did I want from her? In good conscience, I couldn't even answer her preliminary questions. No information without signing. I had hoped my refusing to give even the smallest amount of information would intensify her curiosity, and encourage her to sign the agreement. In the end, we both walked away. No confidentiality, no discussion; worse, no money.

A few days after returning to Vegas, I flew to Colorado Springs solely to meet with Carolyn Kruse, a very gracious, influential, and respected figure-skating supporter who had ties to the Colorado Springs community. I needed to get an appointment with the El Pomar Foundation, a well-known supporter of figure-skating in Colorado, and I knew that Carolyn had the connections to get me in the door.

She met me in the lobby of the Doubletree Hotel. Carolyn and I had a long conversation, and after explaining our goals, I asked if she would arrange a meeting with Bill Hybl, a former USOC president and the current chair of the El Pomar Foundation. I hoped he could offer us some guidance and perhaps pledge financial support. Carolyn, seeming supportive of our plan, agreed to see what she could do, and wished me the best. I returned to Las Vegas that afternoon, without even staying the night in Colorado.

Carolyn was successful in arranging the meeting. I flew back to Colorado Springs; Ron Pfenning flew out from Boston. We met with Mr. Hybl in his posh offices located on the grounds of Colorado Springs' magnificent Broadmoor Hotel. He was very hospitable and agreed to sign our confidentiality statement without giving it a second thought, and then spent a lot of time with us sharing advice. Hybl appreciated immediately the need for drastic change in figure-skating. He himself had been instrumental in reorganizing the Tae Kwan Do Federation, and was optimistic that we could do the same for skating.

On the financial front, the news was not so heartening. The El Pomar Foundation limited itself by charter to the support of only Colorado-based organizations. We had no presence in Colorado Springs, so El Pomar could not help us out. He agreed, though, to call "concerned friends" of figure-skating whom he had been hearing from, to see if perhaps they would dig into their pockets. We needed $200,000, and knowing that they would have to be pretty deep pockets, he said he would see what he could do. He also encouraged us to keep him informed and invited us to seek his advice in the future.

I then traveled to Los Angeles to meet with 1992 Olympic silver medalist Paul Wylie. He was working for Disney at the time. I made the trip from Vegas by car, met Paul for lunch at a country club near the Disney offices, then drove back home. The meeting with Paul went very well. He was thrilled to learn of our efforts. He questioned, though, why we had given up on changing the sport from within. I told him my perspective on that issue, and then the perspectives of Ron, Sally, Katsu, and so on, as I understood them.

Paul asked if we had any problem with him continuing his work with U.S. Figure Skating. He said he wasn't quite ready to give up on a more traditional manner of making change. I told him to be active in any way he wanted, being mindful that we might have to cut off our efforts at any time. I didn't want Paul to lose any opportunities to make change elsewhere. With that, we shook hands and he agreed to come aboard. Paul was invaluable in structuring our organization with an athletic perspective. He was a feather in the WSF cap, and we were thrilled to have his input.

At about this time, U.S. Figure Skating organized a task force to institute change within the ISU. Christine Brennan, the USA Today reporter I had met with in Salt Lake City, ran a story on the topic, and quoted a number of my views. More than one of these quotes upset the applecart, infuriating several in U.S. Figure Skating. First, I accurately said that "the U.S. response [to the scandal in Salt Lake] has been nothing short of pathetic." The country-club elite that is U.S. Figure Skating didn't care for my word choice, and didn't care to have the kitchen light turned on while the cockroaches fed. Evidently, "pathetic" was too strong a word for them.

Phyllis was furious. It didn't help either that I was also quoted as saying that Phyllis "is between a rock and a hard place by being both [U.S. Figure Skating] president and on the [ISU] council . . . as long as she wears the ISU albatross, she can't be a strong leader on this issue."

To add to the furor, other judges, Joe Inman key among them, were upset that I had called the judges "props." I had explained to Brennan that I had turned down all judging assignments for the season in disgust over what was going on. Brennan prodded, why? I responded "If you're judging, you're a prop in Cinquanta's ice follies." I stand by the statement. At that time, we were all simply props. Later, I would find out that many were much worse, but I will get to that a bit later.

With controversy in the air, I traveled to Spokane for Skate America. It was also a great opportunity to meet with Sally again. We invited Carolyn Kruse to join us as well, though she was unable to make our little powwow. When we met, Sally, Ron, and I toyed with the idea of asking U.S. judge Bob Horen to join our group. He had approached me earlier that evening, and said he knew I was up to something, and wanted to know what. Phyllis had recently named him chair of the previously mentioned ad hoc committee to formulate a U.S. strategy to help change the ISU. I told him I would meet him for breakfast the next morning when we could talk.

Bob was a friend of mine, and a very close friend of Ron's. Therefore, Bob was part of what many in figure-skating prone to jealousy call the

"Gay Mafia," though no such thing actually exists. Just because a couple of gay men get together and talk does not a mafia make.

"I got a job for one of youse. I need you to go down and pay that judge from Oklahoma a little visit. Really mess her up! Arrange her furniture on angles, put up some of that fancy gingham wallpaper stuff, give her a bad haircut, and dye it a color out of her season. I'm guessing she's a spring—and then dress her in a tube top and a hoochy skirt. Leave a vase of black cala lilies. Her husband will get the message!" Gay mafia. Right.

When I told Sally that Bob had approached me, and relayed to her what he said (leaving out the part about the cala lilies and gingham wallpaper!), she was convinced our little secret was out. I assured her that I was "up to" a number of things, and not to be worried. I didn't think Bob really knew anything, and refocused our discussion. "Wouldn't it be a coup to have Bob, the chair of the U.S. committee to change the ISU, support our cause?" Ron and Sally countered that it might make our group look too much like a U.S. movement.

In the end, we decided instead to ask Gale Tanger to join us. Though also an American, she was the United States Olympic Committee representative for U.S. Figure Skating. We needed connections to the USOC, at least according to Bill Hybl, and Gale seemed to fit the bill.

At that point, we were being careful only to enlighten individuals who were essential to our movement. We thought that the fewer the people who knew, the better our chances to remain clandestine. While there were plenty of friends I would liked to have told, I knew I couldn't. Bob Horen would be one of them.

I met with Bob for breakfast as planned, and instead of talking about the WSF, went on to tell him all about the new elite athlete committee being chaired by Paul Wylie, which I was instrumental in organizing and assisting as chair of the International Committee. Bob was a bit skeptical. "That is what you are up to?" he said. "Yep," I assured him, going on to explain how Phyllis had fought its organization, initially refusing to allow them to meet, and finally agreeing to move it forward, but only after putting it under the Athletes Advisory Committee instead of the International Committee, where she thought she would have more control. I also told him that the athletes were still keeping me informed and involved in their activities. He seemed pleased.

Later in the day, Sally, Ron, and I secretly met with Dick Button behind the arena. Dick was immediately supportive of our idea. He wanted to come aboard our group, and arranged for us to meet Curt Gowdy, who was also very supportive. With feathers like these in our caps, we'd have a whole headdress in no time!

We then met Gale Tanger for dinner, and before getting into any details, asked her to sign the confidentiality agreement. She was reluctant, but agreed to take it home with her, review it, and get back to us. She assured us that she would keep secret whatever we had to tell her. So, without an agreement, we broke our own rule and told her everything. She was flattered that we would ask her to join us, and seemed concerned when we told her that she would be risking everything. If our plans were exposed, it might spell the end to all our careers in figure-skating. She encouraged our success, but her discomfort was obvious. The next day, she returned the confidentiality agreement still unsigned to Ron, and told him that she was just too busy to take on any additional projects.

AFTER SKATE AMERICA, I was literally skipping around the globe looking for money. I don't think I'd ever worked so hard with so little return. The most fundraising I had ever done was when I committed to raise money for the San Francisco AIDS Foundation to participate in the California AIDSRide, a 580-mile bike ride from San Francisco to Los Angeles, and this was already a tougher turnip to squeeze blood from. By November, I was still flying to various parts of the country and doing my best to raise funds. Though I had several "good luck, pal" comments and a few blank stares, I was not having much luck so far. We had about $75,000.00 pledged at this point, none of it coming in the form of cold hard cash. Bill Hybl called to let us know that his contacts were dead-ends as well. Things were not looking good.

Sally convinced us that we should bring aboard Italian Sonia Bianchetti, the former chair of the ISU Technical Committee who was instrumental in removing figures from the sport back in the late eighties. She had publicly expressed disgust over the ISU's handling of the Salt Lake scandal. Sonia signed the confidentiality agreement and joined us in our work, exchanging E-mails, joining telephone conference calls, and the like. Soon, we also had Don McKnight, an Australian with a straight-shooting reputation, and Judith Furst-Tomber, a respected judge from Hungary, the first of our members from behind the former Iron Curtain.

We seemed to be building momentum in every area except one of the more important ones, financial support. Dick Button had offered to arrange a meeting with ABC Sports executives, something we still needed to do. ABC held the television contract with the ISU. For the WSF to be successful, we needed to know than any transition from the ISU to the WSF would be seamless. We decided to plan one last trip to New York to meet with ABC, and then coordinate a final fundraising effort. If we came up short, or if ABC gave us the thumbs-down, we agreed it would be the end. If on the other hand, we were successful, then we would continue pushing forward.

Our first stop was another meeting with Dick Button at his fashionable full-floor apartment in one of New York's more exclusive neighborhoods. A door attendant greeted us and escorted us to an elevator that stopped at Dick's front door. The apartment was mind-blowing in decoration and finery. Truly one of the more luxurious homes I'd ever visited. After showing us around, Dick was all business and, without delay, was on the phone with Howard Katz, president of ABC Sports to confirm a tentative appointment he had arranged earlier. Given the green light, we jumped into a cab and headed for Katz's offices on 66th Street.

Our meeting with the ABC brass was very, very enlightening. We learned that he would love to see figure-skating changed, and that ABC feared that over time, figure-skating would lose its audience if nothing were done. ABC did not like its contract with the ISU, mostly because Cinquanta had forced them to take speed-skating as part of the deal, a loser that caused them to hemorrhage money faster than a Las Vegas slot machine. He said that the next ISU deal would include only the figure-skating World Championships, and he thought they were not going to pay more than $3 million for it. Up until then, ABC had paid the ISU well over $18 million a year, so it would be a substantial cut.

However, we also learned that ABC was very happy with its contract with U.S. Figure Skating. Katz indicated that the dollar exchange was fair and the National Championships retained its prestigious status. He mentioned some concern with three made-for-TV events, and said that he had met with John LeFevre, Phyllis Howard, and Jerry Lace, the U.S. Figure Skating marketing director, to discuss changing the events. ABC preferred to make the three events part of a series, tying them together, to build viewership throughout the season.

Phyllis was opposed to the change, fearing that it would infringe on the ISU's Grand Prix Series concept. Katz had warned her that if they didn't try something new, it might lead to the end of those events altogether and a lower financial contract for U.S. Figure Skating. That didn't seem to matter to ISU council member Phyllis Howard. She must have forgotten her role as U.S. Figure Skating president. In the end, Phyllis got her way: U.S. Figure Skating kept their events as they were.

Katz asked, "Can you believe she was more concerned about the ISU than her own contract with ABC?" We certainly could. Phyllis had once again placed her ISU priorities ahead of those of U.S. Figure Skating, yet somehow the conflict of interest was lost on her.

Katz concluded the meeting by offering to have an internal meeting at ABC. He would get together his brightest-figure skating people, including Dick, to discuss figure-skating's future, and the ideal programming for it. He then promised to get back to us, so that we could position the World Skating Federation in such a way that both ABC and the WSF would benefit.

We had television behind us! While we didn't have any kind of contract, we had our foot in the door, and there was some real interest, which reenergized Ron and me to go out and raise some money.

Over the next couple of days, now on a mission, we met with several potential backers. Our travels took us to fabulous, posh Manhattan apartments and a mountain, literally an entire mountain, owned by a very successful businessperson. I was blown away over the amount of wealth I was seeing, and more so by their willingness to meet with us.

In the end, we had pledges of another $50,000. It was beginning to look like we were finally headed in the right direction.

Ron left the next morning. I hopped on an Amtrak train to Washington, D.C., and met two longtime friends of skating for lunch, Howard and Barbara Silby. Howard, a doctor, had been very influential in sports and medicine for U.S. Figure Skating. Barbara, his wife, was influential in Democratic politics. Together, they had earned a name for themselves in figure-skating as having been strong supporters and advocates for the athletes. I was finding that advocates for athletes do not fare well in U.S. Figure Skating politics and soon find themselves as outcasts. This would prove to be the case with the Silbys. I went to D.C. to see if they would be interested in renewing their involvement by helping out the WSF.

The Silbys were delighted, to say the least, to hear about our plans. Their daughter Caroline was still involved in U.S. Figure Skating, so they remained linked and aware of figure-skating's goings-on, and they weren't happy with what they were seeing. They were also troubled over what had happened in Salt Lake, with U.S. Figure Skating's apparent failure to do anything about it. The recent arrest of the Russian mobster put them in a frame of mind to do something to help.

I invited them to put their skating knowledge, their organizational skills, and their political acumen to work on behalf of the WSF, and happily, they agreed. They also agreed not to tell their daughter Caroline. Both signed the confidentiality agreements.

After lunch, I hopped on Amtrak and headed back to New York to catch my flight home. Reflecting back, the trip had been very successful. Now we had a varied group of individuals involved, some financial backing, and the cooperation of ABC Television. We began to plan a meeting of all of those involved; after all, we now had the funds to implement our plan.

We decided to plan a meeting in Copenhagen during the European Championships, which were being held across the sea in Malmö, Sweden. Many of those in our group would be there for the championships, making it a perfect opportunity for a meeting.

In early January, I met up again with Sally Stapleford. She was in Palm Springs visiting Steve Winkler, as was Joe Inman. I was in Palm

Springs to complete the continuing education requirements required of all California attorneys. My boyfriend Sandy and I met up with Joe, Steve and Sally at one of Palm Springs' finer restaurants. With Sally leading the charge, we all lambasted Cinquanta's New Judging System. Steve and Joe were just as adamant in their feelings against the system.

Much to my surprise, a week later in Dallas at the National Championships, Joe Inman paraded out at a seminar on the New Judging System. I could not believe my ears, as Joe, the expert panelist for the system, touted its finer points. My disbelief was not based solely on the dinner conversation I shared with him not one week before, but also on the fact that Joe Inman had *never used* or even tried the new judging system. He had attended three different events that fall where it was tested, but he had not been in on the testing. Apparently, he learned his expertise by osmosis.

The new system requires the judge to grade each technical element on a scale of +3 to −3, and then put in 5 separate marks, on a scale of 1 to 10, for presentation. I started to become a believer in its ease of use. After all, if system was easy enough to learn by osmosis, the chimpanzees down at the zoo could learn it too.

Later in the day, I saw Steve Winkler. I sat down next to him and expressed my disbelief over Joe's new Armani turncoat. Did Steve know Joe was now an "expert" on the New Judging System? "I guess Phyllis got to him," was Steve's only reply. I decided then and there that the judges supporting this new system were much worse than simple props in Cinquanta's ice follies. In my mind, they were his chimpanzees, trained to do and say whatever Cinquanta wanted. The army of Cinquanta's chimps would grow over the next few years, as Cinquanta created committees and education groups, involving as many of his chimps as he could.

A few of the chimps were rewarded with bananas. Charlie Cyr, who was also an "expert" speaking on the New Judging System at Nationals, was nominated to take the World Exam for Singles and Pairs. Joe Inman was rewarded later in the year, receiving financial payment for speaking at a judges' school in May, something that had never been done in U.S. Figure Skating: paying a volunteer for his time.

In the meantime, I was still trying to raise additional funds, and felt that it was also time to begin finding lawyers willing to donate their time for our cause. One of my meetings was with Ron Hershberger, U.S. Figure Skating vice president sitting on the Executive Committee. Ted Clarke, the vice president of the East, had given us his support a few weeks before. Ron Pfenning met with Ted after we had learned that Ted was taking a tough stand against the ISU on the Executive Committee, much to the irritation of Phyllis Howard. He was more than eager to help out, and pleased to find others who shared his views of the corrupt ISU.

Ron Hershberger came aboard just as readily. I had a tough time at first, with him not wanting to sign the confidentiality agreement for fear that it would compromise his obligations to U.S. Figure Skating. He did not want any ethical conflict to exist. I modified the agreement to allow him to break it at any time if he felt there was a conflict of interest, so he agreed to sign. He also never broke the agreement.

Hershberger was a probate lawyer with a respected firm in Palo Alto. I asked him to help the WSF find legal counsel to represent us in the event of any fight with the ISU, and specifically to file a class-action consumer fraud lawsuit. He agreed to help out, and we stayed in touch over the next few months.

I met with a few other potential backers, securing one more $50,000 pledge.

As International Chair, I had several responsibilities during Nationals week. I was troubled that my budget only allowed the U.S. to send two skaters in each discipline to the Four Continents Championships, when we were entitled to send three in each. I put together a proposal to request the additional funds to send the three, and submitted it to the treasurer, Joan Rozolis, for approval by the Executive Committee. It was returned to me with "no action" stamped on it. Ms. Rozolis indicated that as chair, I could spend my budget as I saw fit. If I wanted to send three skaters in each discipline, I would have to find a way to cut spots elsewhere.

This "inaction" was objectionable to me. How could the Executive Committee shirk their responsibilities to the athletes like that? I went ahead and assigned three athletes in each discipline. If I could spend my budget as I saw fit, then I would do so. If she came back and said she had told me I would have to make cuts elsewhere, I'd just tell her

I didn't recall her saying that, in the style of American Olympic Pair judge Lucy Brennan.

Then I asked Denise Thomas, my contact at headquarters, to figure out exactly how much money was in the athlete-support budget account. I went ahead and divided it up between the World, Junior World, and Four Continents teams to help with their training. It was a great way to spend the money: on the athletes. Joan Rozolis was furious!

U.S. Figure Skating puts more money aside each year than it spends on its athletes, by almost twofold! In a 16-million-plus-dollar budget, U.S. Figure Skating spends about 1.6 million of it on its athletes, and runs a surplus of over three million. The question is, where does the rest of the money go?

A few weeks later, I was off to the WSF meeting in Copenhagen. It was more than a heady experience for me, with high-level international figure-skating officials coming together for an honorable goal. I met Sonia Bianchetti for the first time, and was immediately taken by her charm and charisma. I was educated by Hungarian Judith Furst-Tomber on geography; Hungary was not in Eastern Europe: it's in Central Europe! Each person brought a needed perspective to the meetings. Haig Oundjian, an English businessman with a keen interest in football and a former figure-skater, attended as well. His naïveté about figure-skating politics was refreshing. He simply could not understand how Cinquanta got away with the things he did. He too couldn't understand how Jacques Rogge, the IOC president, turned a blind eye to Cinquanta's shenanigans.

We hashed out budgets; discussed the constitution, which Sonia and Don McKnight had been hammering out; and divided up the countries of the world into numerous regions, adding a group of developing countries to eliminate the fraud that goes on with the ISU purchasing their votes.

Purchasing votes? Indeed. In the ISU, Andorra, for example, with one ice rink, gets one vote just as Canada gets with its thousands of ice rinks. The ISU doles out a great deal of money, in the name of "developing figure-skating," to very small countries throughout the world to secure their votes in close elections. Cinquanta would use this very method to get his New Judging System passed, even approving obscure countries for membership simply to get additional votes.

Under the WSF constitution, such countries, obscure in the sense of their figure-skating visibility, would be grouped together, minimizing their importance in an election to eliminate the graft in the distribution of funds to them. It was just one of the more innovative approaches we took, the most important of which was the placing of a coach and an athlete on each committee and council of the WSF. The ISU has since taken our lead on that one, the difference being that Cinquanta appoints the ISU athlete and coach representatives. The fact that those appointees are beholden to him is not lost on anybody. The WSF's athlete and coach representatives were to be elected by the athletes and the coaches themselves. We wanted them to serve the master whom they were intended to represent.

The meetings had a humorous angle to them, as Sonia's son Fabio was officiating across the sound in Malmö while she met with us in secret. When she would receive a call from Fabio, she pretended to be back in Italy. It was a lot of fun, as she asked about the skating, the weather, and all the other things she already knew about, being almost right there herself!

We finished our meetings in Copenhagen, agreeing to get together again in Beijing during the Four Continents Championships. I still didn't have any lawyers lined up for the class-action lawsuit; now we needed a lawyer to assist us in the drafting the constitution as well. I returned home to Las Vegas determined to find both.

I knew just the person to help with the constitution, and flew to meet him at his offices. He was skeptical, but agreed to help us if we would keep his identity secret. He was to be called "Boxford" when referred to, and only I was to know his real identity. I agreed to his batty comic-book request, knowing that he had a history of intelligence procedures and clandestine operations prior to his becoming a lawyer. I thought at the time that his Bat Cave–like identity was his way of making it interesting, and I could live with that. Ultimately, he eventually did lift his own mask and reveal his identity to a few other WSFers, but most never knew who he really was.

Again, I contacted Ron Hershberger and asked if he had had any luck in locating any *pro bono* attorneys. He said he had found me two firms, one in San Francisco, the other in Los Angeles, and gave me their phone numbers. I spoke with both, but neither of them panned out.

I then traveled to Beijing in the role of assistant team leader at the Four Continents Championships. A third of the U.S. athletes attending wouldn't have been there had Joan Rozolis and her welded-shut purse had their way. I was saddened to learn that our top Pairs team, Tiffany Scott and Philip Dulebohn, didn't have enough financial support from the association, even with the extra money they received from the ASUPP funds, to bring along their coach. The national champions of a multi-million-dollar association with a known cash surplus; yet, incredibly, there were no funds for their coach.

In any event, after completing my assistant team leading duties, which included running personal errands for the team leader, such as locating a set of expensively priced black pearl earrings, I met with the others at a hotel across town. Paul Wylie and Sonia Bianchetti had healthy discussions regarding athlete involvement and the value of professional skaters. Sonia was from the old school of thought, where only the amateurs mattered; Paul had skated professionally in an environment (post-Tonya) that allowed them to continue improving and honing their skills. Each left the meeting with a better understanding of the other, and our organization was stronger for it.

The coaches who joined us in Beijing, John Nicks and Kathy Casey, provided valuable insight from their years in the sport. Their perspective was at times different than that of the officials in our group. Whenever we reached loggerheads, Nicks seemed to have the solution, always delivered in proper English and with wry humor and usually in five words or less. He was instrumental on more than one occasion in keeping our meetings moving forward.

We finalized the constitution, thanks to Sonia's, Don's, and Boxford's dedication to the work. We were just about set to make a public announcement when a couple of problems presented themselves. First, we still didn't have a television contract. Howard Katz got back to us, and the news was good, but ABC wasn't interested in signing a "contingent" contract. He did wish us, however, the best and assured us there would be a contract should we get recognition from the IOC.

The other problem was that, Boxford aside, we still didn't have proper legal representation.

Despite these two important shortcomings, we began debating the "when," not the "if," of a WSF public announcement. The easiest and most obvious place would be at the 2003 World Championships in Washington, D.C. It would of course provide the most publicity for us, but some thought its proximity didn't provide enough time for us to prepare.

The debate continued after the meeting by E-mail. In the end, Paul Wylie wrote a compelling "if not now, when?" E-mail that got everyone aboard the idea of having a press conference at the D.C. Worlds. Joyce Hisey chimed in her agreement. Cinquanta had assigned her to be the technical representative at the Worlds. She assured us that she would be prepared, and not to worry about creating a disruption of the event.

The only problem with having the announcement at Worlds would be that Joyce would not be a part of it. As the technical representative, she would be too busy to participate. In addition, the ISU was throwing a party for her to celebrate her years of contribution to the sport. She did not want to detract from that by appearing at a press conference in attempt to overthrow her hosts, and rightly so.

We made the decision to go forward without her. Joyce prepared to make sure we didn't adversely affect the events and the athletes. Barbara Silby arranged for a room at the press hotel to host a "press conference." We carefully chose the speakers, who each prepared their own well-thought-out speeches.

I FLEW TO the Bay Area to meet with Mel Weiss, a well respected lawyer from New York, to see if he would act as our *pro bono* counsel, a meeting that John Misha Petkovich, former U.S. National Men's champion, arranged. The meeting was brief, and Weiss agreed to support us.

Ecstatic, I stopped by Ron Hershberger's office, a few blocks away, to give him the good news. He was thrilled for the WSF, but concerned about the U.S. Executive Committee, primarily Phyllis.

One of his concerns was that Phyllis was attempting to put her nemesis Morry Stillwell back on the Executive Committee. Hershberger was running against Phyllis for president. Rightly, his concern was that by Phyllis giving Morry a plum spot, he might throw his support behind her. Up until then, Morry had seemed to be supporting Hershberger.

The plan, hatched between arch two arch-enemies, was apparently made when both Phyllis and Morry attended the Grand Prix final in St. Petersburg. What was Morry doing there, besides being chauffeured to museums and drinking vodka? Got me!

Phyllis returned home and announced she would be putting Morry Stillwell on the Executive Committee as Past President, a position long vacant after the passing of Jimmy Disbrow. The Executive Committee, though chock full of Phyllis friendlies, smelled a rat and didn't let her get away with her plan. Still, if Phyllis were reelected, the door would be open to fill the spot come May. Morry now had a reason to campaign for his enemy Phyllis Howard.

I left the meeting with Hershberger, still high from my meeting with Weiss, but now disturbed by Phyllis's expert political shenanigans. I will give her this: Her Machiavellian instincts border on genius.

I THEN CONTACTED Lorrie Kim, an ardent skating fan and one of the organizers of SkateFair, a fan group planning to protest the judging anonymity at the World Championships in D.C. After persuading Lorrie to sign a confidentiality agreement, I approached her about running the WSF administratively for us. We were getting so large in number, with so many tasks to accomplish, that we desperately needed professional organization. She agreed to join forces. Soon, she contacted another ardent fan, Sandra Loosemore, whose prolific writing about skating on the Internet has earned her notoriety and respect. Sandra agreed to design and administer the WSF Web site. With little time to prepare, she managed to have an extremely professional site up and running in time for the press conference.

IN FINAL PREPARATION for the press conference, Ron Pfenning phoned Mark Mitchell, the athlete member of the Executive Committee, to bring him up to speed on the WSF. John Nicks was assigned to speak to Scott Wendland, the other athlete representative.

I flew to Los Angeles to meet with Sharon Watson, the Secretary of US Figure Skating. We had made the decision not to tell Will Smith and Joan Rozolis about the WSF. I relayed that information to Sharon. Sharon understood why we didn't tell Phyllis; clearly, she had a conflict, and clearly she would not be able to vote on any matter related to the WSF, but why not tell Will Smith and Joan Rozolis? I told her that too many of us didn't trust Rozolis, and that Will Smith seemed to have proven himself as a blind supporter of Phyllis' positions. She asked me to ask the group to reconsider.

I did discuss it with other organizers. No Will Smith, no Joan Rozolis. We couldn't risk them tipping off Phyllis.

After my meeting with Sharon, I met Paul Wylie downtown for a meeting with Anita DeFranz, U.S. member of the IOC. Anita is a bright former athlete who has made a lot of headway in the IOC.

Paul and I shared our plan with her. She shared with us her skepticism, saying something to the effect of: "You are dealing with a good-old-boy's network. Don't expect to be embraced by the IOC." We should have listened more carefully to her warning.

In the meantime, Ron was fighting a battle of his own with Cinquanta over the publishing of the skaters' marks after the event. With the assistance of Boxford, Ron challenged Cinquanta's anonymous scores. The ISU rules still required the publishing of the marks to the skaters after the event. Cinquanta had ignored the rules all season. Ultimately, Ron would resign his role as referee of the Ladies' event prior to the WSF announcement, unwilling to run the event in contradiction to the ISU rules.

We arrived in D.C. feeling as if we were about to save the world. Our spirits were high, and once our secret was out, we looked forward to raising more funds, meeting with the IOC, and taking our message to the member federations in an attempt to gain wider support for our reforms.

We rehearsed the entire evening beforehand. I then called Christine

Brennan at *USA Today*. Tuesday's morning edition would feature a story in her column, with our announcement to follow shortly thereafter. We needed something in the press to ensure an audience at our press conference. How do you call a press conference without telling anyone what it is you are announcing? Getting an exclusive once again, Christine was more than happy to help us out.

∞

PAUL WYLIE BEGAN the press conference by announcing to the press and to the skating world the formation and mission of the World Skating Federation. Barbara Silby, the WSF coordinator for media relations, had packed the place. CNN and ABC had sent camera and lighting crews. Nearly every print journalist attending the Washington, D.C. World Championships was there. The room was packed with interested well-wishers, supporters, and reporters, and nearly every person was wearing a white-and-blue WSF button.

The cameras were directed at the podium where Paul spoke. He was centered on the dais, surrounded by supporters, including:

Dick Button, "Mr. Figure Skating" as he is known throughout the world. Dick is an ABC commentator, businessperson, Harvard graduate, and, most importantly, a repeat World and Olympic Men's Champion.

John Nicks, the British Champion-cum-successful American coach, best known for his straight talk and quick wit—as well as his star pupils, Tai Babilonia and Randy Gardner, Jenny Meno and Todd Sand, and Sasha Cohen.

Scott Hamilton, U.S. National Champion, World and Olympic Champion, cancer survivor, loved by both figure skating fans and the public alike, was also in attendance.

In addition, there was Kathy Casey, the former coach of numerous World and Olympic competitors, now the most well-known skating seminar producer.

The usual suspects from figure-skating officialdom were present, including: Ron Pfenning, Sally Stapleford, Britta Lindgren, Judith Furst-Tomber, the brave and lone former eastern-bloc member of the WSF,

Sonia Bianchetti, the former ISU Technical Committee chair replaced years before so her fellow Italian Ottavio Cinquanta could ascend to his throne, and Don McKnight, the contrarian from Australia who, as longtime president of the Australian federation, was never at a loss to express misgivings about the ISU and its plans.

Appearing via videotape supporting the organization were Todd Eldredge, US National and World Champion, Katarina Witt, German Champion, World Champion and repeat Olympic Champion, and the now-famous Jamie Sale and David Pelletier. Paul Wylie did a top-notch job of arranging in advance to get their comments on videotape, and then worked with Howard Silby to create a short but compelling video containing their wishes of good will to the WSF.

Sending letters of support were: Brian Boitano, U.S. National and Olympic Champion; Kristi Yamaguchi, U.S. National and Olympic Champion; John Misha Petkovich, successful financier and U.S. National and World Champion; and Ted Clarke, first vice-president of the United States Figure Skating Association.

Overall, an impressive group sharing one impressive goal: to replace the ISU with an athlete-dominated organization and to clean up, and ultimately save, the sport of figure-skating.

The press went almost maniacal over the situation, the fans were filled with joy and hope, and the athletes, privately anyway, were emphatic in their support.

The only people we failed to impress that day were Ottavio Cinquanta and his merry band of thieves, suck-ups, and chimps, thick in their arrogance and control of the sport, including those in control of the Canadian and U.S. Associations, Marilyn Chidwell and Phyllis Howard.

We had kicked a hornet's nest, and, in the end, we ourselves would wind up stung. But in that moment, we had taken a courageous and momentous step. We were doing what we believed was the right thing for the sport, for the athletes, for the fans—despite the consequences. We had demanded a place at the table, but those tables would soon be turned.

The first fallout came later in the afternoon. While U.S. Figure Skating had endorsed our principles earlier in the day, they released a statement making it appear as though they had not. When Ron and I attempted to clarify the situation, and asked that the earlier endorsement and vote of the Executive Committee be released to the press, we got nowhere. Phyllis was intent on hiding the actions of the Executive Committee until the press had gone home. She succeeded in casting confusion over the matter, hiding her own vote (which was, as usual, a clear conflict, even U.S. Figure Skating Secretary Sharon Watson agreeing on that point), and denying the press the truth: that U.S. Figure Skating had endorsed the principles of the WSF, just as I had announced in the press conference.

The next day, IOC president Jacques Rogge publicly refused the WSF's request to meet with him. In my mind, what could be characterized as a "calling in of a chit" by Cinquanta from his fellow IOC Executive Committee member, we were denied any opportunity even to present our alternative position to the supposedly unbiased International Olympic Committee. For so long, many have believed that the IOC president, Jacques Rogge, was a progressive leader and on the athlete's side. We were instead reminded of the widespread corruption within the IOC itself. Was it going on here too? The only thing possibly worse than Cinquanta's coverup was Rogge's turning of his head.

Judith Furst-Tomber was the first to experience the consequences of supporting our cause. She was removed from judging her event at Worlds. The Hungarian federation president did the dirty deed, though it was obvious that Cinquanta had put him up to it. It was unjustified and unnecessary, and Judith would never judge again.

Later in the week, the nominating committee for U.S. Figure Skating handed Phyllis Howard a defeat in her reelection attempt, unable to stomach the conflict of interest she had created by trying to serve her ISU master while simultaneously steering U.S. Figure Skating. I leaked the information to the press. I say "leaked," because the nominating committee is supposed to do its work in secrecy. Somehow, the nominating committee must act democratically while conducting its work in secret. How can it accomplish any democratic semblance while remaining shrouded in secrecy? It doesn't, on either account. Its not democratic, even remotely so, and there are no secrets in figure-skating. I wasn't on the nominating committee, so I was not bound by any oath of confidentiality.

I learned of Phyllis's defeat from someone who also wasn't on the nominating committee. I confirmed it with Ron Hershberger, who was on the committee. I congratulated him on his now being in the running. He confirmed that Phyllis was out. The committee had deadlocked between him and Chuck Foster. With the confirmation in hand, I went to the press, specifically a reporter who had been asking me about my chances of replacing Phyllis. Up until that time, I had been in the running for president. With Phyllis out, I no longer saw a need to run, though I had previously considered and publicly expressed a desire to run from the floor of the Governing Council against the nominating committee slate.

The publishing of Phyllis's defeat, together with the Christine Brennan column that sarcastically characterized Phyllis as the president of the figure-skating club of Guam, sent Phyllis and her supporters over the edge, wrongly concluding that this was a personal attack on them. It wasn't. It was an attack against their policies and their political ambitions.

Thursday evening, the Executive Committee met in secret without Ted Clarke. They discussed possible disciplinary actions against him for his involvement with the WSF. For some reason, they didn't appear concerned about Ron Hershberger's involvement with the WSF.

The next morning, Ted Clarke learned of the illegal meeting, and another one, this time one that he was invited to. He appeared, with an attorney accompanying him. After the meetings, Ron Hershberger approached Mary Clarke, Ted's wife, while I was standing with her. He assured us that he knew that no one had done anything unethical by participating in the creation of the WSF, and he was not about to allow anyone's ethics to be questioned. He never made good on his promises.

U.S. Figure Skating soon began a disciplinary process against Ted Clarke, and they did it on an expedited basis. The reason for this is because of the Executive Committee's secret meeting. By meeting to discuss Ted's involvement, they now had a conflict which would prevent them from hearing any appeal. Without anyone to hear an appeal, Ted would be denied due process. The solution to this problem was an expedited hearing because the rules do not provide for an appeal from an expedited decision. Therefore, in order to cover their own illegal action, they used a procedural maneuver to avoid it.

Tom James, the U.S. Figure Skating lawyer, represented the hearing panel, another very clear conflict. The hearing panel not surprisingly found wrongdoing, declaring Ted Clarke "ineligible." This meant that he could not judge or officiate until reinstated as "eligible." Drew Patterson, the chair of the hearing panel, tracked down Ted afterward to tell him that the punishment was meant for one day. He could apply for reinstatement immediately, and he did so. But Joan Rozolis, Phyllis Howard, and several of their cronies interfered, inserting the Board of Directors in the process, none of which the rules allowed for. Drew Patterson immediately clammed up; Ted Clarke ultimately received what was a one-year suspension for his role in the WSF. Drew Patterson was promoted to chair of the Ethics Committee, and that just about sums up the ethics or lack thereof that exists in U.S. Figure Skating.

The situation deteriorated, with veritable vendettas being levied against anyone believed to have been involved in the WSF. One of Phyllis's lackeys, Deborah Weidman, had initiated the grievance against Ted Clarke. Deborah would be rewarded for her actions with a plum team leader assignment.

I learned of Ted Clarke's punishment when I attended the Governing Council meeting of U.S. Figure Skating in Virginia. Ron Pfenning and I scheduled a rally-style meeting to present our case for the WSF to the U.S. delegates. The rally was well attended and a huge success. However, we weren't asking the delegates to approve anything, only to get them to understand where we stood against the ISU.

The day before, Phyllis had suspended the Board of Directors meeting to present her own dog-and-pony show against the WSF. Head clown Joan Rozolis led off the circus act with a funhouse mirror distortion of the imaginary ABC television "contract." Bob Horen rallied support for the ISU, and in the center ring was Gale Tanger adding the USOC's perspective.

After the presentation, I got up to speak, passionately explaining that the WSF had nothing to do with U.S. Figure Skating. I was able to calm a few minds, and Phyllis Howard didn't like it one bit. The same circus act, presented to the hundreds of delegates the next day, would not allow for comment afterward. It was to be one-sided. Phyllis wasn't going to give anyone, let alone me, the chance to disagree with her ridiculous and orchestrated positions.

Ron Pfenning and I wanted to get a vote of support for the WSF. But we already had the vote of the Executive Committee. The Governing Council could vote to overturn that, and we were reluctant to draw attention to that. So, instead, with an endorsement already in hand, and with the advice from the hired parliamentarian, we attempted instead to get a vote renouncing the fear and intimidation tactics of U.S. Figure Skating.

Paul Wylie spoke eloquently on the subject, and was shocked when the body condoned the tactics of U.S. Figure Skating by voting against our motion. Fear and intimidation would remain alive and well, as Ron and I would soon learn.

The meeting concluded with Todd Eldredge, former National and World Champion, running for a position on the Executive Committee, the Midwest vice president. Finally, an elite athlete was running for a top spot within U.S. Figure Skating. While the voting was being conducted, Tom James informed him that even though he was living in the Midwest, that as a member of the Los Angeles Figure Skating Club, he was not eligible for the position. If Todd were to win, the election would be invalidated, according to the bylaws.

I learned of the James legal posturing from Drew Patterson, of all people. I quickly grabbed my rulebook, sending Drew to speak to James, pointing out the rule *requires* the vice presidents to run from the Section where they reside, not where their home club is located. One bullet dodged.

Next, Todd was told that if he won, U.S. Figure Skating would bring a grievance against him to remove him from office. Tom James knew, though, from the Ted Clarke grievance, that only the electorate could remove corporate officers under Colorado law. The threat of a grievance was a red herring. Why were they fighting so hard against Todd Eldredge?

Then, in a move any Florida resident could easily understand with their hanging-chad incident, U.S. Figure Skating allegedly threw out some athletes' ballots for being improperly filled out. U.S. Figure

Skating does not exist for its athletes. If that is not clear by now, it never will be. Not surprisingly, Todd lost the vote.

The WSF also lost that week. The only winner that week seemed to be Chuck Foster, the new president. He would soon find out that it wasn't much of a prize.

> *Chinese pair skaters Xue Shen and Hongbo Zhao repeat as World Champions in Washington, D.C. Though a Russian couple finishes second, the dynasty has lost its stronghold.*

Counsel's Concluding Remarks

*A*T THE BEGINNING of the summer, the New York law firm of Milberg, Weiss, Bershad and Schulman began charting a legal recourse by the World Skating Federation against the ISU. Initially, it was the WSF's intention to bring a class-action lawsuit against the ISU, based on the shady shenanigans in Salt Lake City, so we could utilize the discovery process fully in investigating the French–Russian deal and the subsequent ISU coverup. We set our sights on a settlement that would reimburse the consumers who had been defrauded by the ISU's actions, together with a plan to replace the figure-skating portion of the ISU with the new WSF. The ISU could retain its oversight of speed-skating, which was what they should have been doing in the first place. This plan of action met both the goals of the WSF, while at the same time finally allowing for a full investigation of just what went wrong in Salt Lake.

The old saying about the best-laid plans of mice and men often going awry was never truer. When our lead attorney, Ann Lipton, began preparing the complaint, assembling the necessary facts and researching the various laws that were in violation, she came across a new Utah law that had given complete immunity to the IOC and each of its members.

Negligence? Forget it. Utah law protected them. Intentional harm? Forget it again. Consumer fraud? No way, no how, Utah wasn't going to allow it.

In its first quest to secure the bid to host the Olympic Games, the Utah legislature had passed into law a shield for the IOC. The ISU literally got away with murder because of the shortsightedness of a few state senators and representatives, ironically the very group for which I once interned. We were suddenly stuck without grounds for a lawsuit.

Ann Lipton, in her generosity, tried to help us explore where the WSF might turn next. We explained that we had already been blackballed from the ISU, U.S. Figure Skating, and Skate Canada, and so were our supporters. We were still trying to put on a professional event to raise more money, but no one would take our calls. People in the skating industry feared doing business with us, afraid of retribution, and rightly so, from the ISU and its underlings.

Ann's sharp mind sprung into action. She thought the blackballing sounded a lot like antitrust. As luck would have it, Michael Buckman, a specialist in antitrust law, had recently joined the firm where she worked. She said she would run the facts past Michael and Mel Weiss, and get back to me. When she did, the news was encouraging, and she began preparing an antitrust lawsuit against the ISU.

The ISU provided us with all sorts of great incriminating facts and incidents while marshalling its own forces in an attempt to put the WSF out of business. Earlier that spring, they had sent form letters to each WSFer threatening to throw us out of the organization. Morry Stillwell, a former president of U.S. Figure Skating and a sustained Russian ally, jumped in, alleviating the need for the ISU to come after Ron Pfenning and me, by filing a grievance with U.S. Figure Skating against us. The ISU did not execute the actions it initially threatened against us back in June 2003 until March 2005, and remained curiously silent during the eighteen months that Stillwell and the leadership of U.S. Figure Skating were coming after us.

The grievances were dragged out because U.S. Figure Skating refused to follow its own rules and bylaws. The Stillwell grievance was filed with the chair of the Grievance Committee, Ms. Ann O'Keefe, a woman sporting a Dorothy Hamill-length mullet, a real fireplug of a woman.

O'Keefe forwarded it to the chair of the Ethics Committee. Ms. Patricia (Pat) St. Peter, a diminutive gal with her own version of Dorothy's bob. I always thought she looked a lot like Velma Dinkley from *Scooby-Doo*. Zoinks! She notified Ron and me of the grievances, and then pinched Daphne on the ass and ate a Scooby snack.

Never once did this halfwit court-of-fools ever ask themselves the most obvious of questions before moving forward on Stillwell's grievance, such as: What exactly, if anything, did the WSF's actions have to do with Morry Stillwell in the first place? How was he personally aggrieved by our actions? I raised these legitimate questions to Ms. O'Keefe, pointing out that U.S. Figure Skating bylaws *require* an allegation of harm, something Morry had failed to claim in his grievance, and, for that matter, could not claim. We would find out over the next eighteen months, and as others have found out during her rule, that Ann O'Keefe doesn't pay much attention to rules or bylaws.

Unfortunately, neither does Pat St. Peter. When O'Keefe forwarded the grievances to St. Peter (even though it had not been proper to do so), it was then St. Peter's obligation under U.S. Figure Skating rules to notify us with a separate grievance statement under her signature. This she simply refused to do. O'Keefe stepped in and forced her to do it. When she did so, she laid out a bold lie, under penalty of perjury.

St. Peter stated that I had retracted a statement I had made at the WSF press conference. I had informed the press assembled that U.S. Figure Skating had endorsed the principles of the WSF. This statement was true. Pat claimed that I had lied at the press conference (not true) and then later retracted that statement (not true again). She did not make her bold lie as an "allegation," like some of the other statements she made, couching them in the legal catch-phrase of "based on information and belief," but rather made her lie outright. By career, Pat is herself an attorney, and ought to know better than to lie under oath. So why did she do it? A year later, she became an ISU official, now serving on the ISU Disciplinary Commission! I'll let that speak for itself.

This of course begs the point that Morry Stillwell still had no right to bring the action in the first place. I knew by this time that similar procedures had been ignored in a grievance against Ted Clarke. Deborah Weidman, another loyal crony and front-woman of Phyllis Howard, filed that action. The WSF, Ted Clarke, and their respective actions, had nothing to do with Weidman, but that didn't stop U.S. Figure Skating, Ms. O'Keefe, and St. Peter from proceeding against Ted, and it was not going to stop them from proceeding against us. But why would Weidman do it?

Weidman was rewarded with a team leader assignment, and I had the proof on this one, so I filed my own grievance against Phyllis Howard and Deborah Weidman. I was merely trying to point out how ludicrous it was to allow Weidman to bring a case against Clarke, and Stillwell the case against Ron and me, by bringing a grievance that did not relate at all to him. In the end, as the facts played out, it turned out to be a very legitimate grievance, and U.S. Figure Skating could not move to dismiss it fast enough.

As chair of the International Committee, I also sat on the Selections Committee, charged with choosing the team leaders for the upcoming events. I knew that, prior to the Ted Clarke grievance, Weidman had never been considered for a team-leading spot. I had saved the prior drafts of the assignments, and I could prove it. Weidman's name appeared only in the final document, and was mysteriously put in at the last minute.

I sent the grievance to Ann O'Keefe, together with the evidence. A few weeks later, she sent me a letter telling me that she had brought it to the attention of Lucy "I can't recall a goddamn thing about the Pair Event at the Olympics" Brennan, the current chair of the Selections Committee. She said that Lucy told her the team-leader spot was very difficult to fill because of the Regional Championships being held that week, and that Weidman was a last minute fill-in, put in essentially out of necessity.

Well, the rules don't allow O'Keefe to investigate the matter. The bylaws require her to review a grievance for completeness only (making sure it contains an allegation of harm, for example) and then they require her to forward it on to Ms. St. Peter. Only the hearing panel has the power to make the investigation.

Before pointing out another bylaw violation to O'Keefe, I did my own investigation. First, I determined that the so-called difficulty in making this particular selection because of Regionals was a complete ruse. There were two Regionals being held that week, compared to five Regionals held during a week when there was apparently no difficulty assigning a team leader. Next, I contacted by E-mail each of the three "tentative" team leaders who had once held the spot given to Weidman. Had Lucy contacted them to see what their availability was for that week? Were they available? All three E-mailed me back stating that Lucy had not contacted them, and yes, two of them were still available.

I wrote again to Ms. O'Keefe, outlining what I had learned, demanding that she immediately forward the grievance to St. Peter. Finally, she did. St. Peter dismissed it on the same day she received it from O'Keefe. It was a coordinated effort to insulate Phyllis Howard, Deborah Weidman, and Lucy Brennan.

It was starting to become very clear that we weren't ever going to get a fair shake from the bubble, bubble, toil and trouble antics of U.S. Figure Skating. The Witches of Eastwick would see to that! Ron and I called on a higher power, our dear friend and lawyer Ben Kaplan, who immediately went to work defending us. He was understandably outraged over the complete failure of U.S. Figure Skating to follow its own rules and bylaws—rules that obviously meant nothing to the hard-hearted fiends and the knights of black magic in charge.

In the meantime, Ted Clarke, having once been assured by Drew Patterson that his sanction was only to last for one day, immediately applied for reinstatement. U.S. Figure Skating refused to grant his request. Instead, they put it before the Board of Directors for a decision. Do the bylaws allow for the Board of Directors to get involved in the disciplinary process? No. Did Drew Patterson speak out on Ted's behalf, letting them know that the hearing panel intended for the sanction to last only one day? No, of course not.

The Board then voted to make Ted Clarke ineligible for one year, with his replacement as vice president, Joan Rozolis, arguing for an even longer sanction. It wasn't enough that she got his job; she wanted to be sure he would not get it back. What more could this woman want? Stay tuned. . . .

During the procedural battle that ensued between our attorney, Ben Kaplan, and U.S. Figure Skating, O'Keefe requested an extension of the time for her to process the various grievances from the chairs of the hearing panels. This extension was granted by the chair of Ron's grievance, but was not granted by the chair of my grievance, David Hamula. Kaplan demanded an immediate dismissal, whereupon O'Keefe told him that Hamula did in fact grant the extension and that I must have somehow missed being notified. When Kaplan demanded proof, she of course couldn't produce it. Hamula simply failed to grant the extension on a timely basis.

To cover up this failure, O'Keefe simply removed Hamula as the chair of my hearing panel. She used the guise that Kaplan had improperly contacted him with a procedural matter (something the bylaws required him to do). In response to a request by Ms. St. Peter to dismiss Hamula and the chair of Ron's panel, she granted their removal and allowed no opportunity for Kaplan to respond to Ms. St. Peter's request, wherein he would have pointed out that the bylaws required him to do exactly what Ms. St. Peter was complaining about.

At about this same time, WSF attorney Ann Lipton had completed the preparation for the lawsuit against the ISU, based on antitrust. We were advised to file the lawsuit in New York, assured that the ISU contacts with ABC, mainly the payments they received from them, amounted to substantial contacts in the State of New York that would give the New York courts jurisdiction. Besides, it was a convenient place for our lawyers to oversee the lawsuit. The ISU and Cinquanta were named in the lawsuit, and it included allegations that Cinquanta had profited from the ABC contracts through kickbacks without disclosing such compensation.

Cinquanta is a trained bookkeeper. He comes from a modest Italian family. Yet, since the time he took over as the ISU chief, he has purchased at least one flat in Milan and a beachside villa worth millions of dollars. No longer employed, and serving in a volunteer position, where exactly is he getting all his money? That was one question we hoped would be answered and one that Cinquanta was anxious to avoid.

To initiate the lawsuit, it was necessary that Cinquanta be served papers on U.S. soil. He was going to be attending the Grand Prix final in Colorado Springs, so the process server tracked him down there. He was staying at Colorado Springs' five-star Broadmoor Hotel and Resort, with all the skaters and coaches. Oops! Strike that. The skaters and coaches were all at the budget Doubletree Inn.

One afternoon, just before Cinquanta plunked down into his chauffeured limousine (no doubt to visit the skaters on the other side of the tracks), the process server handed him the papers. He closed the door, and then threw the papers out the window of the limousine, littering the sidewalk with debris and then proceeded to have his driver speed off. He must have thought better of it, because they then backed up, and Cinquanta got out and picked up the papers himself, and then sped off to gab with his gofers.

Meanwhile, O'Keefe and St. Peter were busily trying to find party-line replacements for their hand-picked, but now fired, hearing-panel chairs. In this turmoil, two-sided Tom James, who up until this time insisted he could represent both U.S. Figure Skating and the hearing panels, was also removed. He had already been representing both, so he was finally replaced (at least for our purposes) by the equally objectionable Ed Williams, a sports attorney who originally made his name defending athletes, but was now profiting from the wealthy federations who had acted against them.

Williams decided to bring in an independent party to chair each hearing panel, which I admit was a very good move, and one that we welcomed. Ron and I knew all too well how figure-skating insiders give and receive—and, more importantly, come to accept—"facts," even when untrue. Though we were disappointed that O'Keefe had fired the two impartial previous chairs, we were pleased that two outsiders would now hear the matter. One independent on Ron's panel, one independent on my panel.

In the meantime, the ISU continued to sit on its hands in the action it had initiated against us. Why bother to throw us out when U.S. Figure Skating was carrying out its dirty work?

U.S. Figure Skating then went on to name a couple of independent individuals with experience in Olympic sport arbitration to our panels. We asked U.S. Figure Skating to provide information on any potential conflicts that might exist that would prevent the independent panelists from serving. U.S. Figure Skating refused, telling us only that we could be assured that there was no conflict. Knowing we could never trust a single word any of those amulet-rubbing coven mates uttered, and having fallen victim to their boldfaced lies in the past, we jumped onto the Internet and start making phone calls ourselves.

What we turned up was staggering. The "independents" had numerous conflicts, none of them disclosed to us. Between the two of them, one had served side by side on committees with Phyllis Howard's husband; one had served on committees with Tom James, and was the husband of one of Tom James's clients; one was the CEO of a corporation that Tom James served as a member of the board, and had also been a previous client of Williams. All the while, U.S. Figure Skating assured us that there was no conflict of interest! Pinocchio, you'll never be a real boy!

The stacked deck was changed once again; O'Keefe removed the conflicted hearing panelists, but only after our attorney raised hell about it. U.S. Figure Skating then named James Holbrook and Laura McPherson to serve as the chairs of our hearing panels. Again, we were assured by U.S. Figure Skating that there were no conflicts of interest. We were provided nothing to tell us otherwise, so we went back to the Internet and the phones. Holbrook was easy to track down. A simple Google search and we discovered that he was a well-respected sports mediator out of Salt Lake City who served on the faculty of the University of Utah Law School. One phone call to my friend and former professor, Terry Kogan, who had hosted the Olympic party at his home, put to rest any concerns about him.

McPherson's background was more difficult to check out. In the process of gathering information about her, I spoke to John Ruger, the USOC athlete ombudsman. When he learned what was going on, he asked, "Why don't you ask for independent arbitration by the USOC?" Up until then, I didn't know that we had that option. Ruger explained to me that the USOC and its constitution protected officials the same way they protect the athletes. We had the right to ask the American Arbitration Association (AAA) to intervene and give us an independent arbitration.

Ron and I wrote to the USOC, asking for their assistance, while simultaneously filing a request for arbitration with the AAA. We notified U.S. Figure Skating; they informed us that they were going to proceed with their own hearings, with or without us, notwithstanding the AAA action or our rights under the USOC and its constitution. Absolutely unbelievable!

We realized that we needed yet another attorney, and brought in Jimmy Nguyen, a partner with Foley and Lardner's Los Angeles office, who came aboard on a *pro bono* basis. Jimmy was heaven-sent, as Ron and I had already collectively spent over $35,000 on legal fees and costs fending off U.S. Figure Skating's witch-hunt. By the time it was all over, even with Jimmy's free legal services, we wound up spending over $50,000.

Jimmy asked the AAA to intervene on an emergency basis; they did so, holding an expedited telephone hearing. While the arbitrator agreed that we had a right to arbitrate, he found that he did not have the power to stop U.S. Figure Skating from going ahead. John Ruger in his tenure as ombudsman for the USOC had never seen a single instance where a federation ignored the USOC rights of its athletes, coaches, and officials, choosing instead to forge a hearing. Then again, Ruger had never met likes of the meddling O'Keefe and St. Peter.

Ron and I were faced with a difficult choice. We could simply not attend the U.S. Figure Skating hearing, take the heat of an adverse judgment while waiting out the AAA arbitration to clear our name. On the other hand, we could roll the dice, and then, if we lost at U.S. Figure Skating, move on to the fair tribunal of the AAA. In the end, Jimmy orchestrated a brilliant legal maneuver, persuading U.S. Figure Skating to combine Ron's hearing panel with mine, with the two independent chairs serving with one athlete on the new hearing panel.

This meant that instead of having two separate hearings, each before two skating insiders and one independent, Ron and I would have one hearing together before two independents and one skating insider. Best of all, the skating insider would be an athlete.

The athlete chosen was Ryan Jahnke. This put Ron and me in another difficult position. I knew that Sandra Loosemore, one of the WSF supporters, had given financial support to Ryan and a number of other skaters. While neither Ron nor I, or Sandra for that matter, saw any potential conflict, and despite the fact that U.S. Figure Skating never once disclosed a single conflict on the part of their patsies, Jimmy sent O'Keefe a note notifying her of the "potential" for conflict.

Keep in mind that Ryan had received a great deal of financial support from U.S. Figure Skating as well. In fact, every athlete that could have been named to the panel had received funds from them at one time or another. So this "potential" conflict was actually more sided toward U.S. Figure Skating than with Ron or me. Additionally, it was not the WSF, Ron, or me that had given Ryan the money; there was little "potential" for conflict. When U.S. Figure Skating contacted Ryan, he confirmed that he could be completely objective about the hearing.

So, on one hand, we have undisclosed, direct financial support from U.S. Figure Skating to Ryan, and on the other, we have not even indirect, yet disclosed financial support from a WSF supporter. O'Keefe and St. Peter chose to select an athlete that had only received money from their side. Ryan was out, and a new athlete was brought in. Typical buffoonery with legal routines more suited to Larry, Curly, and Moe.

Speaking of conflicts of interest, around this same time, St. Peter became a member of the ISU Disciplinary Commission. I began referring to St. Peter as ISU Pat. Remember Drew Patterson, the chair of the Ted Clarke hearing panel? He became the new chair of the Ethics committee. Patterson my back, I'll Pat St. Peter yours!

The hearing was scheduled to take place in Salem. Oops, I mean Colorado Springs. Ron, Jimmy, and I chose to stay at the Doubletree Inn. The hearing would be held at the Sheraton, where U.S. Figure Skating had already installed a gasoline-soaked wooden stake.

We arrived to find the recently anointed ISU Disciplinary Commission member, Pat St. Peter, lips licked and ready to "act" as prosecutor for U.S. Figure Skating. Now, one would think that the conflict of interest would be obvious even to a rotting skull. Ron and I had allegedly acted against the ISU. Yet it was U.S. Figure Skating punishing us for it, and the top lead on the case is a card-carrying ISU member. Drew Patterson was there too. Not as a witness, not as a party-liner, just there. Oh, he did try to help out ISU Pat near the end of the hearing, when she was so clearly going down in flames, but his purpose at the hearing was otherwise unnecessary. Except I guess for some extra frequent flier miles he scored out to Colorado from Detroit!

The hearing began with an argument posed by ISU Pat over whether or not the transcript of the hearing would be confidential. The U.S. Figure Skating rule reads:

"Confidentiality concerning the subject of a grievance is to be maintained by all parties until the grievance process has been completed."

It's a very simple rule, so I'm not sure why the hearing started with an argument over the hearing transcript. It's true; Ted Clarke had been denied his. The USOC's due process rights (written by Ed Williams, the U.S. Figure Skating attorney and the attorney present to represent the hearing panel—again, no conflict!) require that a hearing be recorded and that the athlete or official be given a copy of the transcript. We knew in advance of ISU Pat's preposterous position, so we were prepared to bring in our own court reporter. That's a lot of P's!

We thought the matter was resolved, but here was ISU Pat making her argument that the hearing needed to be held in the "strictest of secrecy." She argued it at the beginning of the hearing. Hearing panel chair McPherson ruled against her. ISU Pat argued it again after losing. McPherson ruled against her again. ISU Pat argued it yet a third time at the conclusion of the hearing. She lost again. Why do the ISU and U.S. Figure Skating not want anyone to see the hearing transcript? Since when has anything in figure skating ever been done in secrecy? Who does she think she is, Secret Squirrel? The answer can be gleaned by reading the transcript in its entirety, now widely available on the Web and at www.worldskating.org.

The first witness up for U.S. Figure Skating was Joan Rozolis. Her clenched jaw did little to soften her pointed face as she answered as politely as she could each of the softball questions lobbed her way by ISU Pat.

When our lawyer, Jimmy Nguyen, took his turn on cross-examination, the hearing really became interesting. Joan simply could not hide her bitterness for not having been told of the WSF's formation in advance. As one of the only three untrusted odd-members-out on the Executive Committee, Our Lady of Intense Suffering clearly considered herself a victim of our alleged crimes.

Oh, and just what were the crimes Ron and I had committed, Jimmy asked? Joan was, for once in her life, speechless. What rules were violated? She couldn't point to even one. By the way, how much had this discipline cost U.S. Figure Skating? She had a neatly packaged answer for that. According to Joan, it was well "over $200,000" (money better spent on the athletes, I might add). Yet, instead of being embarrassed, she was proud of her testimony. She thought of course that the world would never see how ridiculous her answers were because she had no idea that ISU Pat had already lost her foolish argument on confidentiality.

However, the biggest smile on my face came when Jimmy asked Joan whether she would have told Phyllis Howard if she had been told in advance about the WSF. Joan's response: "Is this going to [my being a] the puppet of Phyllis Howard?"

"Never mind. Let's take that off the record." Too late Joan.

Puppet? That's not the word I was thinking of. Oh, never mind.

Next up for U.S. Figure Skating cavalcade was its secretary, Sharon Watson. I had told Sharon in advance of the WSF formation, but she claimed to resent the fact that she couldn't talk to Joan, Phyllis Howard, or Will Smith about it. Of course, she was free to speak to the other four members of the Executive Committee, and one of them, Ron Hershberger, was free to speak to Joan, Phyllis, and Will, if he concluded that there had been a conflict, but he didn't. There simply was no conflict. Did Sharon speak to any of the other executive committee members about the WSF? No. So why was she so upset that she couldn't speak to Phyllis, Joan, and Will about it? Because there's nothing more worthless than a secret you can't blab.

Sharon's most revealing testimony came when she discussed my attendance at the National Championships in Atlanta. The rumor in Atlanta, and still believed to this day as fact by some, was that I was sharing a room with my friend, former World Team member and International judge Doug Williams. According to Sharon, she warned him privately that people were upset that he was allowing me to share his room. Doug was also a member of the Executive Committee, so his room was paid for by U.S. Figure Skating. Apparently, the insiders and the ISU didn't appreciate my being in Atlanta with Doug allowing me to share a room paid for by U.S. Figure Skating.

She had been misinformed; Doug provided with her the truth. He was not sharing a room with me. In fact, I had my own room, and it was being paid for by U.S. Figure Skating. As past chair of the International Committee, I was required to be there. Had I shared a room with Doug, it would have saved them money! Of course, U.S. Figure Skating could have checked their own records to see that I had my own room, and that they were paying for it. Instead, they attacked me and my friends without the facts, something they were now getting good at. U.S. Figure Skating has some of the most dysfunctional, unqualified people running a multi-million-dollar operation anywhere. As Sharon's testimony continued, it became obvious the keystone kops were much more calculating than one might think. According to Sharon, in Atlanta people were watching me with binoculars to see whom I was sitting with and talking to.

"Oh, my god, now he's talking to so-and-so, and now he's talking to so-and-so" were her exact words in reenacting what took place by U.S. Figure Skating's binoculared spies. Her next quote could summarize this entire book: in fact, check the back cover, I might have used it as an endorsement:

"Skating is a very incestuous, internal inbred world. Everybody talks to everybody. There's gossip galore," she testified, on behalf of U.S. Figure Skating. I have to thank O'Keefe and ISU Pat for inviting that witness!

John LeFevre was the next witness. We had called him to testify. The USOC rules of due process require that the federation produce any witness under their control. So we took advantage of that, requesting that U.S. Figure Skating produce LeFevre, its executive director; Carol Brown, his secretary; Phyllis Howard, its past president and Executive Committee member; Gale Tanger, its vice president; and Claire Ferguson, also a past president.

U.S. Figure Skating refused to produce Carol Brown and Gale Tanger. Carol Brown actually lives in Colorado Springs! Why would U.S. Figure Skating refuse to produce her? Another rumor that went around for many years was that when U.S. Figure Skating "bought" votes to elect Claire Ferguson to the ISU Council, allegedly it was Carol Brown who delivered the cash to the various delegates. We intended to find out whether or not this long-standing rumor was true, and just how much money U.S. Figure Skating had spent to get Ferguson elected.

If that were true, it would also explain why U.S. Figure Skating failed to produce Claire Ferguson as a witness. Arguably, Ferguson was no longer "under the control" of U.S. Figure Skating, as she was a past officer, not a present one. We asked U.S. Figure Skating to produce her anyway, and also sent Ferguson a letter requesting her voluntary attendance. She was a no-show.

Gale Tanger, the Midwest vice president of U.S. Figure Skating, was, however, under the control of U.S. Figure Skating. Like Carol Brown, U.S. Figure Skating was obliged to produce her. We were told that she had a family outing that prevented her attendance. Keep in mind that Ms. Tanger, just like all the other judges, misses family outings and other important obligations all the time for figure-skating. Besides, the hearing was scheduled on a date selected by U.S. Figure Skating. If it were important enough to spend over $200,000 on this hearing, wouldn't it be important enough for Gale Tanger to attend?

Gale was well aware, early on, about the formation of the WSF, yet never once warned either Ron or me that we were acting unethically in forming the WSF, nor did she ever let anyone on the Executive Committee know about our plans, even though she was not bound by any confidentiality agreement. If these facts were to come out, if she were forced to answer difficult questions under oath, or if she were to embarrass herself in the same way the other witnesses had, her future aspirations might quickly fall into jeopardy.

John LeFevre's testimony was significant. He confirmed the statements he had made at the country club judges' dinner regarding the deals made to get Phyllis Howard elected. He also confirmed my meeting with Phyllis and himself in Salt Lake where I asked them to challenge the result of Kyoko Ina and John Zimmerman, as well as their subsequent meeting with the athletes and the team leader.

Jimmy asked him, "So Phyllis decided no challenge should be made?"

LeFevre answered, "Yeah."

He also confirmed that Phyllis had nixed the deal with ABC to turn the U.S. skating events into a series of events because "the International Skating Union would not have been in favor of our developing a series that conflicted with the Grand Prix series."

When ISU Pat got her turn to ask John a few questions, she focused in on an article Christine Brennan wrote: "Do you remember [Brennan] referring to Phyllis, characterizing her as being unable to be the president of the Figure Skating in Guam?" She asked with a poker face despite herself. So this is what this grievance was all about, 200 thousand dollars later? Because Phyllis got her feelings hurt by Christine Brennan, her U.S. Figure Skating administration comes after Ron and me?

Of course, they weren't counting on a court reporter to confirm every detail of U.S. Figure Skating's misbehavior from its highest-level officers and directors. What were Anne O'Keefe and ISU Pat thinking? Vindictiveness can be so clouding, they must not have been thinking at all.

Next up for testimony was Morry Stillwell, who "appeared" via telephone. As part of his testimony, Morry claimed that before the date of the hearing, he was not aware that Ron and I had ever spoken to the FBI. He also claimed that he had suffered harm because his figure-skating association was discredited. Then after giving a lengthy legal analysis of why a member of U.S. Figure Skating cannot act against the ISU, including rules, bylaws, and complex ethical issues, he refused to discuss the alleged deal he and Phyllis had made to put him back onto the Executive Committee as a past president, stating "I do not have a legal background. I'm only an engineer." He went on to testify that the discussion of this subject was a "dead end," and didn't answer the question. Clearly, he did not want the details of his deal with Phyllis investigated.

Jimmy subsequently asked, "And you are aware that the World Skating Federation is a coalition of people from other countries as well, right?"

Stillwell misled with, "I am not aware of that."

Morry wanted this committee to believe that when he filed this grievance his sole reason for doing so was Ron's and my involvement in the WSF, and that he knew nothing more than that the two of us were involved. His only knowledge of the WSF was "only what I read through the pronouncements of the two gentlemen in question." H'mmm. Nearly every pronouncement we ever made was alongside numerous International individuals involved with the WSF. "I do not know who else is involved," he stated emphatically.

How could Morry Stillwell read the so-called WSF pronouncements without noticing any statements made by others? How could he look at the "public pronouncements in the paper" and at the WSF Web site, and find only the quotes attributed to Ron and me and not read the text which would refer to others and to the WSF's international makeup, while he was generating his grievance? Morry wanted this hearing panel to believe that he was hearing for the first time that the WSF involved others besides Ron and me. This was unmitigated audacity at its finest.

Ron Pfenning began his testimony, and was shortly interrupted. Phyllis Howard joined us from Ireland by telephone for her testimony. I'm not exactly sure what she was doing in Ireland, outside of stepping on leprechauns and pressing her lips against the Blarney Stone.

So, let's recap. So far, Morry Stillwell broke away long enough to join us from a turnip truck in California. Phyllis Howard joined us by international technology over a bowl of Lucky Charms in Ireland—yet Carol Brown, who lives right there in Colorado Springs, could not be produced. Not to mention that Gale Tanger and Claire Ferguson were nowhere to be found. No phones in Wisconsin, I suppose, nor Who-ville for that matter.

During ISU Pat's "examination" of Phyllis, it was clear that ISU Pat was starting to go down in flames. "I lost my train of thought," she even said at one point. Clearly unable to get herself back together, Drew Patterson leaned over and whispered something in her ear. It didn't seem to me that she had fully recovered, but what followed was a series of softball questions designed to give Phyllis the opportunity to rave about all the things she and the ISU had done following the Salt Lake Olympic scandal to better the sport.

The "sweeping changes," as Phyllis described them, included "another layer of governance," the "council has given up some power, and even the president has given up a little power." She said, "And of course there is a new disciplinary commission." Yeah, Phyllis, we know about that, with ISU Pat as a card-carrying member.

New layers of governance and new committees! Wow, Phyllis and her ilk are quite the revolutionaries!

However, what did she say in response to Jimmy's questions regarding any rules and bylaws that she believed Ron and I had broken?

"I'm not going to go there because I don't have anything. I have not investigated that," she said.

Okay, let's recap again. Phyllis sits on the ISU Council, who at that time had sent letters threatening to take away our eligibility; but she didn't have anything, she didn't investigate that? She sits on the Executive Committee of U.S. Figure Skating, which, according to Joan Rozolis, was spending over $200,000 to throw us out, and she didn't have anything, she didn't investigate that? *She didn't have anything. She didn't investigate that.*

James Holbrook, one of the hearing panelists, joined in on the questioning of Phyllis, possibly showing concern over how Phyllis, acting as president, voted to endorse the principles of the WSF, then withheld this vote from the press and public and issued a public statement confusing the U.S. position.

"Procedures" had to be followed, according to Phyllis, procedures which apparently allowed for the release of some votes immediately to the press, but not others. Certainly, it made a difference that Phyllis as an ISU member released only the vote favorable to the ISU, and not the one unfavorable. The hearing panelists listened very closely.

ISU Pat then concluded her remarks with one simple question. "Do you and Ottavio Cinquanta always agree on everything?" To which Phyllis replied, "Absolutely not!" Wow, it's a good thing she got that one in!

The hearing concluded with my testimony, and it was a relief finally to get the whole story off my shoulders.

At the end of the hearing, we took stock in our position as the hearing panelists filed out of the room to have a private meeting. I had one of those "For everything else, there's MasterCard" moments.

Amount paid by Morry Stillwell to file the Stillwell Grievance? $ 0.00.

Cost of the legal fees and expenses incurred by Ron and me to defend ourselves? Over $50,000.

Amount wasted by U.S. Figure Skating just to screw us, when they could have been screwing the athletes? Over $200,000.

Value of seeing the haggard, worn-out, and dejected looks on the aging faces of O'Keefe and her two Pats (ISU Pat and Drew "Pat"terson) after the hearing? Priceless!

For everything else, there's Karma.

The hearing panel decision would not come to us until a month or so later. When it did, it was a complete vindication. The matter was behind us. We had won! The hearing panel, in its ruling, required us to keep the transcript confidential until all appeals were exhausted. Given the bloodshed loss, and the over $200,000 already wasted, surely no appeal would be coming. Besides, any appeal would go to the U.S. Figure Skating Executive Committee. How could they appeal to themselves?

Interestingly, soon after the release of the decision (which, keep in mind, was supposedly confidential at that point), the dormant ISU, who had been sitting on their threats to sanction us, sent us a letter letting us know that they would now be holding a hearing to revoke our ISU eligibility.

Therefore, the ISU, spent very little, while U.S. Figure Skating spent hundreds of thousands of dollars to do the ISU's dirty work; then, when that was unsuccessful, the ISU sprung back into action, determined to take us down by hook or crook.

Just how did the ISU learn of U.S. Figure Skating's loss? Was it ISU Pat or ISU Phyllis who broke that confidential order of the hearing panel? There's no way of knowing for sure, but that's why they call it a conflict of interest, Pat & Phyllis.

After thirty days and then some, I called Jimmy and received his permission to post the transcript on the World Skating Federation Web site. And because of that, all hell broke loose. Anne O'Keefe called Jimmy, and she was furious. U.S. Figure Skating had appealed. O'Keefe dropped the ball again by failing to notify us of that, no surprise there, but she was now blaming Jimmy for breaching the confidentiality. We agreed to take the transcript off the Web site during the appeal, even though it made no sense, as there were no longer any confidences to protect. For, as they say, once the kittens are out of the bag. . . .

The Executive Committee who ruled on the appeal was made up of three members: Tony Morici, treasurer, and the two athlete members. Phyllis Howard could not serve on the panel because of a conflict of interest (finally, a conflict Phyllis could understand), so too Gale Tanger and Ron Hershberger. Chuck Foster also had a conflict of interest because in his election to become president, he had offered Ron and me a deal for positions in his administration if the WSF gave him its endorsement. The WSF declined his offer.

So three members reviewed the transcript, well, they were supposed to review the transcript, and then they made a ruling. They upheld the decision of the hearing panel as it related to Ron, but remanded it back to the hearing panel as it related to me, claiming that the panel had failed to consider fully the conflict of interest statement I had signed.

In the meantime, O'Keefe and Pat #2 (Drew Patterson) were at it again. They filed a grievance against me for violating the rule on confidentiality. By filing for arbitration with the AAA and the USOC earlier in the year, I had attached a copy of the grievance filed against me, and only the grievance. It was necessary for the AAA and the USOC to understand what the arbitration was about. The filing of an AAA request is not confidential, so I shared the filing, and only the filing, with Lois Elfman, a reporter for *International Skating*.

Did Patterson honestly believe that exercising my USOC rights was a violation of the U.S. Figure Skating confidentiality rule? After a few months of battling with them, the USOC intervened to try to mediate the situation. In one of the mediation phone calls, Patterson expressed his belief that the filing with the USOC violated the confidentiality clause in and of itself. Then, in an attempt to prevent the AAA from hearing the matter, putting it solidly back inside the crumbling walls of U.S. Figure Skating, Patterson claimed the only penalty they were seeking was a letter of reprimand. Because my eligibility was not threatened, the AAA no longer had jurisdiction, he argued.

What's with these people? A letter of reprimand?

Here is *my* letter of reprimand: Dear Mr. Patterson, Please send your letter of reprimand ASAP, along with a check for the umpteen thousands you forced me to spend defending myself!

The original hearing panel was not able to hear the remand of the grievance against me right away. Fearful of having to educate an entire new panel, and seeing the anxiousness in O'Keefe's E-mails to find every way possible to let them out of their obligations, we accommodated the hearing panel's every request.

The remand process was quite simple. Each side agreed to brief the issue, rather than hold an in-person hearing. In his brief, Jimmy correctly pointed out that the issue was in fact already resolved, and the remand was merely a ruse by U.S. Figure Skating to get a second chance at me.

The hearing panel's decision was the most thorough I have ever seen in my entire legal career. They dissected the rules and the conflict-of-interest statement, line-by-line, nearly word-by-word, finding no violation on my part on every phrase, paragraph, and sentence. It was if they were sending a clear message: "Mr. Jackson has done nothing wrong! Don't waste any more time appealing this matter."

When Jimmy asked O'Keefe if the matter was resolved, she informed him that they had thirty days to make the decision whether to appeal. Another appeal? When would they give it a rest?

Now, if one were to believe that O'Keefe, her two Pats (St. Peter and Patterson), and their song and dance, together with the whole of the Executive Committee, was an isolated instance directed at two whistle-blowers, Ron and me, one ought to rethink stink.

During this time, I learned that they had also methodically abused the process in grievance filings against a coach, Joey Mero. His crime? His wife had slept with a student. Yep, *his wife!*

Still, they punished him; he "served his time." Done, finished, over. Wrong. After taking his punishment for his wife's crime, the real injustice came next. The student, the one that slept with Joey's wife in the first place, filed another separate grievance against Joey. O'Keefe, ISU Pat, and Patterson had a field day with it; all the while, the Executive Committee looked the other way. Mero's pleas to them were ignored.

Mr. Mero, as you might expect, is now suing U.S. Figure Skating for defamation of character. I have read the complaint he filed. Systematically, in much the same way O'Keefe and the two "Pats" came after Ron and me, they allegedly ignored their own rules, failed to provide due process, and to this day still insist that the entire matter remains confidential, even though the hearings are over, the matter resolved.

Their intentional actions cost Ron and me a great deal of money. It has now cost a coach his reputation. What will it cost an athlete when they turn on one of them?

While I was awaiting word on the remand, Ron and I packed up and traveled with Ben Kaplan to Geneva, Switzerland. The ISU was holding a kangaroo court of its own, since U.S. Figure Skating was unable to find even a koala. The ISU kangaroos gave us only an hour and a half to defend ourselves. The koalas gave us eleven hours. The kangaroos refused to allow us to call a single witness. The koalas conceded a few. The kangaroos refused to allow the hearings to be recorded. What kind of hearing is an unrecorded hearing? The Aussies have a term for it: a setup.

Ron went up first. To my surprise, but not his, every speed-skating member of the ISU council warmly received him. It was clear that they still trusted and respected this honorable man. The many years of working together with them far surpassed the few he had worked against them. I think they actually understood that it wasn't them he was working against. It was the figure-skating members, and Mr. Cinquanta.

When the ISU invited me into the hearing, I used the opportunity to climb aboard my soapbox one last time, detailing every injustice I had witnessed the figure-skating Council members inflict on the sport since the Olympic scandal. The speed-skating members of the sport were all ears. When I was finished, Ben, Ron, and I gathered our things and walked out without answering a single question. Cinquanta told us in advance that we would not be allowed to call witnesses, no examination whatsoever. So, just as Cinquanta specified, we were not going to be witnesses either, no examination allowed. Cinquanta was furious.

I shared my statement with the press. Cinquanta's chimps, and the rest of his U.S. Figure Skating lackeys, were beside themselves in fury. When would I shut up already?

When?

Maybe I will silence the rhetoric when Jacques Rogge and the IOC finally take responsibility for their neglected duties owed to the world of sport by stepping in and cleaning figure skating's house. It's clear that the ISU is not going to do anything, not if it costs them a comfortable lifestyle. Only the IOC can save figure-skating.

After the hearing, I spent a lot of time thinking about simply moving on. Maybe it was time to shut up. Three years of fighting to correct a system and a handful of corrupt, evil witches was enough. I could now walk away from the sport feeling as though I had tried to fix it before abandoning it. I could move on with my life without figure-skating, something I had been looking forward to for at least two years, but I sensed that Ron was not yet ready to leave the sport.

Ron and I discussed dismissing the WSF lawsuit. The ISU had previously offered to hold off reprimanding any WSFer if we did so, and we thought maybe they would still be amenable to such a settlement. Chuck Foster had recently resigned as U.S. Figure Skating president. He couldn't take the personalities any better than we could. Maybe if the WSF dismissed the lawsuit and then dissolved, Ron could run for U.S. Figure Skating president.

I could move on; Ron could stay on.

It was a perfect solution, and I believed I could help deliver votes of the athletes, who had always stood by my side.

Before we could reach any kind of settlement with the ISU, the New York court threw out our lawsuit. It turns out that we had filed in the wrong place. Washington or Denver, the court felt, might be a better place, but we had no jurisdiction in New York. In the dismissal, the judge used some strong language to criticize the WSF attorney's efforts to create a legal argument that would give the New York court jurisdiction, saying that their arguments "bordered on the frivolous." Cinquanta's chimps had a field day with this language, as though it related to the whole of the lawsuit. It didn't. It merely related to filing the complaint in the wrong place.

Michael Buckman called me with the bad news. He also let me know they were ready to refile the claims in Washington or Denver, and wanted to know which jurisdiction we felt the ISU had more ties to. At this point, I was ready to move on, and Ron was ready to make a run for the presidency. We decided not to file again.

∞

RON PFENNING, U.S. Figure Skating president. It has a nice ring to it. Ron thought I was crazy. I brought up the possibility anyway with a few members of the nominating committee. They also thought I was crazy. Eventually I persuaded Ron to go for it, and persuaded five of the twelve nominating committee members to vote for him. This was a remarkable accomplishment because Joan Rozolis, Morry Stillwell, Ron Hershberger, Gale Tanger, and Debbie Weidman were five of the nominating committee's twelve members. The witness against him (Rozolis), the grievant against him (Stillwell), his opponent (Hershberger), the witness who refused to testify (Tanger), and the team-leader grievant against Ted Clarke (Weidman) all sat on the committee that would determine Ron's fate in his run for president. Of the seven "neutral" members of that committee, Ron received five of their votes, including all three of the athletes. And he did so even after Richard Dalley, the nominating committee chair, refused to allow him to appear before the committee, even though Ron Hershberger had appeared before the committee numerous times, as did Joan Rozolis. Yes, unbelievably, even she, the woman of endless gall, was running for president!

Despite all our efforts and the five votes, Ron Pfenning lost. Initially, when Ron decided to run, he agreed to go after the nominating committee's vote only. He was opposed to running from the floor of the Governing Council against the nominating committee's pick. This would require an actual vote of the delegates at the Governing Council meeting. Running from the floor was not only considered in poor form by old-schoolers, it was also an uphill battle. Those same old-schoolers who turn up their noses at a democratic election also hold numerous proxy votes that allow them to control the outcome when someone does make an attempt to run from the floor. Ron Pfenning was not interested in fighting this battle.

However, a funny thing happened while the nominating committee was considering him. The nominating committee is like a group of Masons, usually conducting all their business in complete secrecy. Despite this secrecy, everyone in figure-skating soon learned of Ron's run for president, and he was soon overwhelmed with people calling for him to run from the floor of the Governing Council to be held in Columbus, Ohio in May 2005.

So he decided to run from the floor. As soon as he made his decision, I let him know that I was stepping out of the campaign. I was too much of a lightning rod, and could hamper his hard work. I was the Howard Dean lambasting the Republicans, or the Jeb Bush clinging to the Schiavo case. I simply could not shut up about the Salt Lake Olympics, and skating insiders—even beyond Cinquanta's chimps—were beginning to tire of my rhetoric. "I will still deliver the athletes," I promised him.

Ron set up a Web site, and soon delegates were choosing up sides. Many anonymous letters were sent out, mostly through the Internet, endorsing Ron Hershberger. All of the letters sent endorsing Ron Pfenning were signed, and proudly so. One anonymous Hershberger letter can be traced to another nut case in the Skating Club of New York. What's with those skating crazies in Manhattan? How did Sarah Hughes ever survive?

One letter against Ron Pfenning was written by Morry Stillwell. Morry claimed outright to have been a witness to Marie-Reine's confession in Salt Lake, placing him directly at the scene of the crime. His lies were so confused that he put Ron Pfenning and Joyce Hisey there with him, neither of whom were in that hallway when LeGougne confessed. But then again, neither was Morry. How was he to know? Fortunately, his letter exposed himself for all the delegates to see. It seems that just about everyone knows by now the details of the French confession, and they know that Morry was not there.

Another letter went out endorsing Ron Hershberger as the candidate we "can trust." At that point, I had had more than I could take in silence. It was time to out Ron Hershberger.

My letter was written directly to Hershberger himself, outlining just how involved he was with the WSF, and just how fast he ran for the door when the shit started hitting the fan. I made sure my letter was distributed widely. Most delegates were unaware that Hershberger was as involved in the WSF as Ted Clarke. I had long since learned that my former friend Hershberger would not come to my defense, as he had promised. What made others think he could be trusted with the entire federation?

The initial response to my letter came from Joan Burns. She questioned whether my letter included numerous "twisted facts." Joan Burns and twisted facts. I'm not sure whether she knows the difference between a twisted fact and a triple lutz. No, I take that back. She doesn't know the difference, though she can spot tie-dye a mile away!

A week or so later, Hershberger sent out a letter in response drafted for him by, who else, Anne O'Keefe. It went out to every delegate. Up until this time, U.S. Figure Skating took the position that the delegate list was confidential under Colorado law. Ron Pfenning was denied the list. There was an exception to the rule, but Ron Pfenning did not fit under that exception, and neither did Hershberger. The list remained unavailable, at least until Ron Hershberger needed it. How did Hershberger get the list? The rules and bylaws, and apparently Colorado law, are read and interpreted differently by U.S. Figure Skating lawyer Tom James, depending on who it applies to. We were used to this behavior by U.S. Figure Skating, so we moved on.

During the peak of battle preceding the elections in Columbus, the ISU announced that the WSFers were no longer eligible under ISU rules. It was a lifelong ban. Marie-Reine LeGougne and Didier Gailhaguet had received a three-year punishment for the most grievous crime ever committed in figure skating. The Russians had received no punishment. Yet Sally Stapleford, Judith Furst-Tomber, Britta Lindgren, Ron Pfenning, and I are out for life. No surprise there, I suppose.

I focused my efforts back on the athletes.

In the end, though, the athletes abandoned me. I took it very personally, mainly because I was not able to honor my promise to Ron. Initially, the athlete vote appeared solid. Soon, though, it became obvious that the two athletes on the Executive Committee, Danielle Hartsell and Brittney Bottoms, had decided to play ball with the insiders. But all the athletes had not.

Dan Hollander, a former World Team member and showstopping "audience favorite," was upset by what he saw as the athletes abandoning ship for an administration that had repeatedly done the athletes wrong. He decided to get involved.

He wrote a strong letter of endorsement, pledging his support for Ron Pfenning. In the letter, he outlined how U.S. Figure Skating had abandoned Kyoko Ina and John Zimmerman at the Olympics, as he understood it after hearing about it from John. He then phoned U.S. Figure Skating to let them know he was no longer going to proxy his votes, but would appear in person at the meeting to vote them himself.

What happened next, while outrageous, was not surprising. He received a phone call telling him that he was not eligible to be a delegate to the Governing Council. The insiders were taking away his votes, and his voice. They were all to happy to have his proxy votes, so long as they were in the hands of one of their own, Danielle Hartsell, but not if he was going to vote in person for Ron Pfenning.

Dan Hollander appeared in Columbus, with his lawyer in tow, Chicago's John Collins, to fight for his right to vote. He had a second fight as well: his right to vote the proxies of two other athletes that U.S. Figure Skating was claiming weren't eligible to vote: John Zimmerman and Todd Eldredge. Eventually U.S. Figure Skating caved. They agreed to follow their own rules, thanks to an honest reading of them by Ed Mann, the Rules Committee chair. Either that, or they wanted to take away what could have been an explosive and divisive issue from the Pfenning camp that might have turned the tide his way. It was probably the latter.

The tide did turn, but in Hershberger's favor. Tanger, Howard, and the rest of the Chimps had successfully scared the athletes into believing that if Ron Pfenning were elected, Cinquanta would not allow the U.S. athletes into the Turin Olympic Games. This is almost as preposterous as the Russians not supporting Skate America if Kyoko Ina and John Zimmerman fought for their rightful placement at the previous Olympics. As absurd a tactic as it was, it worked.

Gale Tanger and Charlie Cyr, the Team Leader at the Salt Lake City Olympic Games, hammered the nail in Pfenning's coffin at the meeting of the athletes. Traditionally, the athletes meet with only athletes. It is their chance to discuss their issues, alone and without the influence of the officials. Not this time. Gale Tanger and Charlie Cyr pushed their way into the athletes' private meeting and made their appearances. Gale gave an academy award–winning performance, full of histrionics and arm-flailing. Charlie was there simply to fall on a sword.

Charlie disputed Hollander's account of what had happened at the Olympics to Ina and Zimmerman.

He explained that as Team Leader to the Olympics, it was his responsibility, not Phyllis's, to make any protest. (Wrong. For a standard protest, maybe, but the one Ina and Zimmerman were seeking was not a traditional one. The time to file that protest expired the night of the competition. Like the Canadians, if the U.S. wanted to make a protest of Ina and Zimmerman's placement, they would have to request arbitration, something well outside the realm of a Team Leader's responsibility.)

He then went on to say that he informed John and Kyoko of a pending midnight deadline, and that they decided not to make the protest even knowing that U.S. Figure Skating would have supported them. (Wrong again, and again. There is no midnight deadline. And John and Kyoko did not have the support of U.S. Figure Skating.)

He went on to say that Phyllis had nothing to do with it. (Wrong. He obviously had not read the hearing transcript, and John LeFevre's testimony, and he gambled that these athletes had not either, a gamble that paid off in spades.)

Initially, Hollander didn't know any better. Charlie is an outgoing, enthusiastic guy, one who the athletes like and respect. So Dan apologized for getting his facts wrong and offered to stand up in front of the Governing Council with Charlie to retract his statements. After the meeting, Hollander called me to tell me the meeting was a disaster, that every athlete was going to be voting for Hershberger, including probably him, and that he would be retracting his letter in front of the entire Governing Council. The fight was over.

When I asked him to clarify what had happened, I simply said to him, "You know that's not true. Call Zimmerman." He did, and soon, he began seeing through Charlie Cyr. In fact, he started questioning other things Charlie had told him. Apparently, Charlie told him that the Russians had withdrawn their protest regarding Slutskaya in the Ladies' event. Not true, it was ruled upon as meritless, not withdrawn. Hollander soon found that out too, with a simple Internet search proving otherwise.

What made Hollander different from the other athletes is that he didn't accept the party line, hook and sinker. He took the time to investigate their lies. He read the transcripts. He sought out reputable news stories on the Internet. It wasn't long before he was solidly back in the Pfenning camp, as were the other athletes I had direct contact with. Unfortunately, I did not know the majority of the athletes personally, and it was too late to organize an effort to inform them in the way that Hollander had informed himself.

In the end, Pfenning's margin of loss was less than the athlete vote. He had won a majority of the delegates attending; he lost the proxies held by the head table (Hershberger, Rozolis, et al) and the athletes. I had let down my good friend. I had failed to deliver the athletes. The athletes bought into the scare tactics, the brainwashing orchestrated beautifully by Tanger and Cyr, and pledged their support for Hershberger, Howard, and the rest of Cinquanta's Chimps.

The athletes, for maybe the first time in figure-skating history, were instrumental in electing the U.S. Figure Skating president. They had elected a probate, trusts and estates lawyer, Ron Hershberger. Who better to oversee the death of U.S. Figure Skating?

But Hershberger's election, no matter how ill-conceived, will not be the only gavel brought down on U.S. Figure Skating. Fans are dropping off by the truckload. Interest in skating after the obvious coverup in Salt Lake is now at a low. Sports fans, even skating fans, like to know that the sport they are enjoying is fair, that the athlete who rises to the top did so out of skill, and the best performance of the day will win. They also like a scoring system they understand. Figure skating's target audience, women and gay men, absolutely love the perfect 6.0. But now, even U.S. Figure Skating has trashed that valuable brand.

Until U.S. Figure Skating can restore confidence in fans and spectators, it certainly has doom on the horizon. Lucrative contracts will disappear, as viewers tune out, until eventually the multimillion-dollar well runs dry. While the culture of corruption continues to thrive within bowels of figure-skating, the interest on the outside is disappearing. Yes, it's true that there will always be skaters on the ice, but will there be anyone to watch them?

Russians Tatiana Totmianina and Maxim Marinin bring
back the World Pair title to the homeland by winning in

Dortmund at the 2004 Worlds, edging the Chinese pair. At the Moscow Worlds in 2005, they won again; the Chinese team was out with an injury. The Soviet-Russian Olympic dynasty may be alive and well in 2006.

Jon Jackson in the Year 1, A.S. (After Skating)

WEEK AFTER THE Governing Council summit in Columbus, Ohio, I traveled to Hyannis, Massachusetts with my boyfriend, Sandy Miller, to attend Ron Pfenning's Massachusetts-legalized marriage to Don Rocchio. The wedding was held in a small church in Hyannis not far from Ron and Don's house. Ron had asked me to be his best man.

After spending the previous week in the midst of phonies, chimps, and pats, it was a welcome reprieve, and an opportunity to celebrate amongst friends. By now, both Ron and I knew exactly who our real friends were. Sadly, of the hundreds of people I have met during my twenty-year tenure as a figure-skating official, the number of true friends I made can be counted perhaps in a baker's dozen. Not that there aren't hundreds of good-hearted people within the sport, many of whom remain good acquaintances, but lifelong friends, those that survive outside the ice rink, number few.

Happily, a lot of those friends were able to make it to Cape Cod for the wedding. The Silbys came up from Washington. Both Howard and Barbara came to the rehearsal reception prepared with a light-hearted, warm toast to Ron and Don, bringing down the house with their prepared oratorical theatrics. Ron's neighbor and friend of decades, Caroline Pierce, one of my new best friends, attended with her husband.

On the wedding day, Ted and Mary Clarke came to the wedding. It was great to catch up with both of them at the reception. Friend and French judge Gilles Vandenbroek and his partner Jean-Pascal Julien traveled from Paris for the occasion. Mark Mitchell and Peter Johansen, esteemed coaches and good friends, arrived with Ann Greenthal, a friend who has remained so for many years.

It was also great to meet many of Ron's friends and family from outside the skating world. And Don's family and friends were in attendance too, a group of tight-knit, warm-hearted people equal to Ron's collection of friends and family. All in all, it was a wonderful group of people.

The warmth that weekend in Cape Cod was in sharp contrast to the frigid convention halls of the Columbus Hyatt Regency from just weeks before, where backstabbing and slobbering viciousness ran rampant. It was a wonderful time for celebration, but also for reflection. I had known Ron Pfenning now since 1990. Our friendship didn't begin until many years later. Similar to other skating officials I met, we started out merely as acquaintances. Over the years, we found that we had many things in common. Our friendship was solidified in Salt Lake City at the Winter Games, though I would like to think that it was on a good foundation before that.

Ron had asked me to read a poem or story of my choosing as his best man. I fretted for months, trying to find something perfect that was not only relevant to the wedding but also held special meaning for our friendship. What I found also encapsulated my figure-skating story. I took a bit of poetic license to one on Joni Mitchell's popular recordings, *Both Sides Now*. The revised version reflected upon my friendship with Ron and Don, our paths in figure skating, and their future union. It's a beautiful song, and I thought it clearly summed up how I felt about them both and where I was at the moment. In a small historic church, on an overcast Cape Cod day, I celebrated a lasting friendship, while toasting a new one.

Just shy of six months preceding the Turin Winter Olympics, the gun-shot bloodied body of Chevalier Nusuyev was found in a Moscow apartment. Chevalier was the co-conspirator with Russian mobster Alimzhan Toktakhounov in the 2002 Olympic Pair Scandal. The preparations for Russian Gold in 2006 begin.

INDEX